SILKROADS

AXEL MADSEN

SILK ROADS

THE ASIAN ADVENTURES OF

CLARA & ANDRÉ MALRAUX

PHAROS BOOKS
A SCRIPPS HOWARD COMPANY
NEW YORK

Interior design: Elyse Strongin
Jacket design: Nancy Eato
Cartography: Marilyn Post

First published in 1989.

Library of Congress Cataloging-in-Publication Data:
Madsen, Axel.
    Silk roads : the Asian adventures of Clara and André Malraux / by Axel Madsen.
    p.   cm.
    "Books by Clara and André Malraux": p.
    Bibliography: p.
    Includes index.
    ISBN 0-88687-433-5 : $18.95
    1. Malraux, André, 1901-1976--Journeys--Indochina. 2. Malraux, Clara, 1897-1982--
Journeys--Indochina. 3. Authors, French--20th century-Journeys--Indochina. 4.
French--Indochina--History--20th century. 5. Indochina--Civilization--20th century. I.
Title.
PQ2625.A716Z6984 1989
843'.912--dc19
[B]   88-34325
            CIP

Printed in the United States of America

Pharos Books
A Scripps Howard Company
200 Park Avenue
New York, N.Y. 10166

10 9 8 7 6 5 4 3 2 1

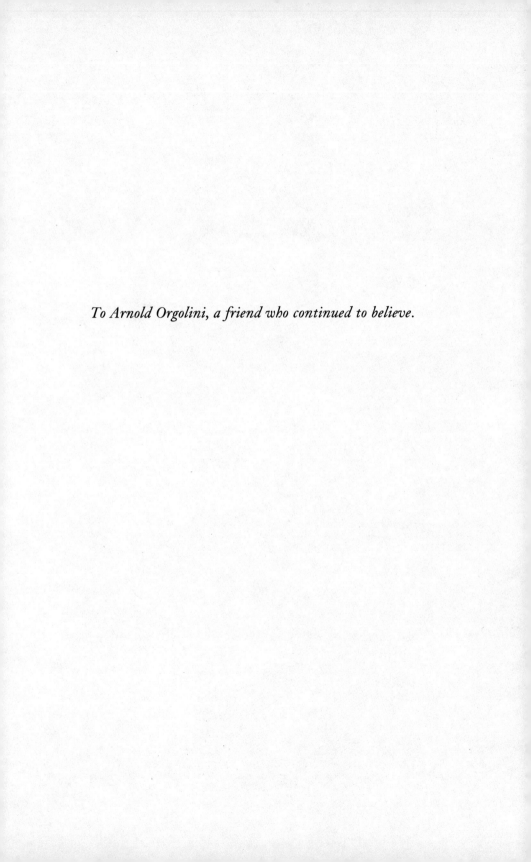

To Arnold Orgolini, a friend who continued to believe.

CONTENTS

Part Two

SILKROADS

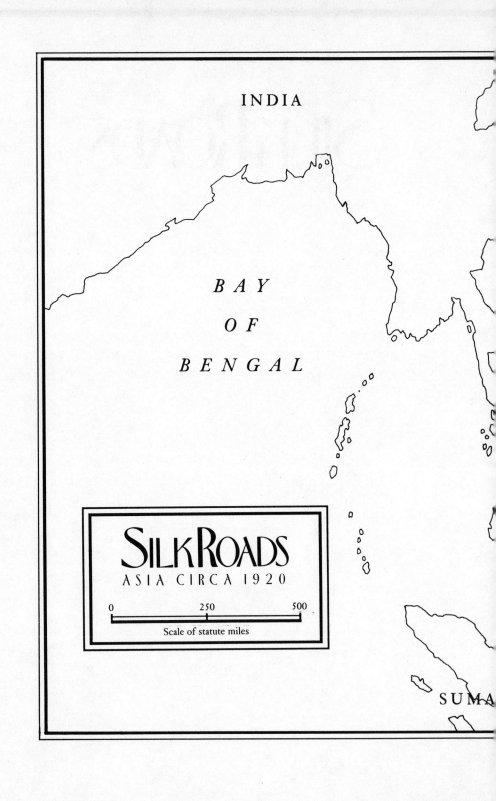

INDIA

B A Y

O F

B E N G A L

SILKROADS

ASIA CIRCA 1920

0   250   500

Scale of statute miles

SUMA

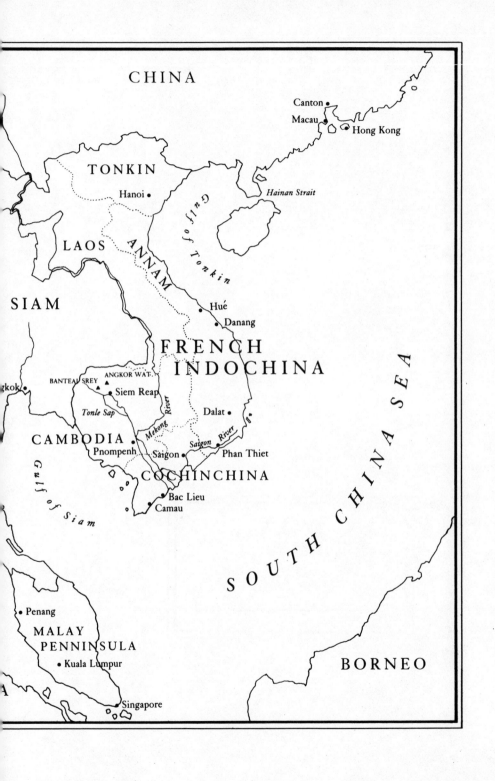

FOREWORD

In the years just after the Great War, adventure in faraway places was *the* thing for smart young people. André Malraux had been spared, not because of luck in the trenches but because the slaughter had stopped at his toes. By 1918 boys a year older were being called up, and when it was all over France had suffered nearly a million and a half killed in action, a third of them young men between eighteen and twenty-eight. Having been born in November 1901 instead of November 1900 made him and many of his contemporaries want to prove themselves by seeking perilous action and bracing ventures. Nor was Clara Goldschmidt much different. When the two of them got married (on a dare and to scandalize their elders) she, too, wanted to show her mettle. To go on a treasure hunt in the jungles of Southeast Asia was a sporting way of showing one belonged to the new Reckless Twenties.

This uncommon couple found more than they bargained for in colonial French Indochina, and their story is a tale of romance, crime, and political awakening. Clara's nonchalant Jewishness and an upbringing that embraced antagonistic nationalities made her sympathetic to the grievances of Vietnamese, Cambodians, and Laotians.

15

Because André was all French and because he modishly dismissed all political action, his reaction to the clammy paternalism of Indochina's French rulers was one of principle. Clara found racial injustice immoral; he scorned a society based on conformity, exclusion, and the surrender of principles.

Together and separately, Clara and André lived to see the yearnings, aspirations and defiance they encountered in Cambodia and Vietnam defeat the will of Western powers. They lived to see the follies of French colonialism, of one people ruling another, inflame American passions and pain. A year after President Lyndon Johnson threw America's might into the rice paddies of Vietnam, André's visit to a forbidden China in the throes of its cultural revolution was also a covert mission to sound out Mao Zedong on the possibility of rapprochement with the Americans. In 1972, on the eve of President Richard Nixon's historic trip to China, André was flown to Washington to brief the President.

In Paris three years later, the author speculated with André on the grand and collective *Whither humanity?* Helicopters were plucking Americans from the roof of the Saigon embassy while, at the end of his long and tumultuous life, André Malraux told his visitor that the major facts of our time are not events, not even such admittedly shattering occurrences as the advent of the nuclear age, but the shifts in the way we think, in the relentless way we question who we are.

We are, André Malraux believed, at the end of the empires because the sense of manifest destiny is disappearing everywhere, even in communism. "It has never happened before that the world's most powerful nation has no sense of what it wants. Yet the United States no longer has any manifest destiny, nor does Russia. The Chinese don't have it either. Domestically, yes; the national will power is very real. But when they say they want to change Tanzania, they're talking propaganda." What will happen after the empires fall is hard to foretell, because profound change is, by definition, subterranean and because we have a tendency to take our problems for examples. "The question is not one of morality but of destiny; we're not looking for a new Moses to give us new laws, we're trying to find out what we can be." He found it stupefying that the era that discovered nuclear physics and unlocked the genetic code is satisfied with conceiving man somewhere between Marx and Freud.

A few years later, an octogenarian Clara thought back to the time André and she were together, when she hated her own semifailures and resented the way André began to write her out of the novels that detailed their Asian adventures. In the name of their total commitment she had cut herself off from her family and accepted misery. He had felt no need to excuse himself. He not only insisted he had every right to transpose personal experiences into fiction but also believed that, rearranged in this fashion, events appeared more plausible. "I was the repudiated wife of the great man and after that, through the peculiar independence that World War II gave me, I recovered my contours and stopped being someone you could see through." Vietnam, she would say, "both wrecked and enriched us. With the weapons that were only his, André would try to dominate the world that, until then, had resisted him. Through his writing he would impose his vision. Our Indochina escapade, exploits, and enterprises would result in books that gave the adventures meaning." She too became a writer, first of fiction inspired by the Indochina ventures and, late in life, of a multivolume autobiography that earned her wide recognition.

If there is a challenge to writing about famous people it is to sketch the portraits while faces and traits are still fleeting and motives still tentative, to catch them *before* they know who they are, before the features are chiseled in accomplishments, fame, and guile. It is before we are somebody that we are interesting.

Here is André Malraux before he could talk about what Mao Zedong told him and what he told Trotsky and Kennedy; before the musings about history's finer ironies; before evocative memories of camels coming down the Pamirs, bellowing through the clouds; before his intuition that what makes humanity awesome and culture a great epic is not our own saying so but our questioning everything. Here is Clara before her difficult journey through life, a young woman of privilege and shining intelligence who would come to believe that her true drama—and that of many women—was that to be fulfilled she needed the contact, stimulation, and embrace of a masculine mind stronger than hers.

This book is one of those looking-glass stories that both re-create an exotic world and illuminate the way we change. It is not American flaws and failure that are exposed here, but another people's mistakes and failure to capture hearts and minds. Yet, unlike the missed opportunities of the British in India, the French failures in Indochina would come to haunt the American conscience. This book is both a prophetic journey and a backward glance, an evocation of a vanished world and a reflection on its consequences. It is a story of love, of emotional liabilities, and of commitments to a cause. Above all, it is the story of youth, a time before fame, when all was possible.

PART ONE

ᏉᏨ 1. LORELEI

They stood leaning on the port-side railing, a smart young couple in wispy summer clothes. She told him they'd hear the legendary echo when they got right under the cliff. He wondered whether the people living along the banks were as much influenced by the river as they were separated by it.

To fellow passengers they were a somewhat incongruous pair: he a lanky, nervously elegant youth, she a vivacious brunette barely tall enough to reach his shoulder. He was a pale and intense twenty-two-year-old with a flair for mocking gestures and a surly hauteur people found attractive because he looked even younger than he was. She was a diminutive woman of twenty-five whose plainness was forgotten in her elan, her sea-green eyes, her resonant laughter, and the movements of her butterfly hands.

"The rhetorical question is whether there is such a thing as a Rhenish culture," he said.

"Lorelei hurled herself into the river in despair over a faithless lover."

"Do you think we'll *see* her?" he asked, looking down. The waters were deep and the current formed small whitecaps.

She held on to her velvet-trimmed taffeta hat. "She's not down there. She's supposed to sit on top of the cliff and lure ships to their destruction."

"Excursion boats, too?"

"Heine said nothing about tourists."

He shielded his face with his coat to light a cigarette. "The ballad of the Lorelei made Heine famous before he was thirty."

"Which means you can still beat him." She remembered their honeymoon visit to family in Magdeburg, her grandfather after dinner asking her to take down the works of Heine so he could read a few poems to this new French grandson-in-law.

"You were moved to tears when Grandpa Goldschmidt read to you," she smiled.

"It was the Gothic lettering that made me all emotional."

"How about my lyrical translation?"

He straightened up and watched the riverbank. A railway line ran parallel to the river.

She continued. "When Grandpa saw how touched you were, he told me, 'You see, you shouldn't worry. Your husband and I understand each other perfectly, even though he speaks no German and I no French.' "

The headwind was stronger as the little steamer entered the gorge. The mountains on the left bank were the Hunsrucks, she explained; the Taunus Mountains with the Lorelei cliff were on the right. Anyone who had grown up with a German nanny knew that. Sightseers with Kodaks took up position along the railing.

It was a beautiful afternoon, the second Saturday in June 1923. The steep hills were terraced and heavy with wine grapes. During prehistoric times the same culture groups existed on both banks, he said. The Romans were the first both to build bridges and to make the river a state boundary. The Rhine was a classic example of rivers alternately unifying the regions through which they flow and making political barriers. Behind them a French voice in a deck chair said this was the most beautiful stretch of the river. She thought of her late father, who had first showed her the Rhine, upstream, where the river formed the border between German and Switzerland. The bell clanged on the bridge. Black smoke belched from the funnel as the engine went into reverse, making the ship float motionless below the Lorelei. The cliff towering above the starboard jutted into the river. One hundred thirty-two meters of sheer cliff, someone quoted from Baedeker. The sun slanted, picture-postcard perfect, through the gorge.

German voices shouted from the stern, echoing back to the ship.

"Hello!"

"Peter!"

"Ich liebe dich!"

The shouts bounced back from the vertical rock with exemplary fidelity. At the railing, a couple in lederhosen and dirndl were the first to have themselves photographed against the romantic back-drop. A war veteran limped onto the deck on crutches.

Clara recited an approximate translation of Heine's famous poem about the scorned Lorelei maiden. André said it was obvious that the Lorelei had always been a danger to navigation.

The ship's whistle blew and children on deck squealed in delight at the piercing reverberation. The bell clanged again, and the ship resumed its downstream cruise.

"What I'd like," he said, "is a newspaper."

She knew he wanted to check their investment in the stock market listings and suggested that the newsstand at Cologne's central station would have French papers.

They took a walk along the deck.

Since their marriage ten months earlier they had lived a nonchalant Bohemian existence. Clara's dowry was substantial. In Paris, they occupied the top floor of her widowed mother's townhouse. Between feverish literary activities—to write, André had discovered, was a way of "making it"—they visited their stockbroker and went to all the museums, movie houses, and nightclubs that everybody talked about.

In tune with a time that was passionately in love with the outrageous, André wanted to be different and loved to provoke. Clara saw herself as a young woman sometimes comically bold, with a taste for the quaint, the striking, and for what surprised her. Traveling was their favorite activity.

Sailing down the Rhine was their latest cultural pilgrimage. Their honeymoon had taken them on their first airplane ride to Prague. In the clouds above the Black Forest they told each other they'd one day fly over sunnier vistas. The women of Prague had red headscarves, and the confectioners exhibited their whipped cream marvels in their shopwindows. They walked among the graves at the old Jewish cemetery where the Golem once defended the dead. André was moved by the orthodox Jews with their mossy beards. Clara said she, too, was discovering them. Which wasn't quite true. She had seen them in Karlsbad before the war and had been embarrassed by their long robes, their curls, skullcaps, and the way they talked with their hands. From Prague they had traveled to Berlin and to Magdeburg to meet the Goldschmidt patriarch with a taste for Heine. The Versailles Treaty that had made Alsace a part of France again had divided the Goldschmidt assets and made Maurice, Clara's elder brother, the head of considerable family interests in the biggest Alsatian tannery. Clara's younger brother, Paul, was still a moody teenager.

"You've married your younger brother," one of her two uncles said in German when they met André and her at the Madgeburg station.

"A blond goy," said the other.

Since then, Clara and André had been to Dunkirk to meet members of the Malraux clan, to Athens to climb the Acropolis and to Tunis to retrace the steps of Gustave Flaubert's *Salammbô*.

The trip down the Rhine agreeably fused their passion for travel and art. Today they were watching the vine-covered hills glide by and speculating about a culture stretching the length of the river. Tomorrow they would be in Cologne for a second meeting with a man whose ideas set André afire.

Three months ago, after attending a guest performance at the Paris Opera of the Pnompenh Royal Ballet—a company whose spare grace of gestures, tone, and costumes enchanted them—André had met Alfred Salmony in an art gallery in the Rue d'Astorg. Salmony was a heavily built German only a few years older than Clara and André who lost all ponderousness in the presence of art, especially Asian art from the dawn of time. A director of the Cologne museum, Salmony was preparing a comparative art show that wouldn't be limited to classical masterpieces but fearlessly included the art forms of all kinds of people.

André had invited Salmony for dinner. He arrived with an enormous briefcase and, after dessert, spread hundreds of art photos on the floor. Without talking, he juggled stills around, bringing certain photos together with others—a Thai torso with a classical Greek head, a Han-dynasty head with a Romanesque bas-relief.

Primitive art raised stupendous questions. Juxtaposing photographs or parts of photographs made it seem as if artists of all ages and all cultures worked in diverse ways toward the same ends. Why did a Wei-dynasty bodhisattva chiseled in northern China in the early sixth century resemble a Romanesque statue carved six centuries later in medieval Europe? Maybe art was a bond, a kind of shared nervous system that linked all people across the chasms of culture and time. After Salmony finally said good night, leaving behind a few of his photographs, Clara and André talked all night, feeling there might be a new way of grasping culture.

And of understanding themselves.

They always talked about who they were. Theirs was a union of carnal intelligence and give-and-take; of mutual discovery, aspirations, and shared complicity. To him, she was the necessary partner, his sounding board and ideal woman. To her, he was manifest destiny, playmate, and dazzling example. There were moments, Clara would later write, when their discussions of the sexes escalated to questions of what each expected of the other, moments when "we climbed together I don't know what abstract mountain, not always with him playing the leader but mostly with both of us egging each other other on and developing such a taste for intellectual jousting that the playfulness of the body asserted itself and physical pleasure seemed the natural result of the pleasures of the mind."

Their families had not approved. After the civil marriage—she in a black Poiret squirrel dress, he in a tuxedo he couldn't quite fill out—they had laughingly told the families not to take them too seriously: within six months they'd divorce.

When the six months were up, Clara brought up the question, to test him. "Shouldn't we divorce, at least legally?"

"How about using the money we'll spend on divorce lawyers in a more constructive fashion?"

"What do you have in mind?"

"A trip to Tunisia, for example."

They had returned via Italy, and in Naples wanted to see the famous *Sicilian Vespers* puppet show. *"No e descente,"* said the hotel concierge.

"Decent or not, I want to go,' said Clara.

They were taken to a tiny theater full of street urchins who were everywhere, in all the seats, even hanging under the balconies like bats. At the climatic moment when the Sicilian populace murdered the French, the beggar children jumped in their seats and shouted bloodthirsty epithets at the stage. Clara and André never found out whether it was the anti-French spectacle or the sight of street kids that was supposed to be indecent.

Their backgrounds were different, but they knew how to interpret their pasts for each other. From the beginning, he felt she was a kindred soul, someone he could *talk* to—about Nietzsche, the meaning of life, the inanity of conventional ideas. From their first date, phrases and subjects caught fire between them. They divided everybody they knew into "fun" and "no fun" people and agreed the surrealists were beginning to take themselves too seriously. "I wasn't even sixteen when I first decided I wanted to be a great writer," he told her on their second date. "Except of course that a great writer, like a great painter, is supposed to suffer a lot." She introduced him to his first horse race at Longchamp; he showed her African art and, for the thrill of it, took her dancing in one of the lowest dives in the tenderloin district of Paris.

Lately she had discovered that although he had been brought up by a single mother, a grandmother, and a spinster aunt, he knew little about women. Challenged, he said a man wanted the woman he loved to live up to the image he had of her.

"A woman," she replied, "wants the man of her dreams to live up to the image he has of himself."

One day he thought that, since the values of society were masculine, it would be fun to imagine those of a feminine civilization. They spent hours compiling various hypotheses, sparring and testing each other's territory.

"I was brought up to believe that women aren't necessarily inferior," she told him. "The men in my family took care of business, and their sons divided their time between business and sports. Matters of the heart and consciousness were certainly respected but belonged to the women."

The division was still true. Maurice might have become the head of the Goldschmidt family's French interests, but he was still less gifted than his sister. It had always been like that in the family. Each generation of Goldschmidts and Heynemanns had spawned one daughter surrounded by several sons—Margrete Heynemann, Clara's mother, had four brothers. So much love was lavished on each generation's unique feminine specimen that the boys concluded females were ungrateful and the girls thought of themselves as precious things. Maurice had grown up unpredictable, brilliant in school and in college in England but full of repressed hostility. In 1914, he went off to war to prove himself. His sister admired the gesture because the family was not yet French enough for the supreme sacrifice, and so many others of their milieu and fortune found ways to shelter their sons from the horrors of the front. Maurice came back a flier with fifteen sorties over enemy lines and was now a crafty and touchy war veteran. Clara's younger brother Paul was an impulsive nineteen-year-old with gorgeous blue eyes who had been left largely in his sister's emotional care during their father's long terminal illness and Maurice's wartime absence. Their compatibility made him believe that life's more difficult moments could be resolved with words, a smile, or a studied pout.

Investing a hefty sum of Clara's inheritance in a Mexican mining company was André's idea. Stock market speculation was something he had learned from his father.

Clara felt investing resembled betting on horses. Once she had overcome her distaste for an activity where, as she would say, "the sweat of one's brow didn't intervene sufficiently to satisfy my ethics as a child of diverse Bibles," she admitted that for women speculation had one advantage over the Longchamp race track—it didn't require a particularly smart wardrobe. Members of the Pedrazzini family who ran the mining company had come to Paris and André had been invited to attend a stockholders' meeting. The Mexicans, he reported back to Clara, were magnificently tanned and sported handlebar mustaches that made them *muy simpático.*

The stock exchange confirmed André's judgment. Clara and André saw their stock climb to feverish heights that, in inflationary francs, made them halfway millionaires. Their first extravagance for the supermodern apartment they had in mind made them the proud owners of a Picasso.

The mountains forced the Rhine into a sharp right turn. The boat trip would end in Koblenz, the ancient royal seat of the Franks, where the Moselle flowed into the Rhine Clara and André strolled the deck again and stood by the railing.

The way the late afternoon sun hit the pine stands on the summit peaks reminded her of Baden-Baden and the sanatorium where her father had spent his last months. She remembered the woman doctor who took her into her father's room and told her to be very quiet. Dr. Fraenkel was Russian. She hated the czar and was the first to tell Clara about Russian sufferings, Jewish sufferings. Clara imagined that her father loved Dostoevsky because of Dr. Fraenkel. Five weeks before he passed away Clara understood that he might die, although she couldn't imagine that her mother's lungs would continue to breathe while Otto Goldschmidt's lungs had turned into sponges. He looked so handsome when he was dead. She had been thirteen.

For André the river evoked memories of Allied victory, Armistice Day, and the rightful return of Alsace. His father had returned from the war as a tank commander, physically unscathed but with deep psychic scars. Like so many veterans, he didn't like or understand the postwar era and was turning into a fiercely nationalistic and vaguely anti-Semitic Frenchman. Patriotism had never attracted André. Even as an adolescent there had been something derisive and reckless about him.

Until he met Clara he had never been out of France. If anything had impressed him besides her ability to talk freely about her most intimate feelings it was her command of languages and her upbringing in the grander liberal tradition of settled German-Jewish wealth, spending a coddled childhood between the big house in the Avenue des Châlets with a German nanny and, until the war, summers in Magdeburg and trips to Italy. As a child, André couldn't grow up fast enough. He still believed that to be young was to be held back.

Koblenz and the confluence of the Moselle River were up ahead. For a glimpse of the Ehrenbreitstein fortress, a tour guide drew a group of sightseers to the starboard next to Clara and André. As the medieval castle came into view high up on the precipitous rock, Clara translated the statistics and the story of how German ingenuity had rebuilt the fortress after the French had blown it up in 1801.

They were rounding the stern and heading toward the prow on the starboard side when André's eyes fell on a French newspaper abandoned in a deck chair.

"What do you know?" he grinned, picking it up.

After a perfunctory glimpse of the headlines, he flipped to the financial pages. As they had done many times before, they followed his finger running down the stock listings.

The tiny figure after the Pedrazzini entry informed them that they were ruined.

⮂ 2. AT THE GUIMET

Decisions had to be made. Rushing back to Paris after their meeting with Alfred Salmony, they learned not only that their stock was worthless but also that the members of the tawny and engaging Pedrazzini clan had disappeared. Clara's confrontation with her family had been pained. Maurice said there were terms to describe her husband: rake, arriviste, parvenu, fortune-hunter. Her kid brother Paul was all snickers and spiteful glee when she tried to stand up to Maurice's wounding accusations. She knew nothing about the real world, he sneered, and she and her husband lived in a fantasy land. Margrete Goldschmidt reminded her daughter of the family's misgivings about André, his testy airs, evasive attitude, his time frittered away in galleries and museums.

The plight was classic and usually ended with the family forgiving and discreetly subsidizing the humbled progress toward responsibility of the prodigal son or son-in-law. In André's case, however, failure made him more audacious. Clara and André were rambling through the Guimet Museum of Oriental Art the next day discussing the predicament when he suddenly asked, "You don't expect me to work, do you?"

His words rang strangely in the museum stillness. Yet they made her realize she couldn't imagine him selling cars or stock certificates. "No, but then?"

He pointed to the Buddha head behind the glass partition and asked if she knew anything about the pilgrims' road from Flanders to Santiago de Compostela.

"We have to be serious," insisted Clara.

He said nothing, staring intently at the Buddha face with its closed eyes and puzzling smile.

"The film import didn't work."

He kept his eyes on the Buddha. "The road through France," he said finally, "was staked out with cathedrals, sanctuaries, and small chapels, just like centuries later the Spaniards in California set out the route along the Pacific Coast by missions, one day's ride from each other. Similarly. . . "

"We ended up projecting the picture for our friends in a private screening room."

The museum was eerily quiet.

"Similarly," he said in a lowered voice, "temples marked out the Royal Way from Siam to Cambodia. From Dangrek to Angkor Wat, there are shrines that have been reclaimed from the jungle and inventoried. But there must be others, smaller way stations, not yet discovered, swallowed up by the jungle."

Clara knew how he loved the museum's fascinating but confusing heaps of Asian art and artifacts—carved Buddhas, stuffed paradise birds, rickshaws—that Emile Guimet had brought back from the Orient half a century before. But she couldn't see how her husband imagined he could redress their finances by becoming a curator.

In Berlin they had discovered the German avant-garde cinema. Robert Wiene's *Das Kabinett des Dr. Caligari*, with its startling expressionist decor, stylized acting, and story of a sinister scientist, gave André the idea that—in addition to their stock market speculation—they could become film distributors of pioneering movies. Since the French rights to *Caligari* were already being negotiated, André sank a hefty sum into the rights to its new rival, *Das Haus zum Mond*, a "phantasmal drama" by expressionist stage director Karl Heinz Martin, which André retitled simply *La Maison Lunaire*.

André didn't take into account bureacratic *visas de censure*, however. they had discovered once back in Paris that insidious nationalism halted the import of the German avant-garde movies. Like Germany, France both maintained and inflated the myth of war sacrifice and the eternal enemy. The commercial exploitation of *La Maison Lunaire* remained unauthorized.

She watched their mirrored selves in the pane of the display case. André's eyes were riveted on the stone features that so perfectly radiated the bliss the soul could achieve through Buddha. On her own face she saw the pain of last night's scene, Maurice's outrage, Paul's glee, and her mother's tears. Firmly she had defended André while inwardly conceding that their epithets described her husband all too well.

"We will go to little Cambodian temples," he said. "I mean to some little-known, overlooked or forgotten shrine in the jungle."

Her eyes met his in the glassy reflection. His voice was just a whisper, "And we will remove a few Buddhas and Shivas and sell them to museums in America."

She felt a shiver run down her spine.

Before she could say anything he grabbed her hand and dragged her to the opposite wall and a glassed-in stone relief of apsaras from Angkor Wat. Known either as the king's heavenly concubines or as girls in heaven who offer sexual delights to the pious or heroic dead, the apsaras were carved with sinuous sensuality. The deep, languid lines of their closed eyes, voluptuous thick lips, and bare breasts were continued in their elaborate hair styles, jewelry, and skirts. One of the standing females had her arm under her companion's. A towering jeweled crown on her head rivaled the locks spread out in a halo of points and loops on the other.

"That," he said, pointing, "will allow us to live comfortably for a couple of years."

What had captivated her when they first met was his restless intellect, his passing for beauty, the ardor of his repartee. Now he had surprised her again.

She followed him to the next room, but when he stopped in front of a sandstone lintel she couldn't quite focus on the carved divas or dancing goddesses.

"What do we know about Cambodia?" she asked.

As a guard walked slowly by them, hands clasped behind his back in civil-service rectitude, André ignored her question. Instead he said that the dancing symbolized divine activity as a source of movement in the universe, particularly as a cosmic function of creation—conservation, destruction, incarnation, liberation. "The object of the divine dance is also to rid humans of illusions."

André kept talking as they walked out of the Guimet and down the Avenue d'Iena. They knew a lot about Southeast Asia. They had read Pierre Loti's sensual, impressionistic novels, with their agonizingly beautiful commentaries. they knew Cambodia was part of French Indochina, that it was a tropical country full of alien diseases. They had enjoyed the splendor of the dancing, costumes, and music of the Pnompenh Royal Ballet. Clara realized that her husband's belief in adventure—adventure as an attitude of life, and as a slap in the face of existing values, and as vindication of personal freedoms—plus his love of art and travel, combined with art dealers' gossip, had made him come up with this crazy yet terribly clever solution.

"We need some sort of official backing," he said.

The way he explained it, they should get some sort of official credentials that established them, if not as heads of a mission, at least as researchers.

"The more official the character of our travels the better. Nobody will find it unusual if a scholar and his wife rent oxcarts to go and explore an archeological site".

"A scholar and his wife?"

He grinned. "We'll have to get permission to study not only the huge Angkor Wat ruins, but to explore smaller unknown relics. The interest in Oriental curios is booming, and apparently there have been no new finds. Carvings of devatas, or guardian goddesses, are considered extremely rare."

He met with Joseph Hackin, the Alsatian-born director of the Guimet Museum, and talked to him about all kinds of ideas. André thought he might interview several cultural types and, on their return, give a lecture at the School of Oriental Languages.

Summer, they discovered, was the wrong time of year for jungle expeditions in Southeast Asia; they would have to wait for the dry season in October.

The Goldschmidts did not take kindly to Clara's ruin. André's lack of remorse, his peremptory eagerness to plunge forward didn't make it any easier on Margrete Goldschmidt, a petite raven-haired widow in her fifties, and her two bachelor sons.

In the next months, however, thanks to André's help in unearthing the bureaucratic figleaf that allowed the family to turn certain German securities into French assets, they managed to suffer his presence in the big house at 10 Avenue des Châlets. Better at ferreting out obscure texts than either of his brothers-in-law, André had found a subparagraph in the decree that allowed turning Grandfather Goldschmidt's prewar holdings in the Muelhauesener Bank into equity in the renamed Banque de Mulhouse.

Between visits to the School of Oriental Languages and to the Guimet André discovered an article in a 1919 issue of the *Revue archéologique* that described how the Fogg Museum of Harvard University had come into possession of an admirable Buddhist head, and how at least eight other Khmer masterpieces somehow had found their way to the United States. "Given the number of Khmer sculptures and the difficult access to the ruins in Angkor," the author wrote, "one can perhaps accept the 'emigration' of a few specimens. Such leaks must not become numerous, however. Let the lawmakers beware."

It was enough to spark André's imagination: a temple containing great treasures stood abandoned in the jungle. Officials were apparently ready to tolerate a few more leaks in the direction of American museums. There was no time to lose, however. An August 21, 1923, mandate by the governor-general of Indochina had set up a commission to study and recommend ways to protect Khmer relics. Legislators might soon pass laws mandating that all abandoned sites be classified historical monuments.

Until their departure in early October, when they were not busy preparing for the expedition, they picked up the literary activities that had occupied them between trips abroad when they were wealthy. For Florent Fels, the publisher of limited editions and of

L'Action, a dynamic little magazine, Clara started translating a Sigmund Freud text she had discovered in Germany, *A Young Girl's Analytical Journal,* while André wrote the foreword to a political book.

Clara had wanted to be part of the postwar effervescence, her generation's excitement and discoveries. An avid reader of the new authors and poets, she was too timid to think she could write herself. She reasoned, however, that her ability to translate was one way of getting close to those who did have literary talent. A family friend had introduced her to a friend who had led her to Fels.

L'Action was a passably "anarchic" magazine—against the established order, patriotism, religion, and traditional attitudes. Among its contributors were Max Jacob, Jean Cocteau, the globetrotting poet Blaise Cendrars, the composer Erik Satie, and the Romanian-born father of Dada, Tristan Tzara. The magazine honored the most modern art, discussed new esthetics in every issue, and reproduced works by Pablo Picasso, Raoul Dufy, Juan Gris, and Suzanne Valadon's alcoholic son Maurice Utrillo. It ran translations of Maxim Gorki, Alexander Blok, and Victor Serge, the Belgian-born anarchist now actively supporting Lenin's new and still-shaky Soviet regime. Even more daring, *L'Action* published the new German expressionists Franz Werfel, Johannes Becher, and Clara's friends Claire and Ivan Goll.

The Golls were a high-voltage couple who loved each other furiously, separated, tried to commit suicide, reconciled, separated again—all accompanied by the fracas of public quarrels. The openhouse Sundays of these Jewish-gentile Alsatians were cosmopolitan gatherings where the newest ideas from Berlin and Vienna, from expressionist cinema to Sigmund Freud, were discussed and where Marc and Bella Chagall and Alexander Archipenko told about the ferment of the new experimental Soviet art.

The Chagalls had just returned from Moscow where, at Lenin's suggestion, the painter had decorated the Jewish Art Theater—mischieviously painting his own likeness in the arms of the drama director. Chagall would remember André of the Goll Sundays as a youth with circles under his feverish green eyes.

Claire was very much the blonde Berlin poetess, who at their gath-

erings preferred to stretch out on a couch. She and Clara were intimate friends. When they were together they said playful things in
frisky, affected phrases.

André had written a piece on André Gide in *L'Action*. In the early
1920s Gide was, with Paul Claudel, the great literary figure. Then in
his early fifties, the novelist, critic, diarist, playwright, and traveler
was a bisexual with a strong tendency toward homosexuality who,
since the turn of the century, had pursued his pleasure and striven to
make it as public as possible; he upbraided Marcel Proust for turning
the men he had loved into women in his novels. The drama of his life
was his marriage to his cousin whose strict Calvinism could not accept his paganism and homosexuality but who was nevertheless the
person he loved most.

When André met the author of *Les Nourritures Terrestres* on the
Boulevard St. Germain for an interview on his views on art, Gide
showed up munching a croissant. The resulting piece called Gide
"the greatest living French author."[1] André's gift for taking quick
and forceful possession of ideas and for speaking without redundan-
cy or hesitation impressed the interviewee as well. When conversing
with Malraux, Gide would say late in life, "one doesn't feel very
clever."

The Cambodian treasure hunt promised to be a bracing mix of risk
on the fuzzy edge of laws governing historical sites and cultural
sleuthing that might lead to important discoveries: Was it possible
that the art of the Khmer civilization, which began to decline in the
thirteenth century, was a hybrid between Indian and Chinese influ-
ences, the kind of cultural overlap that Salmony's juggling of photographs suggested?

The couple read everything they could. Clara read foreign books.
A British encyclopedia said the Angkor Wat complex was nearly ten
times the size of Canterbury Cathedral. German periodicals mentioned Lecoq's recent finds in central Asia, excavations that might
support André's theory that an as-yet undiscovered link between Eu-

---

[1] In *L'Action* No.12, March-April 1922.

ropean and Asian art might exist. André believed he would find the key in the Cambodian jungle.

André had no difficulty locating a Lieutenant Marek's 1914 account of a visit to a small Buddhist temple at Banteai Srey. While Lunet de la Jonquière's three-volume *Inventaire Descriptif des Monuments du Cambodge* of 1911 had excellent detailed descriptions and maps of sites along the Royal Way from Dangrek to Angkor, Lieutenant Marek reported that the Banteai Srey temple was standing abandoned in the jungle.

André also came upon an article by Henri Parmentier, chief of archeology at L'École Française d'Extrême-Orient in Hanoi, who wrote of the remarkable beauty of the Banteai Srey ruins during a visit in 1916. The Far-Eastern French School was the highest institute of learning in Indochina and, André realized, also the Paris government's appointed custodian of Vietnamese, Cambodian, and Laotian archeology. No doubt Parmentier was someone to see once they got there.

Banteai Srey was twelve miles north or Angkor. Everything about it was distinctive. It was the greatest work of Khmer architecture and sculpture in the tenth century. It was founded by Yajnavaraha, a Brahmin of royal descent, and consisted of three tower-shrines in line inside concentric enclosures. The more André delved into the subject the more he realized these could not be the ruins Parmentier had visited seven years earlier. There had to be two sites of the same name, Yajnavaraha's remarkable three-tower shrine near Angkor Wat and the Banteai Srey ruins Parmentier had visited northeast of Angkor Thom on the right bank of the Siem Reap River.

"I don't quite know how, but I bet the confusion can serve our purpose," he told Clara.

While he scanned archeologists' field reports at the School of Oriental Languages library to try to pinpoint where exactly on the right bank of the Siem Reap River they should concentrate their efforts, Clara bought quinine tablets to guard against malaria, snakebite serum, and a dozen hacksaws. The ancient Khmers ignored the use of cement, she had read. It shouldn't be too difficult to dislodge the statuary. With her mother's seamstress she concocted tropical suits of her own design for both of them.

Friends looked upon their upcoming adventure with a mixture of admiration and envy. André knew how to give the story a spin, and Clara had a clever little phrase that always had its effect: they were going to put back into circulation artworks threatened by vegetation and neglect.

But there were moments when they dimly realized their planned adventure was amateurish and improvised. They had always read too much. Their knowledge was all from books, while in reality they would be a couple wandering the jungle with little money and less experience. They ignored such basics as the local language and customs, the hothouse climate, fauna, and the tigers, snake, and mosquitos whose names they could barely pronounce. At night when they were alone in their spare top-floor living room with their lacquered black furniture and lone Picasso on the wall, they talked for hours.

Clara remembered childhood adventure stories full of cruelty. They, too, would be sailing up a river in an exotic land. They, too, could meet people laying claim to supernatural powers, spear-wielding savages, ritual slaughter, slavery, torture. André thought of re-enacting Alexandre Dumas novels in the forest surrounding suburban Bondy with his school chum Louis Chevasson. There was one Dumas novel he had never forgotten—*Georges,* the first book he had ever read. It was the story of a foundling brought up on Mauritius Island in the Indian Ocean by a Taiwanese nurse who taught him Chinese and swordsmanship. Georges Munier spent his brief, tumultuous life searching for his father, traveling through exotic lands, fighting and ensnaring ladies and perfidous villains.

"Ensnaring ladies?"

André ignored her sarcasm. "In the end, Georges returned to his island to lead liberated slaves in an assault on plantation owners who from their hilltop barricades set fire to kegs of rum and sent the flaming barrels down on their assailants."

André decided the way to double their chances of success was to find buyers of Khmer art in advance. He explained to Daniel Kahnweiler, the art dealer, that Clara and he might shortly come into possession of a shipment of Khmer art. The gallery owner promised to write a fellow dealer in New York.

Kahnweiler was a German Jew who had opened his first gallery in

Paris in 1907 and in five years had become the merchant for Derain, Vlaminck, Picasso, Braque, and Gris. He had been in Italy in August 1914 when the war broke out. To avoid both incarceration in France as an enemy alien and service in the Kaiser's army, he had sat out the conflict in Switzerland. He had been permitted to return to France in 1920 only to discover his property confiscated. Eight hundred paintings belonging to this "impresario of cubism," as he was affectionately called, were sold at public auction. With his new gallery in the Rue d'Astorg and a French citizen as his associate to protect him from further "enemy alien" prosecution, he was starting over again.

Kahnweiler's New York correspondent was more than hopeful when it came to selling choice Khmer pieces to American institutions. Kahnweiler suggested André write to his correspondent himself. How much money were we talking about, André wanted to know. Again Kahnweiler obliged and managed to obtain trade figures for Khmer statuary from Paul Cassirer, the famous Berlin art dealer who had first sold impressionists in Germany and had organized the first exhibition of Vincent van Gogh.

In 1930 when André wrote *The Royal Way,* a heroic retelling of their Indochina venture, he would have his two heroes discuss their planned treasure hunt.

Claude Vannec, a trained archeologist who can only think of making a fortune, tells Perken, an older European adventurer in Asia, that if they decided to team up there will be obstacles. French authorities certainly represent hurdles, but there is worse than that. There is the danger of dying:

> "The Mois, you mean?" Perken asks.
> "The Mois, the jungle, the malaria."
> "I'd have guessed as much. Let's talk money."
> "A small bas-relief, almost any statue, will fetch thirty thousand francs or so."*
> "Gold francs?"

---

* After the French financial crisis of 1924-1926, when the franc plunged to 50 francs to the dollar, the dollar stood at 26 francs to $1. In 1923 30,000 francs therefore equaled some $1200 in period dollars or, in 1989 currency, approximately $9000.

till its head of archeology. The ministerial order authorized
é to study Khmer temples and to recruit farmers and carts to
ports his baggage. It specified that "Monsieur Malraux must
all costs and his expedition can have no commercial aim." His
obligation was to give an account of his travels on his return.

lara and André's friends were impressed when they told them
y were now in possession of a ministerial authorization. In a letter
Kahnweiler, Max Jacob made fun of the Malraux mission, saying
dré would end up professor of Asian studies.

It was decided that Chevasson would follow Clara and André to
igon three weeks later. When the moment came to say goodbye,
lara saw only apprehension on her mother's face. Clara felt a shiver
f premonition. She was sure a part of her life was over.

In the taxi taking them through the Paris evening traffic to the
Gare de Lyon and the overnight boat train to Marseille, she curled up
in a corner and sobbed.

"Why are you crying?" André asked.

"Because nothing will be the same again."

She felt the bitterness of parting; he talked about a future that
would be more beautiful yet still look like the past.

Their ship would make a stop in Siam. Maybe they should get off
there, she suggested. Siam was an independent country; maybe
things would be easier there. Thai art was beautiful too, less perfect
than Khmer art in architectural lines perhaps, less solemn but more
beguiling.

"There must be antique dealers in Bangkok; maybe we can manage
to buy art pieces," she said on the train.

André assured her that their New York art dealer would advance
money once they were in possession of the statuary.

They saw the ship. On the dockside in the gray October morning
light the SS *Angkor*, they agreed, bore a name that was foreordained.

They sailed Friday the thirteenth, in first class and without return
tickets. Their plan was to travel east around the world. Once in possession of their treasures, they would proceed to Hong Kong and to
Yokohama. From the Japanese port they would cross the Pacific and
see America "backwards," from San Francisco to New York, where
they would deliver their cargo before sailing home across the
Atlantic.

"That's asking too much."

"A pity. Then I'll want ten at least, and te‌ all told."

"Twenty sculptures."

"Feasible, I think."

"Don't forget that a single bas-relief, if it's firs‌ for instance, sells for at least 200,000 francs."†

"How many stones would it take?"

"Three or four."[2]

Somewhat against Clara's will, it was decided tha‌ hood friend Louis Chevasson would join them on‌ Clara didn't like the short and good-looking bachel‌ André had gone to school for six years and acted out Du‌ the Bondy forest. She thought Chevasson too impractic‌ lous for a jungle expedition and called him "the colorle‌ cause he never seemed to have any opinion. She had to a‌ ever, that once in the bush with the hacksaws, a third pai‌ might be more than useful.

André asked Joseph Hackin and the Guimet Museum boa‌ bers for a meeting. When the administrators and curators he‌ outline his desire to study Khmer art in Indochina, entirely‌ own cost, they were amazed by his knowledge. This young ‌ who lived in a townhouse in Passy and was the author of a numl‌ articles and a whimsical little *édition de luxe* novel in the c‌ vein—wanted to undertake an expedition that wouldn't cost the g‌ ernment anything, yet might eventually add to the prestige of Frer‌ scholarship.

"Why should we turn up our noses?" Hackin asked when the tim‌ came for the board to consider the request.

A *charge de mission* dated October 1, 1923, was duly signed by the new minister of colonies and complemented with letters of recommendation to the Far-Eastern School in Hanoi and to Henri Parmen-

---

† About $46,000 in 1989 currency.

[2] *La Voie Royale* (Paris: Grasset, 1930); *The Royal Way*, translated by Stuart Gilbert (New York: Smith and Haas, 1935).

⚈ 3. SEAFARERS

The first time Clara had seen the sea was one summer when Maurice was at camp and Paul stayed behind in the nursery, and her father took his wife and daughter to the Riviera.

Clara was nine years old and thought the ocean was tiny, limited by the coastline and the horizon, which she had imagined bigger and much farther away. A flying machine drifting over Nice and the glittering bay was more surprising. Her mother and she wore dresses, hats, and gloves on the Promenade des Anglais; her father was in striped cotton suits and sported straw hat and cane. On the pier he lifted Clara up to show her the water below.

André was the grandson, great-grandson, and great-great-grandson of seafarers. The Malrauxs were a Flemish clan that had lived between Calais and Dunkirk for centuries. The etymology of the family name perhaps derived via Mallaert from Indo-European *mal-ruk* and made it mean "ill-turned plow."* If André's father was some-

---

* With Malraux pronounced Mal-ro, this book adopts the literate French fashion of forming adjectives from archaic aux noun endings: Malrucian (instead of such unpronounceable ones as Malrauxian or Malrauxesque).

thing of an eccentric, his grandfather Alphonse was a character. The son of Louis Malraux, a commander of fishing fleets who died at sea, Alphonse was a master cooper, outfitter, and ship's chandler, proud of his master title and of his fleet bringing cod from the Grand Banks off Newfoundland. He had married Mathilde Antoine late in life and had three sons and two daughters, with André's father Fernand in the middle.

Like his father, Alphonse apparently never learned French but spoke the Flemish dialect of the Belgian border dunes. He was a querulous and forgetful man. He forgot to insure his boats (some accounts have it that he found insurance somehow immoral) and one night lost several of his ships, including *La Zaca*, his best vessel, in a storm. This brought him close to ruin as he doled out most of his remaining wealth to the widows of his drowned men. He never completely recovered, became secretive, and almost shut himself off from his children. He cursed his fate and, because he was in revolt against his parish priest over some canon-law trespass, could be seen on Sundays kneeling outside the church, railing against God for having brought him to despair but determined to remain within earshot of the house of God.

André was eight years old when, one winter day, grandfather Alphonse (who was in his sixty-seventh year) got so frustrated watching a ship boy's clumsy attempt at splitting wood that he took the axe from the lad to show him. Forgetting it was double-headed, he swung the axe above his head so mightily he split his own skull. He died a few hours later in a hospital.

André would forget the facts but never the legends about the old man. And he would remember the big stone house in Dunkirk with its tiled walls. The house went to Alphonse's eldest son Maurice and stood there above the harbor and the gray Channel until it collapsed in a hail of bombs in 1940, when German air power and armor drove defeated British and French forces into the sea.

André's uncle became deputy mayor of Dunkirk, and his wife recalled André's childhood visits. "Very early, he had a marked personality, but we were never able to get him to talk about his future. 'You will see' was all he'd answer. When he was ten he surprised us one day. He had hurt one knee very badly and for a while we were afraid the leg might have to be amputated. Doctors and surgeons, surrounded by the family, held a hushed consultation. When the physicians were ready to leave, André, from his bed, said, 'I won't see you to the door, gentlemen.' "

Despite his disclaimer that he hated his childhood and couldn't grow up fast enough, Malraux's early years were to ring through his fiction. Like his own father, Grabot's father in *The Royal Way* dabbled in household inventions, and André's grandfather was to be evoked in three of his books. The *Anti-Memoirs*[1] contained savant mixes of transposed memory and acknowledged recollections. Ostensible portraits of the Alsatian Berger family included such paragraphs as the description of the grandfather's funeral:

> As the *foie gras* succeeded the crayfish and trout and raspberry brandy followed the Traminer wine at the funeral dinner, the reunion showed signs of developing into a festivity. Thousands of years have not sufficed to teach people how to observe death. The smell of pine and resin drifting through the open windows, and the innumerable objects of polished wood, united them all in the memories and secrets of a common past, of childhoods spent in the shared surroundings of the family forestry business; and as they recalled my grandfather, they vied with one another in the affectionate deference which death permitted them to show unreservedly toward the rebellious old burgher whose inexplicable suicide seemed to crown his life with a secret.

A page later, the grandfather's falling out with the Church and his stubborn attendance of mass outside the parish church is remembered:

> Thereafter, cut off from the Church but not from Christ, he attended mass every Sunday outside the building, standing in the nettles in an angle made by the nave and the transept, following the service from memory and straining to hear through the stained-glass to catch the frail sound of the handbell announcing the Elevation. Gradually he

[1] *Antimémoires* (Paris: Gallimard, 1967); translated as *Anti-Memoirs* by Terence Kilmartin (New York: Holt, Rinehart and Winston, 1968).

grew deaf and, afraid of missing the bell, ended up spending twenty minutes on his knees in the summer nettles or the winter mud. His enemies said he was no longer in his right mind, but such unyielding perseverance is not readily dismissed, and for most people this figure with the short white beard and frock coat, kneeling in the mud beneath his umbrella, in the same place, at the same time and for the same purpose for so many years, seemed not so much a crackpot as a just man.

Fernand Malraux was a ruggedly handsome inventor of better mousetraps, a director of ephemeral companies, a believer in dizzy financial schemes, a stock market habitué and a ladies' man with few principles but a big heart. Fernand had not wanted to earn his living on the sea. He was going into business for himself, and as a strapping youngster with a flattering mustache and a sonorous laugh he went to Paris. He had visited Spain once, hated it so much he swore never to leave France again—and never did. Something of a dreamer, with a gift for caricature, he knew his way with gourmet foods and the new century's new ideas. His favorite aphorism was "You must always mistrust yourself."

When Fernand was twenty-five, he fell in love with Berthe Lamy, a tall pretty girl who was eighteen but looked younger. Berthe was the daughter of a farmer and came from the Alps. Her widowed mother, who bore the stately name of Adriana Romania, was of Italian descent and lived with an unmarried daughter in Bondy, still a semi-rural working-class suburb, and managed a modest grocery. Berthe was two months pregnant when Fernand and she got married. They moved into a big apartment at 73 Rue Damremont, a long, prosaic street running down the less-than-picturesque northern slope of Montmartre. Georges André Malraux was born there November 3, 1901.

Little André—the Georges was dropped while he was still an infant—was a serious only child. He spent his first years quietly in the big apartment with his mother when his father didn't sweep him off his feet during irregular if boisterous eruptions into his and his mother's life. Fernand was always elsewhere, it seemed, busy making money. Losing it, too, and recouping. The excitements of André's preschool years were playing in the Parc Monceau and visiting his grandmother and aunt in Bondy, a trip that took two hours via Metro and trolley car. The big events were taking the train all the way out to Dunkirk to visit his father's family.

By the time Alphonse felled himself with the twin-blade axe Berthe and Fernand were separated and André and his mother living with his maternal grandmother and aunt in Bondy. If business hadn't lured Fernand from home and hearth, women had. He lived in an apartment in town and, in the absence of parental candor, it took André several adolescent years to realize his parents were divorced and that his father was living with a Mademoiselle named Godard.

Fernand's inventions, which included a necktie hanger and an antisplash faucet, had naturally led him to the most amazing of new creations, the automobile. He had come up with various electrical starters and a fuel-injection shield that he had managed to market, but his crowning feat was a skidproof tire, exhibited at the Concours Lepine, the new annual competition organized by Paris police chief Louis Lepine and endowed with numerous prizes and medals to encourage small manufacturers' ingenuity.

Fernand's heroes were men who quickened the pulse of the century with astounding creations—Edison's incandescent bulb, Roentgen's X-ray tube—but his heart was especially with France's men of progress: Fernand de Lesseps for building the Suez Canal, Gustave Eiffel for his tower, André Citroen (another Lepine exhibitor) for his automobile gear train, and Louis Blériot for being the first man to cross the Channel in a flying machine. The handmaiden of progress was commerce, and even before the war Fernand invested aggressively in the stock market. At one point he seems to have been the Paris agent for an American bank, although the name of the financial institution he represented was never revealed.

It was a heady and flamboyant era, and Paris was its epicurean center, a most fabulous city with its noble architecture, its boulevards, smart shops, adventurous artists, celebrated fashions, elegant women, and racy nightlife. Governments might succeed each other at a dizzy pace, but France was nevertheless politically stable and economically sound. It was optimistic and expansionist—at home democratic reforms, freedom of the press, secularized free education, and abroad new colonies. Everybody sang the ditty about Le Père Bugeau losing his hat conquering Algeria.

Colonial expansion never excited the minds of the French as it did the British, but most of north and central Africa was nevertheless French. Indochina had been French since the 1860s, conquered by a handful of soldiers, Madagascar since 1897. In all, France now counted some three million square miles of overseas territory and a colonial population twice the size of that of France itself—one hundred million people.

Colonialism, for Clara and André, began with the cabin assignments. The rigid class system aboard the SS *Angkor* was both metaphor and premonition of the world beyond the prow, of a society Clara and André had never known. The month-long voyage made a profound impression on them.

With them in first class traveled the top administrators and their wives, beginning or returning to a tour of duty. On the deck below were the middle-rung civil servants and the *colons* or settlers, the French merchants and craftsmen determined to carve their stake out of the colonies. In steerage were the Chinese tradespeople, Vietnamese students, and other polyglot colonials. "Given his habit of speaking his mind," Walter Langlois was to write in a book on Malraux's Asian experiences, "young, brilliant, liberal and haughty André must have made quite a few enemies and very few friends during the long voyage across the Indian Ocean."[2]

Clara and André saw the outline of Sicily as the *Angkor* crossed the Mediterranean to Port Said in four days. The passage through the Suez Canal made Clara look east toward Mount Sinai and wonder whether it would have been any easier to distinguish the tribe of her Hebrew ancestors against the yellow, sienna, and saffron vastness of the desert than to spot a boat on the ocean horizon.

"Between Europe and Asia were a protracted span of days filled with reverie, yearnings, hopes, boredom, weariness and heat that ventilation holes in the sleeves were supposed to alleviate," Clara

---

[2] Walter Langlois, *André Malraux: L'Aventure Indochinoise* (Paris: Mercure de France, 1967)

would write in *Nos Vingt Ans,* the second volume of her memoirs.[3] "There were games on the deck, where quoit replaced *boules.* There were ping-pong matches, festivities, sometimes costume parties, and deck chairs set out next to each other. There were strolls around the deck that you meticulously counted, amusing promenades where you discovered that new twosomes had been formed and that other pairings had been dissolved. And there were boring trots that were good for the health. Bets were laid on how fast we were sailing. On foggy nights there was the melancholy fog horn. There was the news posted at noon, with the attendant surprise that a world existed beyond this ship cruising toward goals that were different for each of its passengers."

And there were the ports of call. In Port Said, little boys offered dirty postcards and their sisters at the quayside. In Djibouti in French Somaliland at the other end of the Red Sea, they plunged into nameless streets deserted in the noonday heat and saw famished goats which, to prevent them from suckling each other to death, had their teats encased in small sacks. The evening cool brought out a polyglot population: Somalis, Isas, Afars, Yemenites, Greeks, Armenians, Italians, and Indians.

An excursion took Clara and André to cliff dwellings that looked like so many human honeycombs. At nightfall, beautiful girls danced naked for them. At first only the girls who had been paid danced, but the rhythms of the drums captivated the gowned female spectators. Carried away, they slipped out of their djellabas and joined. The pungent heat, Clara would remember, felt no longer oppressive but electrifying.

They had always been tourists with a taste for the spicier folklore. On their honeymoon they had toured the sights of vice in Vienna and Berlin, cities haunted by defeat, depravity, war cripples, hyper-

---

[3] Six volumes appeared under the overall title *Le Bruit de Nos Pas: Apprendre a Vivre, Nos Vingt Ans, Les Combats et les Jeux, Voici que Vient l'Eté, La Fin et le Commencement,* and *Et Pourtant J'etais Libre* (Paris: Grasset, 1963-1979). An English translation of selections of the first two volumes, translated by Patrick O'Brian, appeared as *Memoirs* (New York: Farrar, Straus & Giroux, 1967).

inflation, and artists with an acrid, edgy vision. Before they were married, André had dabbled in erotica, an activity that Clara, when they met, had found deliciously naughty.

As a teenager, bookbuying and bookselling had financed André's increasing independence from Bondy, his grandmother, mother, and aunt. At eighteen he bullied permission from his mother to look for a studio apartment in Paris while, to his astonishment, his newly demobilized father not only did not object but agreed to add to grandmother Adriana's monthly support.

Like the eighteenth-century poet Gérard de Nerval he admired, André had browsed through occult books since his early teens. In his wanderings through Paris, he noticed a new bibliophilic emporium near the Madeleine, an elegant rare-book shop called La Connaissance. He ventured in and on a second visit offered his services to the owners, Marcelle and René-Louis Doyon. Doyon was a litterateur of the first order and was soon impressed enough by the young man's expertise to offer him the position of *chineur*—in Parisian argot, a practice somewhere between ragpicking and secondhand dealing. The job consisted of combing secondhand bookstores in obscure sidestreets for volumes that would interest the select booklovers who browsed at La Connaissance. The postwar slide of the franc was beginning and many affluent Parisians found more security in a first-edition Mallarmé than in stocks and municipal bonds. Since he would be strictly on commission with no strings attached, André agreed.

He worked only in the morning and stayed home when it rained. He showed up at La Connaissance at 11:00 A.M. sharp with the previous day's catch—now an original edition of *Cyrano de Bergerac,* now an eighteenth-century bawdy text, fifteenth-century German mystics or poetry collections with signed woodcuts. Once money matters had been disposed of, André melted enough to talk. "He had very definite literary opinions and he wasn't short of sarcasm," Doyon would remember.[4] Doyon believed Malraux would be an art-

---

[4] René-Louis Doyon, *Memoire d'Homme* (Paris: Connaissance, 1953)

ist of some sort, though the young man also seemed to show a developed taste for good printing and an all-round talent for publishing.

André was no ladies' man at eighteen. He was nervously elegant but timid, and his first mistresses were not literary lionesses but easy pickups and little demimondaines. His writer friend Georges Gabory, whose audacious defense of the notorious woman-murderer Landru brought Florent Fels' *L'Action* magazine into trouble with police, was to remember him bragging poetically about one girl who, he said, "possessed the trifling grace of a young monkey."[5]

Evenings were spent on Montmartre. With Gabory and several other young men, André dropped in on a painter or a poet, sometimes Max Jacob in his Rue Gabrielle studio.

André, who earned more than the others and often showed up in a dashing Baudelairean cape, high collar, and moleskin gloves, preferred to dine at flashier tables—Larue's or Noel Peters—but if Jacob was along dinner was at La Mère Anceau, a bistro where Max loved the mutton stew. It was there that André first met the painter Maurice Utrillo. "With his heavy eyelashes rising on the forsaken void of his eyes he asked me, 'Painter or poet?,' sat down and fell asleep," André remembered fifty years later.

Over dessert, Max began to draw—on paper when paper was available, or on napkins or the tablecloth—dozens of sketches of friends and fellow diners in an evening. His sketches of André would all disappear—"transformed," as one of Malraux's French biographers would ask, "into french-fry wrappers or burned when the Gestapo sent Jacob to his death in the Drancy concentration camp in 1944?"[6]

Sometimes they finished the night on the seamier side, at a *bal musette* behind the Bastille; at the noisy Tabarin, where one of them might pick up a girl; at one of the new jazz clubs; or the raunchiest of gay bars on the Place de Ravignan, where Paris' most notorious

---

[5] Georges Gabory, "Souvenirs sur André Malraux," in *Mélanges Malraux Miscellany*, No 11; Lexington: University of Kentucky Press, 1970.

[6] Jean Lacouture, *André Malraux: Une Vie Dans le Siecle* (Paris: Seuil 1972); translated by Alan Sheridan (New York: Praeger, 1976).

"tantes" gathered. "We were young, Malraux and I, and easily impressed by the display of real or put-on depravity," Georges Gabory recalled.

When Doyon decided to expand his literary activities and publish a monthly magazine, he naturally asked his young *chineur* to collaborate. When the first issue appeared in January 1920, *La Connaissance* included an article signed André Malraux, a rather taxing piece of writing on the rage of the day—cubist poetry.[7]

André was also interested in editing, and persuaded the Doyons to let him edit two obscure nineteenth-century texts. André's taste for *le fantastique*—that untranslatable Gallic term meaning as much the surreal and the otherworldly as spine-chilling science fiction and demonology—made him choose a stigmatized Bavarian nun's hallucinatory retracing of the Passion and a supposedly edifying treatise full of divination, black magic, devil worship, and witchcraft.

André didn't feel he owed Doyon any allegiance and he soon met two other marginal publishers. One was Lucien Kra, a former circus hand who dreamed of matching a competitor's success in erotica. André soon found two little-known texts by the Marquis de Sade for him. Published with dadaist drawings, the little volume became a kind of under-the-counter best-seller.[8] Florent Fels, who with his demobilization bonus had founded *L'Action,* brought André under a healthier and more dynamic sway than the semi-clandestine publishers of erotica. It was at a luncheon given by Fels for thirty intimate and not-so-close collaborators that Clara and André met.

The *Angkor* crossed the Indian Ocean along the 5-degree-north latitude line. Although Clara and André told themselves it was bourgeois and silly, they were nevertheless pleased when one night they were invited to the captain's table.

The first Asian landfall of the voyage was in Colombo, Ceylon,

---

[7] See Axel Madsen, *Malraux: A Biography* (New York: Morrow, 1976).

[8] Actually excerpts from de Sade novels, *Les Amis du Crime,* illustrated by a painter named Moras, and *Le Bordel de Venise,* illustrated with "scandalous" watercolors by G.A. Drains, appeared without Kra's publishing imprimateur.

the next in honey-scented Penang on the Malaysian peninsula, where the rains never stopped. Clara and André went ashore in Penang with a newlywed couple, the husband a civil servant, the wife with few illusions about the life awaiting her. On high heels after a Chinese puppet show, Clara walked a little behind the others, her head under a broad-brimmed southwester. Crossing a line of flagstones that served as a bridge, she missed her step and fell into a rain-swollen open sewer.

The current swept her toward a tunnel running under several houses. Floating, sinking, and bobbing up again she knew she was drowning and imagined her body being found on a sandbank where the conduit reached the sea. A second flagstone bridge was coming up. She heard shouts her and saw André and the couple lying flat on the slab reaching down toward her.

They got hold of her and pulled her to safety.

A fire in the *Angkor's* holds delayed their arrival in Singapore, the port city of British Malaya, and made them miss a boat to Bangkok. Too short of funds to wait for the next Bangkok-bound ship, they decided to continue to Saigon aboard the *Angkor*.

"We discovered England through her colonies," Clara would write, "the big breakfast, the afternoon tea, lawns in front of houses, long dresses and white tuxedos."

Singapore was remembered for its Victorian monuments and the Raffles Hotel, one of the most opulent in the Orient, where Somerset Maugham had written *The Moon and Sixpence* in the Palm Court and Asians were not allowed to stay. At the bar they learned to drink Singapore Slings and in their room a "boy" with a string around a toe pulled a huge overhead fan from behind a screen all night. Clara discovered inch-long insects with brilliant brown wing-sheaths in the bathroom one day and called André.

"A kind of cicada," she said, pointing. "And, look, they are not afraid of humans."

He bent over the tub. "They're cockroaches, silly."

Twenty-nine days after leaving Marseille, they were steaming up the Saigon River. The "Indochina French" stood leaning on the railing, telling Clara how happy they were to be home, "talking about the docile 'boys' waiting for them in their houses full of embroidery, chiseled silverware and jade they believed to be antique."

After disembarking Clara and André drank a glass of real pastis, the kind that drove alcoholics blind and was outlawed in France, but was still to be found in the colonies.

4. SAIGON, HANOI, AND PNOMPENH

French Indochina was ruled from Hanoi, not Saigon. After visiting the picturesque Rue Catinat, after seeing Mediterranean-type houses surrounded by iridescent green gardens shaded by tamarind trees with huge brownish pods and royal poincianas with scarlet and orange flowers, and deciding that Saigon reminded them of a French provincial town laid out in geometric patterns, they were off to the administrative capital.

The letters of recommendation from the Guimet Museum and André's own missive had indeed preceded them, but after they checked into a modest European hotel, put on their best tropical white, and showed up at L'École Française d'Extrême-Orient, they were told Henri Parmentier was out of town. In any case, Monsieur Malraux would have to see Monsieur Finot first.

André made an appointment with the director of the college, and at the appointed hour was whisked into the office of Louis Finot—a man in his fifties with the sallow look that, André had noticed, many Europeans seemed to have after living a few years in the tropics.

Finot rose from his desk facing the window, which framed a clump of palms, and a wall stained blue-green by rains and cordially greeted his visitor. The letters of recommendation from Paris were in front of him.

André eased into the conversation by talking about art and the disintegration that was taking place in antique works. Primitive art raised stupendous questions, he said, and challenged the very foundation of Western optimism. He was careful not to sound too obscure nor too eager.

"Archeology is not my discipline," the director warned.

Finot knew little about Khmer art, but after listening to the young amateur archeologist, he was perspicacious enough to find the Malraux "mission" improvised if not a bit shady.

"You intend to explore the regions lying along the line of the ancient Royal Road of the Khmers?" Finot summed up.

"That's right."

"I may as well tell you that the trail—not to mention the road itself—is wiped out over long stretches, and near the Dangrek range disappears completely."

"I am sure I will find it," André smiled.

"Well, let's hope so, for your sake. It is my duty, my official duty, to warn you of the danger you will incur."

As the director read the letters of recommendation in front of him, it occurred to André that the man's pallid and pasty appearance was probably due to an abscess of the liver.

"When will you be starting out?" Finot asked.

"As soon as possible."

Finot said he would of course issue the supply warrant that would allow André to procure native carts and drivers through the resident deputy in Siem Reap.

As the director got up, André realized he could not pretend to be both a detached scholar and a fearless adventurer. Also, he was smart enough to understand the director's warning.

"You can pass by my office tomorrow," Finot said, escorting him to the door. "The supply warrant will be waiting for you."

To while away the week until Professor Parmentier returned, they visited the town, the governor-general's residence behind the old citadel, the mixed quarter at the bottom of the Paul Doumer Bridge, the three European quarters, the elegant Rue Paul Bert with, at the eastern end, the military headquarters, and the Vietnamese and Chinese markets around the Rue de la Soie. Merchants in minuscule stalls steamed, grilled, stewed, broiled, and stir-fried an assortment of food and, to entice customers, wafted the fascinating, spicy smells toward strolling passersby with palmleaf fans. They saw Vietnamese women in silk pajamas and with lacquered teeth, and "boys" who always wore black turbans. Both Clara and André were struck by the pallid faces of the European women. Apparently it was the height of colonial chic to look like a figure in a wax museum. Europeans didn't walk; they had themselves transported in rickshaws pulled by spindly-legged coolies.

When it wasn't raining, Clara and André walked, defiantly. When afternoon downpours threatened, they stayed at the hotel. They were too poor by now to buy the raingear that would protect Clara's spare wardrobe and André's one tropical suit.

They were surprised by the throngs of children and the noise in the street, the corner soup-seller blowing on the charcoal in his brazier, the chauffeurs driving barefooted, an irritated European dressing down a hotel doorman, getting angry at his "boy," at his Vietnamese mistress. They did their tourist shopping, buying beautiful gray bowls and stoneware spoons from street vendors. In one side-street they discovered a freak show. Craning their heads in front of a house with ornate Chinese doorpost carvings, they managed to see windows with odd animals—a three-legged hen, a turtle whose shell had been removed. "Come in, the lady will be happy to see you," an adolescent cried out.

The lady was old but was indeed happy to have a visit. She had shared a French doctor's life once, she said. The ceiling was painted, and in one corner she had a replica of the Eiffel Tower and everywhere wind-up toys.

In the backyard she showed them a mechanical dwarf dressed as a Western youth. Clara touched the automaton's chin and felt the crabbed imitation of human skin. The lady grinned. "I collect monsters," she said.

The hotel room had shutters but no glass panes. The bed, however, came with mosquito netting. Taking an afternoon siesta while André was meeting school officials, Clara felt her fears drain away. Since her dunking in the Malaysian sewer, she felt in an odd way cleansed. They were in the fabulous Orient. Street odors and noises were already familiar. White people complained ritualistically about the climate, but André and she found Vietnam not much more sweltering than Greece. True, it was more clammy, but Clara's fair skin seemed to adapt well to the humidity. If anything, the heat inspired their lovemaking with novel voluptuousness.

Early on, both had been inhibited and sensitive about their physical flaws. Whether André's mother thought she was preparing her son for life's hard knocks or was reacting to her own conjugal disappointments, she had always told André he was ugly. He had big ears and his loose build was sometimes ungainly, but, as the wife of his first publisher would tell Clara, "At thirty, you'll see, he'll be handsome."

The feminine fashion required hip-length jackets flared or waisted over long narrow skirts; hats; muffler; and the new buckled shoes, the accessory of 1922. Clara was keenly aware that she didn't have the boyish figure that the decade demanded. She had tried with low-slung belts and oppressive bras to attain the flat-chested flapper look, but he grazed her most sensitive nerve when, seeing her naked for the first time, he expressed his astonishment at not finding her looking more like an ephebe.

André had lost his virtue the traditional way, with little Montmartre prostitutes, the year before he met Clara; she had tried sex with a boyfriend the year she turned twenty-two. Identified only as Jean in her memoirs, the young man was in the army, a pastor's son from southern France, a friend of her brother Paul.

Clara had her hair cut in the new short fashion and went dancing with Jean in skirts as short as Chanel demanded. Jean called her his "little princess," read poems to her, and had her all flustered when he kissed her and let his hand slide up her new silk stockings.

She had asked Maurice whether she should become engaged. "Why not," he had answered.

From his training camp, Jean wrote her letters every day.

"My parents will never accept us getting married," he told her. He wanted to be important to her, and after their first confused tryst, said, "You must understand, we can't go on like this. I must mean more to you than sex."

"I don't care," she whispered.

He became angry. "I can't be the love of a woman who tells me she doesn't care."

That was not how she had meant it. But after that they quarreled all the time. He was late for their dates and implied that other women were panting after him. When the year-long engagement was over, she told herself she would die of sorrow. Instead she went to Italy and spent four months studying art in Florence.

They sipped rum-sodas, the national drink among expatriates, on faculty verandas and improvised themselves as archaeologists. Suspicions were aroused when André asked about shipping heavy baggage from Pnompenh back down the Mekong River for forwarding from Saigon. Offhandedly, school officials warned them. A governor-general's regulation of 1908 declared that all "discovered and undiscovered" monuments in Siem Reap, Battambang, and Sisiphon provinces must be left in situ. A new decree further protecting Khmer antiquities was not only on the legislative agenda, as André knew all too well, but was supposed to have been enacted in Paris a few weeks before.

The risk only added to André's determination and sense of adventure. Besides, Professor Parmentier turned out to be a delightful old fogy. André had done his homework. The moment he met the chief of archeology, he charmed the goateed scholar with his erudition and enthusiasm. A cocktail party was called for, Parmentier decreed, before the young couple went off to prove their devotion to archeology.

"Perhaps I will accompany you to Angkor," Parmentier beamed.

Finot was at the cocktail party, but it was Parmentier who held forth. He had no high opinion of such steamy authors of exotica as Pierre Loti, whose novels had enchanted Clara and André in Paris.

"Loti speaks of vultures crowding in banana trees," Parmentier cried, "when everybody knows a banana branch will bend too much to support a single vulture."

The professor spoke both authoritatively and lyrically about the

Khmers, of all Asians the only people to show a true genius for architecture. While the Annamese, as the Chinese called the Vietnamese, had been under China's domination for over a thousand years, the Cambodians had fallen under the gentler sway of India.

"The monsoons and the alternating trade winds favored maritime relations," Parmentier said. "Like Burma and Thailand to the east and Malaysia on the other side of the Gulf of Siam, Cambodia virtually owed its existence to the creative influence of India."

"Not conquest or invasion, but trade and, in its wake, Buddhism, the merchants' religion," he continued. "No forced conversions but ideas that various tribes adopted because the people found them useful. Indian Brahmins brought Hindu deities, Sanskrit language and literature, and the Indian alphabet, but not the strict rules of caste and society of their homeland."

More positive than the peoples of India, who avoided any precision that might hinder the flight of the imagination, the ancient Cambodians took literally the idea that a temple should be an image of the cosmos and therefore built their temples in the form of a mountain.

"In the heart of the jungle," Parmentier enthused, "five towers with slender spires dominate the great building of Angkor Wat, a temple of Vishnu that you may call the Parthenon of the East because of the perfect harmony of lines and sculptural decorations. Khmer sculpture is the most exquisite in the Orient. Indeed, it compares favorably to classic Greek art."

André told the professor how he had discovered art when he was seven. What had struck him while walking through the Louvre were Leonardo da Vinci's paintings because they had pretty skies. "for years, I thought Leonardo was a sky specialist."

One Sunday when his mother had visited a friend at the Place d'Iena he had been allowed to cross the square and see the Guimet. What he found were as yet unsorted Asian art and artifacts that Guimet, the industrialist and amateur archeologist and musician, had brought back. Another temple of eccentric exotica where the adolescent André had daydreamed was the Trocadero Museum across the Seine from the Eiffel Tower. Here visitors could see a plumed helmet from the kingdom of Hawaii exhibited next to an absurd miniature of a palace in Cadiz, next to Montezuma's headdress.

André told Parmentier how the famous Angkor "smile" of the Banyon period had struck him at the Guimet. Buddha was carved with his eyes lowered, as though absorbed in meditation, while a faint smile on his lips reveals the serene detachment of those who have given up all worldly things and aspire to nirvana.

"The inner walls of Angkor are decorated with relief panels depicting scenes from the mythological life of Vishnu," the professor said. "The effect is overwhelming. An American has said these reliefs have the character of an exotic, noble, and measured ritual ballet not unlike the dance performed today by the court dancers of Pnompenh." Clara told Parmentier how the performance of the Royal Ballet of Pnompenh had enchanted her and André.

The conversation turned to the apsaras, of which, the professor informed them, there were 1750 life-sized figures at Angkor Wat. "To some observers the celestial dancers seem affected and monotonous," he smiled, "to me they are Grace personified, the highest expression of femininity ever conceived by the human mind."

When André was out of earshot, Parmentier leaned toward Clara and with a nod toward her husband said, "So young and so wealthy. So disinterested too."

The professor gave them his enthusiastic endorsement and said he would telegraph ahead and arrange for his man at Angkor to meet them and perhaps help them get native guides and provisions. Before the evening was over, Parmentier was so infatuated with the young couple that he insisted on coming with them as far as Pnompenh.

The rainy season was exceptionally long in Southeast Asia in 1923, and the Mekong was still swollen in early December when, after picking up Louis Chevasson in Saigon, the quartet sailed up the delta toward Pnompenh.

André and Louis wore identical tropical suits, wing-collared white shirts, black string ties, and pith helmets. The diminutive Clara thought herself too ridiculous in a cork helmet and defiantly wore a Chinese peasant's cone-shaped straw hat. Parmentier, who had his Cambodian "boy" with him, covered his white locks under a tropical helmet that had seen better days.

Louis and André had been friends since the sixth grade in L'École de Bondy, a rather modest private school where the principal and a teacher named Monsieur Malaval taught twenty students in two classes. Louis had been a short, dark boy who lived around the corner from Grandma Adriana Romania's grocery store.

In 1914, they had been only three weeks from the start of their final year at Bondy when the guns of August thundered. The German blow came on the front where French generals had said it couldn't happen—through Belgium. By the third week of August, the main force of the German army was sweeping over the Franco-Belgian border. The German advance wavered before Paris, and on August 30 General Alexander von Kluck turned his army southeast, passing to the east of Paris instead of enveloping the city. The French and the British forces rallied and fresh forces, transported to the front in six hundred Paris taxicabs, rumbled through Bondy to strike the flank of Kluck's army on the Marne. André and Louis saw the taxis roll east on the Meaux highway. At night they could hear the big guns.

On September 6, 1914, when the French and British stood and fought and produced the "miracle" of the Marne, the Germans were less than thirty miles from Bondy.

By then Bondy, France, and Europe had settled into war. André could hold his head as high as any. Fernand Malraux and his mistress Mademoiselle Godard might be the parents of a baby boy, but the thirty-eight-year-old entrepreneur had been among the first to volunteer. André's half-brother was named Roland.

Professor Malaval celebrated the "miracle" of the Marne by taking his class on a tour of the previous week's battlefield. There had been little time to bury the dead; the bodies were piled up, soaked with gasoline and burned—a sight Malaval spared his charges by ordering lunch. "At lunchtime," André would write in the *Antimemoires* forty years later, "bread was handed around to us, which we dropped, terror-stricken, because the wind covered it with a light sprinkling of ash from the dead piled up a little farther off."[1]

Peace gave André a second half-brother. Fernand Malraux re-

---

[1] André Malraux, *Antimemoires*.

turned a tank commander and, true to his promise, married the mother of his two young sons. He did not bring his new wife to Clara and André's wedding, but one weekend, when Clara and André were not invited to the Golls or the Kahnweilers, they took the train to Orleans to visit André's father and family in the house he had bought. For the first time André met his stepmother.

Fernand was in semi-retirement and, with Roland intensely interested in this adult half-brother and little Claude perpetually crying, the war veteran talked endlessly about the pleasures of being French and on lurking alien dangers. Clara didn't try to argue with her father-in-law, but on the way back to Paris tore into André. She might lack Fernand's firsthand experience of German perfidy and her husband's notion that a certain historical perspective was necessary in order to understand this latest conflict, but to her, she said in an angry crescendo, the organized murder of nine million Frenchmen, Germans, Russians, Serbians, Americans, Italians, Englishmen, Turks, and Belgians had been a meaningless if not criminal slaughter.

They were outside the Gare d'Orleans looking for a taxi when André said he had found the charge of the Saint-Cyr cadets in the beginning of the war admirable.

"I know that charge. One of my brother's friends was one of its victims."

André maintained that the gesture had been gallant.

She said he was wasting his rhetoric of fustian chivalry, honor, and sacrifice on her. In fact, she had no trouble imagining Maurice's friend shouting "Follow me!" over his shoulder and running up the hill in his royal blue uniform jacket, scarlet trousers, and silly parade kepi that the dumbest of German infantrymen would have no trouble keeping in his gunsight.

"The gesture was beautiful," André maintained.

"It was useless. It was the gesture of a murderer."

A cab pulled up to them. They got in.

"You have no sense of grandeur, no sense of nuance," André continued.

"When you defend a gesture like that you're as stupid as the Saint-Cyr cadets."

"And you, when you talk like that, you're such a Jewish coward."

Calmly she asked the taxi driver to stop. When he did, she got out. The cab moved off.

She walked. André came running back toward her. "You're crazy."

"You called me a Jewish coward."

"You started it. You told me I was just as dumb as a military cadet."

"I admit I'm wrong there," she sighed. "You're not that stupid. But at least when I insult you, I don't use stereotypes."

They argued the rest of the evening, storming upstairs without saying hello to Mme. Goldschmidt, slamming doors, bickering in the shower. Exhausted, they finally agreed they were saying the same thing, that the war had made them challenge the views they grew up with. The whole of Europe had been lied to. The generals had lied about the nature and the length of the war and the politicians had lied about its causes. That was what separated them from the previous generations, what increased the distance between the old and the young, what made the new artists hate all forms of authority, all traditional modes. They told each other they could never go back to what they repudiated, their parents' burned-out order. Because even if in a weak moment they might be tempted, the lecturing and sermonizing they'd be subjected to would make them run away again.

Parmentier commented on the dense settlements along the Mekong, the Cambodian stilt huts, and on the complicated river itself. The river may start in China and be navigable only below Savannakhet; the most interesting feature was nevertheless the Tonle Sap lake where they were heading. At floodtime, water from the Mekong flowed into the Tonle Sap to make it three times its normal size. As the Mekong floods subsided in early spring, the lake re-established its normal flow, thus acting as a natural flood protection for the entire delta. The Khmers believed the Mekong flowed both toward its source and toward the sea, and on the day they observed the flow change the king went out in a boat to cut a ribbon stretched from shore to shore. "When the waters recede," Parmentier said, "Cambodians walk out and with their bare hands pick up the fish that, when marinated in huge barrels, produce the *nuoc-mam* fish sauce without which no Cambodian or Vietnamese meal is complete."

In Pnompenh, where the professor would leave them, Clara, André, and Louis visited the royal museum and made last purchases before transferring to a riverboat for the trip to Tonle Sap. What they saw at the museum left them speechless—and their tour guide indifferent.

The man's European condescension and asinine commentaries, Clara would remember, made them almost feel good about their planned poaching. "When I asked this 'authority' which artwork he'd prefer—meaning really which one would *he* steal—he told me, 'Oh, I couldn't care less about their beauty. You know, I'm an architect.'"

André found Pnompenh full of rancid odors. Treetrunks along the river's edge had rings of dried froth marking the last monsoon rains. Everything smelled of warm mud drying in the sun and decaying animal matter. After meeting Victor Golubev, however, André and Clara agreed there was at least one clever European in Pnompenh. Only slightly older than they, Victor was a rather delicate intellectual with nervous dark eyes who (as he said) wore two if not three hats. A teacher at the French college and an archeologist, he was also the sometime correspondent for *L'Impartial,* Saigon's major daily. "Don't be fooled by the title," he smiled, "the newspaper cannot write anything with impartiality. It's partially owned by the governor."

They couldn't afford tents. The nights would be warm enough in any case, so they bought field cots and tulle for mosquito netting. Golubev approved of Clara's homemade jungle suits, and his Cambodian servant introduced Clara and André to a young man who said he knew how to cook white people's food, how to bake bread, sew and iron, and wasn't afraid of the jungle.

"What's your name?" André asked.

"Xa," he replied in broken but enthusiastic French. The bright-eyed youth was no more than eighteen, Clara guessed.

She and André reasoned they would surely need someone who spoke the language and wasn't afraid of the bush. Xa was thin but sturdily built. His bare feet in his leather sandals were wide and calloused. His skin was light brown. Around his waist was a *krama*—the Cambodian all-purpose scarf. Clara liked the way he smiled, sure of himself; André sensed his resourcefulness. Xa was hired. After all, the treasure hunt was supposed to make them rich.

To transport their loot back to civilization they bought three huge, coffin-shaped chests made of camphorwood, which, Xa said, was the strongest wood there was.

With Xa helping, Clara, André and Louis were getting their gear aboard the riverboat that would take them to Siem Reap, the debarkation point for the Angkor Wat complex, when a European police captain came running. He exchanged a few words in Annamese with Xa. The boy seemed terrified and moved aside.

"I must warn you that your boy has been in jail," the official told André.

"What for?"

"Gambling, petty theft. You'd better look for another."

"I'll think about it."

"And certainly not give him an advance."

The captain was gray, from his stubbly hair to his canvas shoes. White people in the protectorate could not be imprisoned for debt, he told them. Natives could. "Anyhow, I've explained things to the boy," he continued. "He'll . . . well, he'll transmit your instructions to his successor."

The gendarme opened his mouth as if he had some further message. But with a little grunt, the captain only saluted and slowly strolled away along the dock, looking back to see how the European trio resolved the dilemma he had created.

Xa came over, humbled and anxious. His face had the look of a prematurely aged child, serious beyond his years.

"I don't give a damn about what the police just told me," said André. "All I ask is that you behave yourself with us."

Xa stared at André.

"You understand?"

"Yessir."

"You heard the captain tell me not to give you any advance. Well, here are five piasters."

Clara liked her husband's gesture. But when she looked down the quay, she saw the police captain was watching André handing Xa the money. Clara sensed they had made an enemy of the last white man before the bush.

There was one more representative of the law. At the sleepy anchor-

age of Siem Reap, a police sergeant who introduced himself as Brigadier Cremazy and told them he was also Director Finot's resident
deputy, greeted them with an automobile, offering to take them on a
tour of the Angkor Wat.

André handed the man Finot's warrant for supplies. Siem Reap
was perfumed with rancid fish sauce. Men and women bathed in the
palm-shaded river that meandered through town, lifting up their gar-
ments with extreme modesty as they allowed their bodies to sink into
the brown water. The houses were shacks standing on piles above
their refuse. Beside each was a receptacle raised on a post with offerings for wandering and neglected souls, people who had no descendants to provide for them. The women were dressed in saronglike
skirts of plain colors with a blouse hardly reaching the midriff. They
came sauntering out of the most squalid hovels clean, bright, and
pretty and with a ready smile of welcome.

André couldn't wait to get to Angkor Wat and at each turn of Cremazy's automobile strained to catch a glimpse of the temple towers
beyond the treetops unevenly bent toward the west by the lake
breezes.

Before the tour, however, Cremazy stopped at his residence to offer aperitifs and advice and to have them meet friends who would put
them up at their bungalow for a night or two. The closer they got to
the bush, Clara thought as their gray-bearded host poured Cinzano,
the more punctiliously European rituals were observed.

"You will need oxcarts, drivers," said Cremnazy, lifting his glass.
"And you will need a guide."

The veranda was hot and airless. André sipped his drink and, although he already had Xa, agreed that hiring a local guide might perhaps not be a bad idea.

"Well, you know, what you're out to do isn't an easy little jaunt. I
may as well tell you straight, those supply warrants don't cut much
ice in these parts, Oh, I know the fellows they send out on research
don't like to be told their business. Still. . . "

"Yes?"

"Well, it's just that what you're out to do isn't an easy little jaunt."

When André asked point-blank if Cremazy wouldn't execute the
supply warrant, the resident deputy backed down. "You're sent out

on an exploring job, well and good," Cremazy said. "You'll be given everything you need; don't you fret about that. Orders are orders, as they say."

André was ready to depart immediately, but Cremazy and his friends insisted they spend at least one night at the bungalow while wagons, drivers, and horses were organized. André asked Xa and Louis to get to work on this right away while Clara and he took up their host's offer of visiting the Angkor Wat. A couple of hours spent visiting the grandest and most complete monument left by the Khmers was probably the best initiation they could ask for.

Sitting with his drink at a rattan table, Cremazy added to his growing list of don'ts the suggestion that Monsieur and Madame Malraux call off their trip. "Go back to one of the big towns—Saigon, for example—and wait a bit," he said. "And, mind you, I know what I'm talking about."

André wasn't sure he understood what the man was trying to tell him. "You don't think I've come halfway around the world just to twiddle my thumbs in Saigon like a little tourist?" André said.

"As for coming halfway round the world, we've all done that in our time" was Cremazy's answer.

The more André listened, the more he realized there was little love lost between Cremazy and Finot. At one point the sergeant said he was not paid to give away secrets to André or anybody. Whether this meant he was angry at the administration in Hanoi or that he knew shortcuts he wasn't sure he'd give away for free André never found out, because their host pronounced himself ready for the Angkor Wat visit.

Clara felt the heat and the drinks on the veranda were having their effect on her. By the time she and André piled into Cremazy's car she was pretty tipsy. Honking his way past huts and villagers, the sergeant drove out of town on a road of red clay. The chirping of the cicadas was so shrill as to be audible above the rattle of the engine. Cremazy waved his hand toward a sudden glimpse of the horizon and, quoting Professor Parmentier, said, "Angkor Wat is dedicated to Vishnu, and it is the Parthenon of Southeast Asia."

Rows of stone lions guarded the causeway across the moat to the temple with its central tower and four towers in each corner of the great pyramid, symbolizing the sacred cosmic mountain. Cremazy and his guests began to walk toward the main rectangular enclosure. The aggressive usurper King Suryavarman II, whose rule extended the Khmer empire to encompass Siam and much of the Malay Peninsula, built the temple in the first half of the twelfth century. Clara had the impression she was in front of a baroque Versailles, a masterpiece of elaborate symmetry. André would remember their shoes getting caught in dislocated flagstones.

By the time they followed Finot's deputy through the towering gate pavilion whose winged roof rode down in steps to the level of the enclosure roof, André knew that Cremazy disliked and distrusted Cambodians. By the time they reached the central tower and the Shiva shrine with its enthralling stonework, André could barely contain his sarcasm at the inanities of the brigadier's guided tour.

André escaped the dim-witted observations by overwhelming the police sergeant with his own commentary. The lumpiness and stiffness of the free-standing sculptures clearly showed the genius of the artists who had worked here eight hundred years before.

"Their genius was for relief, sergeant. Every space is filled with pattern, the reliefs of celestial concubines."

"Is that what they are?" Cremazy asked.

"Asparas they are called in the Hindu tradition."

"There are exactly seventeen hundred fifty of them."

"Did you count them?"

'Parmentier did. He told me. I've got a head for figures."

The asparas were all carved standing in only slightly varied postures, hands and arms frozen in one of a dozen correct gestures. Framed in floral decorations, the reliefs illuminated not only the upper walls of the exterior galleries but also every angle and every window of the temple.

"And look," André sighed, "all display the famous smile."

Cremazy nodded.

"When we die," André explained, "we are, according to our merits, either punished in hell or carried off to the mountain peaks of heaven where the asparas, filled with unquenchable lust, await us."

Clara wanted to know what heavenly delights awaited women when they died.

André gave her a queer look. "The Hindu has no difficulty imagining himself born as a woman or bird in his next life."

"Then why does he treat women and birds as inferiors?"

"Societies who believe in reincarnation should not have hierarchies," André said with finality, "but they do."

Cremazy said he was a Catholic.

The temple was incompletely cleared. They wandered down identical passages and through identical courtyards, and then suddenly faced a wall, a wave of vegetation, in which the heavenly goddesses disappeared with decorous gestures. Back to the center, Clara decided to sit down for a minute and to let the two men inspect the open colonnaded gallery with its groups of divinely beautiful female courtiers.

Parmentier had taught Cremazy the exact number of celestial girls, and, as the sergeant said, he had a head for mathematics, because when he followed André's admiring gaze, he grinned and said "Three thousand five hundred gorgeous breasts!"

~~~ 5. INTO THE BUSH

In cork helmets and Clara's tropical getups and leggings, they were off. Water bottles, cameras, and compasses dangled from their necks and belts, while a rifle and two revolvers were hidden in their luggage.

With Xa, a local guide named Svai, and a dozen coolies, they rode into the bush on tough little horses that made André's long legs dangle comically. They were followed by four oxcarts with the camp cots, mosquito netting, stoves, saucepans, axes, crowbars, hacksaws, sledgehammers, ropes, the camphorwood chests, and Clara's pharmaceuticals. The procession advanced slowly along rice paddies, sparkling in the morning sun. Low earthen dikes divided the fields into irregular checkerboards. The men and women of the countryside were dressed in the same drab, saronglike skirt, in the men's case pulled into the shape of breeches by bringing the waist-sash through the legs.

After a while the primitive road entered the forest. Monkeys howled in banyan trees, mosquitos stung, and the slender trail became so narrow they had to ride in single column.

They rode all morning in the green stillness. "Stones hewn in advance can't be easy to find here," André said at one point. The trail wound through wide curves and almost seemed to double back on itself.

Xa, who never stopped smoking André's cigarettes, showed his talents during a noonday break. He set up folding chairs and table for Clara, André, and Louis, brought out glasses and napkins. He lit a fire in an abandoned anthill and, after deftly mixing wheat and water on a palm leaf, had little loaves baking in it.

Waiting for lunch, they talked strategy. According to their maps and hunches, the ruins were near the village of Rohal, thirty miles— two days' march—northwest of Siem Reap in the direction of Sisiphon and the Thai border. As far as they had been able to determine, no official had visited Banteai Srey since Parmentier had inventoried the site seven years ago.

"What we don't know," André said, "is whether the shrine has crumbled under the lianas or whether present-day Cambodians, like Romans during the Dark Ages, use the ruins as a quarry and haul off the masonry from their imperial past to build chimneys."

The state of their financial resources was such that they could no longer pretend to be on a high-minded excursion.

"Let's go directly to our ruins, to Rohal," André suggested.

Xa served them a European meal with the little baguettes baked in the anthill. Clara knew she would have to prove herself, but she was still apprehensive about the enclosing jungle.

"Anything that will make the expedition as short as possible is fine with me," Clara said.

Louis emitted no opinion.

Only Clara had ever ridden a horse before, and by midafternoon André and Louis were complaining of sore buttocks. She was up front following Svai, who walked ahead of the column. He had the handsomest male back she had ever seen. Naked to the waist and with the smoothest of tawny skins, his shoulders were glistening with rivulets of sweat. Svai was, she decided, a nimble-footed Khmer statue.

André became aware of the essential oneness of the forest and was giving up on trying to distinguish animal from vegetable life, life that moved from life that oozed. Everything grew soft and spongy, tended to assimilate itself to its surroundings. People had warned them about tigers, panthers, elephants, and gaurs, the massive wild oxen of Southeast Asia who, according to Cremazy, had a preference for goring white people with their prehistoric horns.

The most dangerous animals, Xa told them, were the high gray anthills that towered up like moonscape peaks. "The termites never show themselves on the surface," Xa said, "but if you fall into the anthill they'll devour you alive."

By late afternoon the biggest game they had seen was a family of bowlegged black pigs.

The column stopped. It took André a while to distinguish the palm-thatched huts on their stilts, to realize they were in a village.

"Thank God we didn't go in the rainy season," Clara said climbing down from her little horse. It was not hard to imagine savage downpours drowning out the jungle and wiping out the road they had traveled so carefully.

Nightfall came quickly. Small fires were visible inside every village hut. André smelled joss sticks burning somewhere before a wooden Buddha. All he saw in the intense darkness was the glow of the cigarettes that Xa and Louis smoked to keep mosquitos away. Svai sat hunched on the ground, stiff-legged, and carried on an involved conversation with a scrawny village elder.

The night was spent in a sala, or travelers' hut, that all Cambodian villages possessed, a structure similar to the other straw huts and surrounded by a huge stagnant pool, coconut trees, and a quasi-impenetrable clump of bamboos. A traveling salesman from China was already occupying the sala.

Linen cloth was suspended in the middle of the hut to give the wayfarers a modicum of privacy. The tropical night and their neighbor's opium-smoking kept Clara awake. All night long she saw a small light shine on the other side of the linen division. "For the first time in my life," she would write, "I smelled the aroma, the best in the world, of poppy seeds adroitly manipulated at the tip of two needles."[1]

[1] Clara Malraux, *Nos Vingt Ans*.

At dawn, when Xa brought her freshly brewed tea, he told her the Chinaman was a trader in tableware, someone who bartered crockery for sticklac, the prized resinous secretion that the tiny lac insect deposited on young soapberry, acacia, and sacred fig trees that the Chinese used to make shellac.

The morning heat was already oppressive under the sheen of greenness. While Clara drank her tea she heard monkeys cry, long ululations that reminded her of the Arab chants they had heard in Djibouti. Buddha had once promised the monkeys to turn them into humans, she was told. The monkeys believed Buddha, but when they wake up in the morning and realize they are still who they are they protest by filling the forest with their indignation.

André was intrigued by Buddhism but had no faith himself. He had lost interest in Christianity at twelve. "After that I studied Catholicism in its relation to art, but I have always been responsive to what religion contains of grandeur," he would say. "Admiration without participation in short."

Clara listened to the monkeys. She had kept her love for childhood fairy tales, her willingness to believe in unreality.

The second day's march was more difficult. The trail narrowed further and the forest became a viscid, emerald steambath. Palms and vines formed such a dense screen overhead that the sunlight had an aquariumlike sheen to it. André joked that it was a mystery to him how anyone could have built a great civilization in these fetid forests.

The humidity could be blamed for many things, Victor Golubev had told them back in Pnompenh. For the need for siestas, corpulence, the use of a car for a hundred-meter journey, the mildew in the shoes, the sweat-rot in the armpits of dresses. Clara thought the jungle with its bewildering fauna made you lose all sense of direction. Mosquitos were everywhere, and leeches began to fasten themselves to clothing.

André suffered less from the heat than did Clara, and he was getting better on his tiny horse. Xa translated Svai's warning that high up in their saddles Clara, André, and Louis might not see lianas strung across the path, vines so sharp they could cut their faces.

The trail ended in a small clearing surrounded by squat palm-thatched huts. They were in Rohal, but no one knew of Banteai Srey, of any ruins.

With André hovering over them, Svai and Xa conducted a veritable inquisition among young and old. Persistence led to an old man whose skin seemed to hang loose on his bones. The patriarch couldn't quite remember whether ruins he had seen in the jungle were the remnants of an old shrine or of an old encampment. A little money was pressed into the gnarled hand to jog the man's memory. Yes, he did remember. For a little more money he would bring his two sons and guide the party to the place.

Leaving Svai, the oxcarts, and their drivers in the village, André, Clara, Louis, Xa, the old man and his sons were off at dawn. The trail soon became so impenetrable that the little horses could not longer be ridden but had to be led. Up front, the old man and his sons hacked at vines and foliage with coupe-coupes, huge machetelike knives. When she looked down on the soft ground, Clara could barely see the tiny leeches and hideous insects before she stepped on them.

The rancid stench of decaying vegetation, the oozing of a planet in its primordial making, played tricks with their senses. Distant overhead shrieks sounded as if the monkeys were in the next treetop.

"Something right out of Nerval,' André grinned.

Clara wasn't sure what book he meant, but it occurred to her the reason Gerard de Nerval was one of André's favored authors might be that the poet, too, had traveled to exotic lands.

"Nerval said of the peerless beauty of his poems that their magic would disappear if anyone tried to explain them."

André had read to Clara *Sylvie*, Nerval's dreamlike story, which hovered between reminiscences of his childhood and his idealized love for an actress that lasted until the poet's first mental breakdown. Madness would possess anyone in this jungle, Clara thought.

"How the old man or his sons can spot temple ruins in this never-ending greenness," Clara shouted to André trudging in front of his horse, "is a mystery to me."

An odor of decay wafted from stagnant bogs and hung in the air.

Mechanically they slapped their cheeks. The mosquitos carried the ever-present threat of fever and insanity.

The column stopped to let the old man and his sons catch their breath.

"I wonder if the track only exists in the old man's imagination," André sighed, wiping his forehead.

"Right now, I think this treasure hunt is crazy," Clara answered.

Starting up again, the clammy air felt even more unbearable than before the halt. It was a world, André thought, where humans had no place.

Ants zigzagged up porous treetrunks. Spiders with grasshopper-like claws sat in the center of webs that were often four meters across. Flies, roaches, and curious little insects with heads protruding from their shells crawled on the moss. Up front, the villager and his sons swung the coupe-coupe with metronome precision.

The old man stopped, his knife high in the air. Directly ahead lay a mass of overgrown rubble.

Bamboo canes formed a natural palisade between the ruins and the forest. The foundation stones were clamped by clawlike roots. In the dank heat dewdrops sparkled in the moss. Above the treetops some large birds flapped away on clumsy wings. André was startled to see a snake.

Clara would remember the decorated pink stone with its mossy blotches as a jungle replica of the Trianon retreat Louis XV had built at the edge of the Versailles garden for his mistress.

We weren't the first to behold it, but we were no doubt the first to see it like this, to have our breath taken away by the grace of its stateliness, by its beauty, superior to any of the temples we had seen so far, all the more moving because forsaken. Seeing only the pink rock face, I moved forward when my eyes caught an emerald snake curled up at my feet. It formed a gleaming hoop larger than a car wheel.

Warned by our presence, it reared its head, which was as elegant as the temple, then slipped away among the stones that might conceal a sculpture fragment. That's how I found myself in Banteai Srey, a temple whose name had the same meaning as the town of my happy childhood holidays: Magdeburg, Banteai Srey both meant the virgin's fortress. Silently, we moved closer, like children who had just been given their dream present. The *devatas* watched us with their slightly bowed heads.[2]

In André's fiction, the encounter was to be much more foreboding. If ever there had been a Royal Way, it only revealed itself in occasional mounds of festering rubble. When, in *The Royal Way*, Claude and Perken discover their coveted ruin, they are not even sure whether the overgrown vestiges spell success or failure:

It looked like a mason's yard invaded by the jungle. There were lengths of wall in slabs of purple sandstone, some carved and others plain, all overgrown with hanging ferns. Some bore a red patina, the aftermath of fire. Facing him were bas-reliefs of the best period, marked by Indian influence—he was close now—but very beautiful. They were grouped around an old shrine, half hidden now beneath a breastwork of fallen stone.

It was difficult to take his eyes off the carvings. Beyond the bas-reliefs were the remains of three towers razed to within six feet of the ground. The mutilated stumps stuck out of such an overwhelming mass of rubble that all the vegetation around them was stunted and the towers looked like candles in their sticks. An imperceptible tremor, a perpetual vibration, began to stir within the leafy depths, even though there was not the faintest breeze.

A loose stone fell and sounded twice in falling, first with a muffled thud, then clearly; and Claude, in his mind's ear caught an echo of the word eer-ie. . .

Something inhuman brooded over all these ruins and the voracious plants which now seemed petrified with apprehension: a presence of supernatural awe guarded with its dead hand these ancient figures holding their lonely court among the centipedes and vermin of the forest. Then Perken stepped past him, and in a flash the world of shimmering sea depths died out, like a jellyfish cast high and dry on the seashore; it lost its spell when faced by two men.

---

[2] Clara Malraux, *Nos Vingt Ans.*

"I'll get the tools," Perken said.

"Why don't we find the entrance first and get our bearings from it?" André said, arming himself with a coupe-coupe.

They pushed their way around broken flagstones and bent aside the tall bamboo that stood in front of the entrance—a portal or stone gateway enveloped by vines, lianas, and thorny furze. It opened onto a little roofless courtyard. The whole thing seemed not so much the work of human hands as of some extinct species inured to a life without horizons, of ceaseless putrid birth and decay. André began to hack away at the vegetation barring the way to the inner courtyard. A layer of viscous moss carpeted the base. André cut his arm on a furze and nearly slipped on the moss. Many of the stones on the ground bore half-obliterated traces of bas-relief.

No Buddha heads, but whole walls of bas-relief devatas, guardian goddesses. The statuary still embedded in the walls was much better preserved than the loose pieces on the ground.

"We've got to get the pieces in the walls," André whispered, awestruck.

The more they looked, the more they convinced themselves these carved goddesses were distant cousins of Greek divinities, that Alfred Salmony's and André's own hunch of one artistic family of man was correct.

Sweat beaded Clara's face, streamed down her neck. "It'll be awfully hard to let go of them, they're so beautiful".

They let their hands run over an end carving and felt the delicate texture of the forms standing out from the plane.

"We'll keep some for ourselves," André said, grinning.

6. CHRISTMAS IN THE TROPICS

Back at the village, the old man was the center of attention. In one bold stroke, André hired the able-bodied men to hack to the temple a trail fit for bullock carts. The men looked to Svai as if for his approval. Xa translated. They would let André know in the morning.

Under their mosquito netting, Clara, André, and Louis caught a few hours sleep before they were up and, with Xa and his strong tea, waiting for dawn. At first light, they, Xa, Svai, the old man, the coolies, and the hired villagers lugged the tools on their shoulders to the site.

With the Cambodians standing timidly aside, André and Louis scrambled into the temple courtyard and, in shirtsleeves and suspenders, began working in the sweltering heat. Clara joined in.

The walls were covered with carvings. Twelfth-century Banyon-style bas-reliefs were visible under vines. Friezes of asparas ran along the top. Baboons in the treetops watched. Snakes slithered over suddenly disturbed surfaces. They decided to attack the most beautiful bas-relief in the wall, a design of devatas composed of four slabs of stone.

The first disappointment was the saws. They were not suited for cutting sandstone. One after the other they broke and, with them, Clara and André's hopes. Since the ancient Khmers had not used cement, they had imagined that separating the sculpted slabs from the supporting wall would be easier than peeling an orange.

When Clara walked outside the courtyard, the Cambodians had vanished. Fearful of divine revenge for such desecration? Ages ago men had piled stones on top of stones in order to communicate with the unknown, she thought. Then they had disappeared, perhaps appeased by their effort, while only the plants and animals lived on, satisfied with reproducing themselves. Until now.

When she reported back to André and Louis, they stopped chiseling.

"I guess they're making camp," André suggested.

As if to confirm his words, they heard footsteps.

"And if nobody comes to pick us up, how will we find our way back?" Louis asked.

As he spoke it occurred to Clara that in their excitement they had left the rifle and the two guns with their gear in the village. Their money, too.

The sound of the footsteps ceased. Only the rasping sound of monkeys on swaying tree branches was to be heard.

"Let's just go on," André suggested.

With crowbars, André and Louis managed lift the top slab a couple of millimeters. Using the chisels as wedges, they kept levering the stone forward. Blinded by sweat and attacked by mosquitos, they worked for what seemed hours until they maneuvered a rope behind and under the loosened block. With André lifting with the crowbar and Louis and Clara pulling, they saw the block move.

"We'll continue tomorrow," said André, exhausted.

Outside the temple, Xa and the guide were waiting for them. The camp was ready. Word from Rohal was that the villagers would hack a bullock trail to the ruins here.

Under a kerosene lamp that evening, Clara bathed André's bruised hands in a water basin. They stretched out, sapped of all strength, listening to the night.

The next day, André and Louis were bare-chested, their backs glistening, their hands wrapped in rags. With their crowbars they moved a slab of devatas to the edge of its niche. To lower the devatas they rigged up a hoist, a rope slung over an upper branch of a tree and tied around the midriff of the first goddess stone. Every hour made the effort more painful, but by the end of the day two slabs had been pried loose and lowered to the ground.

The third evening saw their labors crowned with success. The seven pieces of the bas-relief stood in slings on the courtyard floor.

It was hard to gauge the mood of the local Cambodians. They seemed brooding and afraid. Whether it was their fear of their ancestors' gods or, as André suspected once, of Svai was hard to say. There were moments when Clara and André told each other that the villagers were clearing the trail under duress, and moments when they dismissed their own impression of native sullenness as being a reflection of their own bad consciences.

On the fourth day the oxcarts reached the temple with the camphorwood chests. Less fearful than the others, Xa joined Clara, André, and Louis when it was time to hoist the slabs out of the courtyard. All four hauled together, raising the first slab a few centimeters. Pull by pull, they got the stone above the height of the wall. While Clara and Louis grimly hung on to the end of the rope, André swung the slab over the wall. Xa coerced a pair of villagers to bring an oxcart with the open camphorwood chest under the devatas hanging in midair. The old man from the village had a chill of fright, watching. Svai snarled something briefly, and the clumsy cart lurched forward.

Carefully they lowered the slab.

When the stone rested in the chest, the chassis of the cart sagged onto the wooden axle and the wheels sank into the humid earth. The villagers stared with blank indifference at the stones lashed with ropes. A sunset glow had begun to redden the forest when the last slab was lowered into its chest. The blocks weighed about a thousand pounds. André estimated their slabs would make them a hundred thousand dollars richer once they got it all to New York.

To thwart the myriad of night insects, the kerosene lamp stood between the cot and mosquito mesh Louis was using and Clara and

André's cots. In the lamplight Clara examined her bruised hands with their rope marks. For a dainty upper-class lady, she told herself, she was holding up pretty well.

"All I can imagine is a bathtub," she sighed. She couldn't move her shoulders. "I feel like the people who were tarred and feathered in the Middle Ages. Everything sticks."

Under the sweating night, Xa was putting away pots and pans. André walked over and offered Xa a cigarette, lit one himself, and tried to find out why the villagers were so reluctant to help with the stone.

"I'm not from here," Xa said, his hands and lips voluble with apologies.

Where Xa was from wouldn't mean much to André, so instead he asked about Xa's family and how he had grown up. André learned that Xa had two married sisters and that he had only gone to school two years because his father believed the longer students stayed in school the greater fools they became.

André tried again. His questions elicited no direct answer, but insight. In his rapid approximate French, Xa explained the Cambodian word *kum*. If André understood it right, buried under the beauty and serenity of the Cambodian soul was a peculiar mentality of vengeance that extracted revenge much more damaging than the original injury. "If a government official steals my brother-in-law's chickens and my brother-in-law waits one, maybe two years to put a knife in the thief's back, that is *kum*," Xa explained.

André saw no connection but felt uncomfortable. "We didn't steal anybody's chickens," he said. "They led us to the ruins, they hacked a road for the oxcarts. We paid them."

"Lord Buddha sees everything, but what does anybody care?"

A second cigarette made Xa concede that the villagers' reluctance to help might have nothing to do with Clara, André, and Louis. It might mean they knew Svai and resented him, or that Svai had told them to hold out for more money. "They take advantage all the time," he added, grinding out his cigarette.

"Tell me about it."

"On the other hand, people make promises they can't keep."

They stood there for a moment. Uneasily, André said good night and walked back to the lamp, the mosquito netting, and his cot. Like the jungle, its people were not what they seemed. He stretched out. Clara was asleep. It was all very complicated. There were undercurrents, suggestions, motives, maybe deep infections in the Cambodian soul, emotions he did not understand. He felt his body go limp with physical exhaustion. In less than five minutes he was asleep.

They spent nine harrowing hours getting themselves and the oxcarts back to Rohal. Svai was as handsome as ever, but even he walked more slowly at the head of the column. Clara felt the sweat permeating the leggings, making her legs seem glued to the horse. Her throat felt dry, but neither she nor anyone else wanted to drink the last lukewarm drops in the flasks.

At the first halt, a lanky youth crossed to a palm and clambered up the near-vertical trunk, a coupe-coupe between his teeth. An iridescent bird fluttered off. The youth reached the clusters of green orbs. Coconuts rained down and earthbound blades split them open.

Sweet liquid trickled down Clara's throat as she drank the coconut juice.

"There won't be anything we can't do," André grinned between greedy slurps.

"First let's get out of here," she smiled back.

All she could think of was that this was a country where white men found it natural to beat their servants: "Without the strap, my dear lady, they won't do what they are told." Another way of keeping natives in line, they had told her, was to withhold part of their salary. "That's the only way you can keep your boys." Yet these whites were also the guardians of Cambodia. They would be the first to consider the two of them thieves.

She could live with that. Behind them on the oxcarts, she reasoned, were the proof that André and she found a way of escaping the sterile gestures of intellectual revolt, that they knew how to convert their loathing of society into a solemn gesture.

At Rohal the oxen were unyoked and the camphorwood chests sheltered by a little roof of thatch. Joss sticks were smoldering. Clara and André sank into folding chairs while Xa began preparing the evening meal. "There won't be anything we can't do." Clara repeated

André's phrase and wondered what it meant. "What do you do when everything is possible?" she asked. To read, to absorb, to feel, to love. Perhaps it meant they'd have the chance to be the kind of people she thought they should be after all.

From the beginning they had been sure of themselves. When she had told him on their second date that she would be going to Italy in August, he had said he would come along. Just like that. The third time they went out he had told her gravely he knew only one person more intelligent than she—Max Jacob. In the legendary Montmartre personality, friend of Picasso, poet, visionary, painter, homosexual, recluse, astrologer, and humorist, André admired not only a matchless nonconformist with a boundless creative gift but also an artist in love with perfection, a curiously aware amateur of *le fantastique* who expressed the sharpest pain of his existence with throwaway anecdotes, "cubist" visions, and surrealist texts. That Clara Goldschmidt both knew and appreciated Jacob had made a very deep impression on André. Here was a girl with whom he could talk about everything, even death.

She had lost her father when she was fourteen. "And I'm a Jew and it's not easy for Jews to accept the idea of death because there is nothing in the Bible that really says God has promised salvation."

In reality she knew little about Judaism. She had always been treated like the prodigy in her family, had always felt more gifted than Maurice and Paul. A woman both corseted in the rectitude of Wilhelmine Germany and sufficiently assertive to believe happiness was its own justification, Margrete Goldschmidt had retained her own rather liquid Judaism but brought up her daughter without religion. When Clara told her mother about her new friend, Madame Goldschmidt had not been unduly alarmed but told her daughter it was nice to be intelligent, because intelligent girls obviously pleased intelligent boys.

They had become lovers on Bastille Day, spending the evening in his garconnière while the fireworks set the sky ablaze over L'Etoile. The next day André had not been at the appointed rendezvous. He was seeing his father to ask permission to marry. The request was not so much a gesture of filial respect as a legal necessity. He was not yet twenty-one.

Permission refused. Years later, no one would say whether Fernand Malraux had considered his son too young or Clara Goldschmidt too German—and too Jewish. On her side, she planned another trip to Italy that was suddenly encouraged by her mother. Madame Goldschmidt hoped the holiday would put an end to her infatuation with the young upstart.

When André showed Clara his brand-new passport, he grinningly told her his father preferred to let him have a passport to go to Italy than to get married. Madame Goldschmidt had accompanied her daughter to the Gare de Lyon and saw that she was properly installed in her wagon-lit and that she was alone. As the train pulled out, André slipped into her compartment.

It had been André's first trip outside France. In Florence, they savored the emotions of a first illicit hotel check-in and were given a room with windows on a minuscule inner courtyard. At the Uffizi they discovered the quattrocento masters, and watched Michelangelo's *David* from a trattoria while having ice cream. From the post office they sent telegrams to Paris announcing their engagement, carefully omitting any sender's address. She discovered he had a way of visiting museums—storming through the rooms first and then returning to the canvases he felt worthy of his interest. In front of Uccello's *The Battle*, he told her to watch the painting as if it contained no anecdote. She told him of the four months she had spent in Florence after she broke up with Jean.

Everywhere she translated. Quadrilingual (in German, French, Italian, and English), foreign tongues were one domain where she excelled. The playfulness and sarcasm of his ideas astonished and delighted her, as did the sharpness of his observations. They confronted their divergent pasts one afternoon lying in the grass near the San Miniato al Monte cemetery, their heads against the unfinished wall that Michelangelo had wanted built. With the city spread at their feet and the sun reddening the spires and the rooftops, they told each other they were happy.

By way of Siena they traveled to Venice, where they checked into the Hotel Danieli—the only hotel name Clara could remember because of George Sand novels and visits with her parents. Once the hotel bill and railway tickets to Paris were paid for, they had no more money.

The Simplon Express was twelve hours late that day, making them spend the afternoon on the Lido beach eating grapes. On the Swiss border, they discovered a few Swiss francs in their possession and bought four sandwiches, which lasted them to Paris.

The Goldschmidts were at the station. Clara's spinster aunt asked whether it was worth it, her mother whether she was happy, while Maurice told her she had dishonored the family and that he would emigrate to America. The next day, Maurice and André met formally for lunch at Fouquet's.

Fernand gave in, observing after meeting his future daughter-in-law that for a Jewish girl she dressed with taste. She rather liked Fernand, "a dreamer who takes himself seriously, a handsome man for whom words came easily as they do for men who love women and whom women love."

Clara wanted "something religious" to follow the compulsory civil marriage. André agreed, if "something religious" could be sufficiently pantheist to include ceremonies in a church, a synagogue, a mosque, and a pagoda.

Maurice warmed to his sister and asked Isa, his longtime girlfriend, to go shopping with her. For the civil wedding Clara chose, at Poiret's, a velvet dress edged with fur. Eight hours before the marriage she visited the mayor's secretary at the city hall, and with all the authority she could muster asked that the dates of birth not be read out aloud at the ceremony.

"I see," he said, "the bride is a bit older."

"I'm the bride."

"Ah," he sighed. "It's the groom who's too old."

"No, he's too young.

At the ceremony, the mayor said Clara and André would be happy because they were young. One of Clara's more distant aunts noted that no one read the dates of birth of the bride and groom.

When Clara's Aunt Jeanne kissed the bride she whispered "You should have married the father."

"You wouldn't have interested me, if you hadn't been rich," André had told her on the train taking them to Strasbourg the day he was to join the army.

"You mean what attracted you was the surprise at seeing me work for Florent Fels although I could afford not to."

When he received his induction papers a few days after their marriage, they decided there could be nothing more absurd than eighteen months of playing soldier in Alsace. To their astonishment, brother-in-law Maurice offered to help. Maurice had been mobilized in Alsace and, since the family held considerable interests in the tanning industry, he was not without influential acquaintances.

Together, André, Clara, and Maurice made the trip to Strasbourg. André carried with him a certificate attesting to a childhood rheumatism in the joints. Maurice located a friendly physician. On the fateful day, André presented himself for his medical with the right amount of antimalarial quinine in the bloodstream to make his heart beat dangerously. He was exempted from military service.

From Strasbourg the newlyweds had continued east into Germany, Czechoslovakia, and Austria, discovering expressionist movies and investing in the French-language rights to *Das Haus zum Mond*. With Ivan Goll's help, André had also started negotiating to acquire Ernst Wendt's *Uriel Acosta*, a picture, Clara was to remember, that showed her the synagogue could be as cruel as the church.

Dawn came abruptly over Rohal. André became aware of someone next to him and sat up. It was Xa. André crawled out from under the mosquito netting.

"Svai is gone," Xa said.

"You're sure?"

"Sure."

André crossed to the water bucket and tossed its content over his head. He wasn't sure what it meant that the guide Cremazy had foisted on them had disappeared. "Good riddance," he said, taking the towel Xa handed to him.

Monkeys were chattering in the trees.

Both André and Clara had noticed that the natives deferred to Svai. Maybe the guide was working under orders. Under whose orders? Cremazy's? Parmentier's? The off-hand warnings at the faculty veranda in Hanoi had only added to André's perseverance. Now the possession of the treasures excited him and sharpened his determination. He'd fight anybody to keep the contents of his camphorwood chests.

The carts with the chests and the oxen were still there. "But will the villagers continue without Svai?" André asked.

"The cartmen from Siem Reap, yes," said Xa. "They want to get home."

"And get paid." André remembered the white people's warning to Clara about withholding part of the natives' wages. He also remembered Xa talking about *kum* last night.

Except for the cartmen waiting for orders to move out and a few women, Rohal was empty. Over breakfast, André, Clara, and Louis discussed their next move. They were reasonably sure that with the help of Xa, the cartmen from Siem Reap could find their way back. But there was a strong possibility that Svai was alerting Cremazy and that authorities would be waiting for them at the end of the trail. André told Xa to ask if there were any alternate roads back.

Yes and no. "Yes, there is a trail going through an unknown region, a trail that ends up at the anchorage in Siem Reap," Xa explained. "But with the chests the oxcarts are maybe too heavy for that way."

"Xa, do you know how to drive a cart?"

"Sure, sir."

An hour later Xa had packed the camping gear and the cartmen yoked the oxen. With Xa sharing the seat with the drive of the first cart, they lumbered off. In the fictionalized version of the adventure that André would write in *The Royal Way*, he was on the third cart himself. "Claude made little attempt to drive his oxen, letting them amble on after the others," he would write.

Like successive theater curtains and flats disappearing to reveal a stage decor, the jungle density with its overhead canopy of palms and vines gave way to clearings. Finally, an aperture in the vegetal arch let them see the spires of Angkor Wat. From a pocket in her a jacket, Clara pulled a mirror and a gluey lipstick.

When they saw the first rice paddies, André had Xa ask about the alternate road. When he was told he was only ten minutes off to the south, he had the caravan detour. There was no reason to give Svai, Cremazy, and the Siem Reap constabulary the joy of waiting for them at the end of the trail.

When the anchorage was in sight, they decided that Louis and Xa would lead the bullock carts directly down to the landing so the chests could be slipped on board the first steamer heading for Pnompenh and Saigon while Clara and André paid their respects to the Cremazy and his friends.

Clara and André rode on to the bungalow where they had spent one night ten days ago and with a sigh let themselves slide down from the saddles. They were both exhausted, dirty, and hungry, but since Clara looked especially fragile, they decided that if Cremazy or the couple asked why they were back so soon, they would say Clara had suffered an attack of dysentery.

To their relief, the police sergeant was nowhere to be seen. Nor was Svai.

The couple, however, took the alleged dysentery seriously, forced Clara to bed, and called a Cambodian doctor.

"We must be reasonable," the physician kept saying when she refused the enema and purgatives he wanted to inject with a syringe. André didn't know what to do. The grand adventure threatened to turn into slapstick routine.

Clara gave in. The worst effect of the medical intervention, she would remember, was her loss of faith in injections.

Two days later, their camphorwood chests were loaded into the hold of a river steamer labeled "Chemical Products" and addressed to Berthot & Charrière, forwarders in Saigon. Together with Xa, whose services they decided they could afford until Saigon, they boarded the steamer.

The riverboat tied up at Pnompenh, within sight of the scarletroofed royal palace, in a magnificent sunset. Church bells pealed, and Clara, André, and Louis realized it was Christmas Eve.

Christmas in the tropics. The trio decided to stay on board—the steamer would continue down the Mekong to Saigon in the morning—and turn in early.

Shortly before midnight, heavy banging on their cabin door woke Clara. She shook André.

"Police."

She slipped into her robe. Andé got down from his bunk. She opened the door only to be blinded by a flashlight.

A detective, holding the flashlight, and two uniformed Cambodians stood on the doorstep. After making Clara and André confirm they were Monsieur and Madame Malraux, the detective ordered them to follow him.

"Where?"

"To the hold."

Five minutes later the detective, Clara, and André stood at the very conspicuous camphorwood chests, the detective surveying the dimly lit cargo space.

Behind them the two Cambodian policemen entered with a bathrobed Louis.

With his flashlight, the detective read off the labels of one of the chests. Chemical products. "Are these chests yours?"

"The chests, yes," André answered.

"Open!"

André handed the keys to the padlocks to one of the policemen.

The Cambodian opened the heavy lid.

The detective's flashlight played on the stony dancing of the devatas. Clara sniffed and made a remark about how lovely camphorwood smelled.

The detective ordered the next chest opened. More carved stone was revealed. When they opened the third chest, Louis bravely said "This one is mine."

Addressing himself officially to Clara, André, and Louis Chevasson, the detective explained they were under arrest for being in possession of statuary fragments stripped from an archeological site.

"Meaning what, exactly?" André asked in a surly tone.

"Meaning you cannot continue. Meaning that the chests and their contents will be transferred to the Pnompenh court clerk's office first thing in the morning."

Before it all sank in, the detective added that since they were Europeans, they could go to their cabins and spend the rest of the night there.

They all clambered back on deck.

"Merry Christmas," the detective said, walking toward the gangplank. The policemen saluted as they left the ship.

⟨∾ 7. HOTEL MANOLIS

The detective and his underlings had barely disappeared down the dock when André burst into a hysterical laughter that gradually spread to Louis.

Clara bit her lips. "When you're through laughing," she snapped, "maybe you'll tell me what's so funny."

Suddenly serious, André told her that, under the worst of all possible circumstances, this little interlude might delay their departure for a few days.

Annoyed, Clara stalked off to their cabin. André and Louis went after her down the narrow stairs, André arguing that there was nothing to get all worked up about. They had been found in possession of fragments from a temple so neglected for so many years that trees grew in the middle of the sanctuary. A mile or two to either side they might have stumbled on the ruins of another shrine.

In the narrow cabin, the trio thrashed through it all, going from despair to hilarity to sober evaluation of their situation. Louis was sure their case would proceed in typical colonial fashion, that it would be slow, difficult, and confused. Since he was unmarried, he suggested that he take all the blame and that Clara and André sail back to France. Once there, André would be in a position to find lawyers and exert sufficient influence to bring about his release.

André refused to take the whole thing seriously. The midnight drama had all the staged absurdity of an Alfred Jarry play, the ridicule of *Ubu Roi*. André launched into an impersonation of Jarry's pompous schoolmaster. Clara was in no mood for a burlesque imitation.

"We know the jungle now," André said, lowering his voice.

"What do you mean?"

"I may bungle once. The second time I make damn sure I succeed."

Louis wanted to know what he meant by "a second time."

André said, "I mean we may have to consider the idea of another expedition."

"The monsoon season is coming," Louis commented.

Clara felt almost exhilarated. The worst had happened, but they had foreseen it. She liked her husband for not giving up. "We're practically broke as it is," she said.

"I've thought of that, too," André retorted. "Don't you see? We can talk with such authority to people interested in Khmer art that we'll have no difficulty raising money for the next expedition."

"In the meantime," Louis yawned, "maybe we should try to get some sleep."

He left the cabin as the first light of dawn came through the porthole.

Windlasses hauling the camphorwood chests into police custody on the dock woke them up an hour later. The captain refused to reimburse the unused Pnompenh-Saigon tickets. A law officer told the disembarking trio they were released in their own cognizance pending trial.

"Meaning what?" Clara asked.

"House arrest at a hotel of your choice, Madame. You are free to come and go during daylight hours, but you cannot leave Pnompenh."

The officer saluted and crossed to his automobile. Obviously no court was in session on Christmas Day. Tomorrow, Clara and André kept telling themselves, they would simply ask the judge to return the slabs, to which their labors, if nothing else, conferred ownership.

"In addition, they should apologize for last night," André said.

Clara wondered whether the telegraph office was open so she could send a wire to her mother. She wanted to tell as little as possible, but they needed money. Behind them, the riverboat tooted and the last passengers embarked.

The Hotel Manolis was owned by a Greek with the sonorous name of Aristotle Manolis. The establishment was less than first class, but whirring ceiling fans greeted arriving guests at the front desk and, in the restaurant, tried valiantly to whip up the humid air above the diners.

Louis got a room at the end of a hallway. Clara and André's room had lime-washed walls and possessed, besides the double bed with mosquito netting that a maid lifted into a tester during the day, a round table and one chair.

The inhabitants of Pnompenh washed, dressed, and ate in public, and half-naked families were to be seen squatting and devouring the splendid fish that was the staple. Refuse was thrown out of a window or pushed through the floor, collecting in mounds under the pilings. The city was full of dogs of an ugly yellow variety. Together with pigs and occasional domestic monkeys, they profited from the Buddhist aversion to taking life.

No courts were in session until after the New Year, they were told the next day. André was at the table writing a long letter to his father when Clara burst in. In tears, she handed him the return telegram from her mother. Margrete Goldschmidt suggested her daughter divorce.

Clara couldn't stop crying.

André was cutting. "You're bringing out your portable wailing wall."

For the New Year's Eve festivities, the dining-room tables were pushed toward the walls to make room for a dancing area. Outside, monsoon rains lashed the city.

A small army orchestra played a mixture of bal musette and Cole Porter, and the ceiling fan ruffled the few streamers hanging from lamps.

At five minutes to midnight, most of the *colons*, the French settlers, and their wives and dates were passably tipsy. Some wore funny hats. Ladies managed the appropriate titters at the big plantation owners' crude sense of humor.

Over the music, Louis tried to keep up a conversation with Manolis. "Both Monsieur Malraux and I are expecting postal money orders."

Manolis pushed his great nose, his great eyes, and the cleft of his mustached into Louis' face. "By next week, I hope."

Louis nodded and committed the mistake of adding that André's father was in banking, financing. Manolis had seen deadbeats before.

The owner stopped a waiter with a tray of champagne, lifted a glass off, and handed it to Louis. "You'll settle both accounts on Friday then."

The orchestra stopped. Couples on the dance floor looked at the clock. Manolis crossed to the orchestra for the midnight ceremonies. Sweaty, Louis looked toward the entrance, gulping champagne.

At two minutes to midnight, everybody grabbed glasses from waiters' trays. The musicians were ready.

At the stroke of midnight, Clara and André made their entrance. Unwittingly almost, the crowd turned to see the young couple, sparklingly dressed, Clara in her black Poiret wedding dress, André in a newly pressed white tuxedo.

The orchestra broke into "Auld Lang Syne." People wished each other happy 1924; Louis snatched three glasses off a tray and elbowed his way over to Clara and André.

They were formally charged on January 3. André was haughty and difficult during the hearing. Clara was appalled. As she would write in retrospect, "When you don't want to knuckle under, you either must be very strong or very crafty; we were neither. The values we questioned were easily defended. On the other hand, our defenses caved in—bank statements traced our ruin in sharply declining curves and no previous undertakings justified any sudden passion for Khmer art."[1]

Two days later, the first newspaper account of the Banteai Srey episode appeared in *L'Echo du Cambodge,* the local news sheet. On January 8, a longer piece, headlined VANDALS AND ROBBERS OF RUIN, ran in *L'Impartial,* the big Saigon daily. The article repeated the basic facts of the original news story, accompanied by a roused commentary by publisher Henry Chavigny de Lachevrotière.

The days dragged on. At sunset on Fridays, a military band played in the main square for Frenchmen in colonial white and Frenchwomen in mousseline prints. On Wednesdays, the hotel set up a gramophone in a large upstairs room and *colons* and their ladies from surrounding plantations came in for an evening of socializing. It was here that André first heard about David Mayrena, the legendary king of the Sedangs. This nineteenth-century soldier of fortune, adventurer, and swindler was born Charles David in Toulon, the son of a French naval officer who affected the surname Mayrena to celebrate some vague claim to ancestral distinction. After seeing action in the French Army after it gained a toehold in Indochina and working for a bank in Paris until evaporating funds congealed in a cloud of embezzlement, Mayrena took refuge among the Dutch in Java, was deported as an undesirable—and returned to Paris with apocryphal tales of sultans, gold, and gutta-percha, the milky juice from various Southeast Asian saponaceous trees used in the arts, as a dental filling, and as a finish for canes. A French financier gave Mayrena thirty thousand gold francs to lead an expedition to Indonesia, where rebels fighting the Dutch seemed disposed to trade gutta-percha for guns. Mayrena promptly took a boat—not to Indonesia, but to Cochin China. In April 1888 Mayrena departed Saigon for the highlands of eastern Cambodia on an Arabian horse, followed by two mistresses, three interpreters, four Chinese merchants, eighteen Vietnamese soldiers, and eighty porters. He returned to civilization four months later astride an elephant, the king of the Sedangs. Mayrena ruled his short-

---

[1] Clara Malraux, *Nos Vingt Ans.*

lived kingdom with gusto. He demanded absolute obedience to his slightest command from his Montagnard tribesmen.

Mayrena's borrowing money from the gullible, his duels with local chieftains, audacious scrapes with French officials, his army of elephants and bodyguard of Moi warriors were discussed in the bars of Pnompenh, Saigon, and Hanoi by people who swore they had known Mayrena at the height of his glory thirty years earlier. This Joseph Conrad figure was to become a pathetic has-been in *The Royal Way* and reappear in the *Antimemoires* as the subject of a screenplay that Baron Clappique, a fictional character in André's most famous novel, *Man's Fate,* tries to peddle to Hollywood producers.

The incessant rain and the heat sapped their energy. The event of the day was the trip to the poste restante window at the post office. There were never any letters from the Goldschmidts.

Xa insisted he was still their servant, although they couldn't pay him. When he accompanied André to the post office one afternoon, André tried to explain that Clara, Louis, and he had no money.

"No such thing as white people without money," Xa said.

"Yes, there is such a thing."

European postal patrons gave André and the little Cambodian a peculiar look.

"Madame says when things are okay again, you and she take me to France."

André walked back outside, followed by Xa, to stand under the awning and watch the rain. After a moment, Xa explained he did understand. With cruel innocence, he asked why before they set out for the jungle André hadn't told him what they were looking for. Trying not to hurt Xa, André said it was kind of delicate.

"Me, I found ancient stone carvings, without anybody finding out."

"You say that now."

"You still want?"

To Clara and André, Xa was becoming more interpreter of the country's life than of its language. His comments made André realize that odd superstitions and prejudices, complacency, and tribal pride prevented the races of Indochina from understanding each other.

Xa told them Vietnamese did things like this, Cambodians like that. He insisted that they meet his new mistress and told them his new woman should always walk one meter behind him. "In bed, she would always lie lower than him," Clare would remember. "This last command surprised me a bit."

On evenings the rain stopped, Clara and Xa strolled the main street. "On street corners we bought sugar cane that I gnawed on like I had chewed on licorice as a kid. The charcoal offerings of the street vendors smelled good. In a woman's basket on the ground, I chose what looked like a round eggplant. It was a mangosteen, Xa told me, as he pressed it open and inside the purplish-blue husk showed me the transparent white slices. I learned it was a marvelous fruit. Fritters were tempting also, but I got grease spots on my dress. The Royal Palace reached the trees with its padoga beams. A tiny band stand was used as a school for young dancing girls. In a cage on the square, a tiger that was stronger than a bull walked hopelessly back and forth, unable to forget he was both deadly and a prisoner."[2]

With money his parents sent him Louis paid his hotel bill and spent the rest as a down payment so a lawyer would represent the three of them.

One afternoon in late January, shortly after the newspapers announced the death of Vladimir Lenin, André met with Victor Golubev. The one intelligent European in Pnompenh came to the hotel for an interview. The Saigon editors of *L'Impartial* had found the temple-robbing story colorful and had told their Pnompenh stringer to do a profile on the principal defendant. Besides a Cambodian waiter idly polishing glasses behind the bar, André and Victor were the only people in the hotel bar. André liked the teacher-archeologist and part-time journalist, and told the story of his archeological exploits with gusto.

"The limestone bust of Queen Nefertiti disappeared in 1912 and is still in the Berlin Museum," he said. "If a private collector loots an historical site he's a smuggler. But what if a government does it, or a person steals a work of art and gives it to a museum? Most of the

---

[2] Clara Malraux, *Nos Vingt Ans.*

Louvre's finest Chinese treasures were stolen from Buddhist cave-temples."

Victor grinned and scribbled in his notebook.

"Look, there isn't one top civil servant who doesn't have his private collection of Khmer art," André concluded, finishing his rum-soda. "What Chevasson and I did was to detach a few pretty sculptures left to the admiration of monkeys."

The interviewer's smiles goaded him on.

"The gesture has more class than taking down the chandelier in the governor-general's residence so the outgoing governor can ship it home with him."

Victor ordered another round of rum-sodas.

As they nursed their new drinks, André asked more questions than his interviewer. What kind of people were the settlers he had seen at the New Year's Eve party? How had Victor come to live here? Victor's observations were astute and informative, and contained clever little sketches of the who's who of colonial power. As they talked, André became more and more interested in the politics of colonialism. "And what do the natives want?" he asked.

Native yearnings, Victor said, were ever so feebly incarnated in a few Vietnamese who were either in exile, in prison, or both.

"Or both?"

"The prestigious Phan Chu Trinh is in exile in France, if you can believe it."

"Isn't any of us interested in the natives?"

"Paul Monin, maybe."

As Victor explained it, Paul Monin was that first tentative bridge toward awakening native hopes and dreams. Monin was a lawyer in Saigon, a war veteran in his early thirties who believed France's overseas presence was only justified by higher ideals, not one-way mercantilism. Because he had on several occasions defended Vietnamese, he had been called a traitor to his race.

André was sarcastic. "God created colonies so we can exploit them."

"France is simply how you see it."

"And how do the French in Indochina see it?"

"Very conveniently," Victor said. "The Banque d'Indochine buys it for us. It lends money to the settlers, whereas Vietnamese, Cambodian, and Laotian peasants must rely on moneylenders. When their harvests are in, they pay seventy-five percent in taxes and usury interests. If they can't pay, we grab their land. From the governor-general down, everybody is in on land speculation."

"And your newspaper. . . ?"

Victor interrupted with a cynical smile. "Didn't I tell you my paper is partially *owned* by the governor-general?"

André wouldn't give up. "And what about Vietnamese-language newspapers."

"Quoc-ngu," Victor corrected. "To break Vietnam's cultural continuity, we banned the Chinese characters and replaced them with quoc-ngu, the romanized alphabet. But anyway, you need the governor-general's permission to print in quoc-ngu."

Emptying his glass, Victor said Monin was the exception. Everybody else was in Indochina for one reason only—to enrich themselves.

"We faced a choice thirty years ago when we extended our control over Cochin China," Victor explained. "We could have pursued the policy of 'association,' as the British did in India, governing indirectly through natives. Instead, our specialists pleaded for 'assimilation.' How can anybody not want to become French?"

Which didn't mean life for the seventeen million Vietnamese, Cambodians, and Laotians living under the French flag was any worse than life was for Indians in India, Indonesians under the Dutch, or Filipinos under American rule. Mahatma Gandhi's entry into politics three years earlier had been marked by the jailing of twenty thousand Indians for civil disobedience and sedition, and during one month the year before the British had imprisoned another ten thousand for political offenses.

They got up. André asked about Monin and the Saigon dockworkers' strike the lawyer was supposed to have fomented.

"Monin is a member of the Colonial Council, if you can believe it, someone who thinks the solution to colonialism is not so much a matter of ideology and class as a matter of respect for people."

What Golubev didn't mention during their free-wheeling interview was that he was wearing yet another hat, that the prosecuting attorney had asked him to assist Henri Parmentier in assessing the damage done to the Banteai Srey temple. At Judge Bartet's* urging, the two archeologists, along with Louis Finot, had traveled to Banteai Srey to survey the depredations the defendants had inflicted. Nor did he say that, in a backhanded compliment to André's flair for Khmer art, Finot had decided to have the Banteai Srey shrine restored.

The Mekong rose steadily. Houses along the riverfront were marooned in lakes of brown water. Snakes lodged in the branches of half-submerged trees, and the bazaar was closed. In the Manolis dining room flying ants flew into the electric lamps. Clara wondered how anybody could eat. André discovered the municipal library, got himself a card, and began reading books that, he said, he would never have read otherwise—ungraceful but evocative travel diaries, provincial governors' painstaking reports. In their room at night when the rain drummed on the window, Clara and he discussed the afternoon's reading with the passion of seminary students.

Almost in spite of themselves they discovered a humiliated Asia. Until their involuntary immobility in monsoon-drenched Pnompenh the focus of their interests had been themselves, art, history, and—in a high-flying abstract way—metaphysics. Although Clara needed to identify with others and was affected by suffering, people's daily struggle somehow had never been a subject of their conversation. André especially tended to see the majority of humanity as so many puppets moving about with little motivation and less charm, and, in any case, little inclined to have any sympathy for him.

If Clara looked back at her childhood with fondness, André hated his. "Almost all the writers I know loved their childhoods, I hate mine," he would say. More than Clara, he accepted the harsher realities of life. The rung that individuals occupied on the social ladder

---

* The first name of Judge Bartet as well as those of most lawyers involved in the 1924 trial have not come down to posterity because of the French custom of addressing judges and pleading lawyers as *maître* and making the title part of their professional names.

had to do with how they themselves tackled the business of living. Too many might be subservient, mean, and timid, but if society had a function, it was not so much to help the downtrodden as to act as a seedbed for its achievers. Not that independence, generosity, and self-reliance entitled anyone to an easy life. On the contrary, great men usually led tragic lives. To see adversity for what it is and have the guts to be ruthless toward oneself were the marks of people who had a positive attitude toward life.

Imperceptibly, Clara and André went from self-centered calculation to an awareness of two worlds coming together without melting. They had been traveling amateurs out to make a mark—and a killing. Slowly, the suffocating heat and the encircling semi-poverty which in many ways made life so easy compelled them to become aware of others. The short, tawny people who enchanted both of them loosened up André and taught him, as his wife would say, "not to be ashamed of his own goodness."

They noticed that the shouting market women with their black teeth and hair wrapped around their heads like turbans turned silent when whites were around. They saw piercing native gazes that, when met, pretended indifference. And without quite knowing now, they heard stories—the existence of Colonel Darles, the governor-general's enforcer, who based his power on informers and counter-terror and could be found dining in Saigon's Continental Hotel in Saigon every night. They discovered that a man had tried to shoot Governor-General Martial Merlin in a Shanghai street during an official visit was a Vietnamese whose land had been seized.

They saw the arrogance on their compatriots' faces and heard Europeans groan that they weren't understood by the people they themselves never tried to understand. Of the range of human emotions, Asians responded to only one, they thought—fear. "Without the strap, my dear lady, they won't do what they're told." Clara heard whites wonder what the world was coming to now that a European couple in Siem Reap had been discovered renting their bungalow to a native doctor. Through newspaper accounts of a Cambodian's suicide after he had signed a work contact whose content he did not understand, they sensed the existence of an indentured workforce.

There were fewer than twenty thousand residents born in France, and three quarters of the expatriate population was made up by bureaucrats. Golubev hadn't quite said it, but the way twenty thousand Europeans ruled seventeen million Asians was through informing. Snitches, stool pigeons, squealers permeated society.

That the case against them was based on informing had never really crossed their minds.

"You are free."

"And sick."

In a hushed voice, she told him to listen. Judge Bartet was young, only a few years older then themselves. He had dropped the charges against her, but he had also whispered that senior justices were watching him, that he had to go by the book. "We need help. Your father sent us money; my mother told me to get a divorce."

"The telegram was so obviously dictated to her."

But Clara was back on her idea. "One of us must get back to France, back to Paris to find money for lawyers, to alert people who care about us, sell the Picasso painting. And the one who can do it is me."

"You don't know how to dramatize."

"We have no choice. I'm the only one who *can* leave, legally."

"But can you make people believe?"

She had learned from him, she said, learned how to exaggerate and embellish the truth. She would know how to color and dress up reality and, like him, make herself the center of wonder and surprise.

Her fevered mind trailed off into ruminations about their marriage, the contradictory demands she felt he had put on her. On one hand, he would like her to be brilliant, but on the other he couldn't accept her outshining him. "You saw in me what I couldn't see, which is the reason you have the power to change me." She didn't want to be his mirror only. "When I gave you the little girl I once was, I gave you the biggest proof that I love you."

She talked about her childhood, her grandfather's portrait which distracted her when she had to do her piano exercises. Grandpa Heynemann was crazy, too, she said. He was a chemical engineer who transported explosives from country to country one time too many, because at customs one day, grandfather, customs agent, and customs building blew sky high. If Clara had inherited a taste for rebellion from anyone it was from his widow, Louise Heynemann. "At eighteen, my grandmother eloped with a man who married her but committed suicide. She was going to marry another man when Grandpa Heynemann abducted her. They called her *die schoene Louise,* and she was beautiful. She was lively, open, independent and often defiant."

After a while André sat up behind Clara and cradled her against his chest. He patted her brow with a towel dipped in the glass of water. Her words continued. "You were lucky that you weren't the first man I went to bed with. You dazzled me. And we surprised each other. The way our minds and our bodies floated into each other was our revelation."

She went on. Gently he rocked her in his arms.

Down the hall someone died. Outside the rain continued.

The fever broke after a month. To get her strength back, Clara was encouraged to try short walks on the arm of her husband or a nurse. One Sunday in early June when she leaned on André and the sole Cambodian male nurse on duty accompanied them into the hospital garden, the barefoot Clara almost stepped on a black scorpion.

"You must kill it," André told the nurse while all three bent over the insect, whose sting was deadly.

The nurse kept watching the scorpion.

"Children play here," André insisted.

"I won't kill it," the Cambodian said.

Clara and André tried to make him see the contradiction between his attitude and his nursing job.

Suddenly, the nurse grabbed the scorpion by its carapace with his left hand. Delicately he brought it up and with his right hand broke the stinger. Putting the defanged scorpion back down, he looked at Clara and André with a face expressing only profound confusion. "Was it then," Clara would ask herself many years later, "I suspected for the first time that oppression is not worse than destroying a people's relationship with its environment?"

During the long afternoons when André was in town, Clara pulled out a notebook and in a long cursive handwriting jotted down her thoughts about men and women, about couples, André and herself. Her inspiration was Benjamin Constant, the Swiss-French novelist and politician of the Napoleonic era whose penetrating insights into the couple she admired. Constant's fifteen-year liaison with the older Madame de Staël had been marked by passionate jealousies and reconciliation. In her notebook, Clara analyzed *Adolphe*, Constant's autobiographical story of a man who, out of vanity, seduces an older woman and has her leave her protector and children. When Eleonore realizes Adolphe doesn't love her, she dies of grief.

Clara had started the notebook during the boat trip down the Rhine and imagined she might one day turn her notes into a book. In the meantime, she did not want André to see her sketchings. When she unexpectedly heard him approaching one afternoon, she just had time to hide the notebook under the sheet. She wasn't sure her writing was good enough and she wasn't sure he would approve.

From the city library, André brought her all of Nietzsche, and a book by Emile Durkheim, the sociologist of their fathers' generation who believed people's morals were merely a reflection of their social behavior, and that social facts had nothing to do with a person's conscience. "When we were alone we got all excited discussing things," she would remember. "For days on end, we didn't mention what had preceded our hospital stay, the indictment or how we thought we'd get out of it all. Another adventure interested us—the brilliant way in which I challenged him and he tested me."

A second money order arrived from Fernand Malraux, with enough money to buy a steamship ticket for Clara and to retain a separate lawyer for André. A court date was set. André and Louis would go on trial July 16.

Maître Parcevaux insisted he could only represent one of the two defendants, that one of them would have to find his own counsel. André and Louis flipped a coin. André won, and Parcevaux suggested Louis go see a colleague of his, Maître Dufond.

They decided that Clara should go back to France immediately to try to drum up support. André was optimistic about the hearing. "They've got nothing serious against us," he kept telling her.

In the evening, when the heat was less oppressive, she walked a few paces in the hospital garden, leaning on André and listening to his reasoned talk about the necessity of understanding Asians. As long as he talked, she knew where she was.

Looking better, Clara was sitting up in bed and having her hair combed by Tuit. The nurse smiled a lot and told Clara that under the Mekong is a city, a city where all the inhabitants are women. Each time a child is born, it is a girl.

"But Tuit! Who do they make the babies with if they are all women?"

"With the wind," Tuit smiled.

André was at the door, dripping outside rain. The two women thought he looked comical in his wet clothes.

Coming over the bed, André said with a gesture toward the empty flower vase that he could see Xa hadn't been there yet. Tuit handed him a towel to wipe his hair and face, and returned to combing Clara's hair.

"So what did Victor say?" Clara asked, following Tuit's combing in a pocket mirror.

"If nothing else, I found out that the reason the preliminary investigation took so long is that Bartet requested—and received—police reports from Paris. The one on Chevasson, Louis, couldn't be better. It takes note of his 'modesty' and talks about his exemplary conduct."

Clara couldn't believe the prosecution would leak such details to Golubev.

"As long as he doesn't write about us in his Saigon rag," André smiled.

Golubev was a sore point between them. Clara couldn't get over the fact that their friend was part of the prosecutions' team of experts; André appreciated that Victor had actually come clean and told him. André also like the idea of having an informant in Judge Bartet's office.

"What does *your* dossier say?" she asked, to change the subject.

Evasively, he answered that it was not the kind that would endear a defendant to colonial magistrates.

"Now I really want to know."

André cast a glance toward Tuit, who sensed she wasn't wanted. She finished Clara's hair and left, closing the door behind her.

André spoke about himself in the third person. "The dossier on Malraux, Georges André, describes him as an associate of avant-garde anarchists. It details his collaboration with Florent Fels' marginal magazine and notes he is married to a naturalized German Jew, that he's the archetype of the asocial, if not amoral, postwar intellectual."

There was worse, but André didn't tell her. He had met with Parcevaux, and the lawyer was not happy with what he had learned from the prosecutor's office. "Awful" was Parcevaux's repeated word as he read from a dossier that revealed police had tried to obtain a statement from one Margrete Goldschmidt in Avenue des Châlets. That meant Clara's mother knew a lot more than what Clara had disclosed in her telegram last Christmas. Bartet also possessed evidence that showed André had solicited eventual buyers for his loot.

"That means premeditation," the lawyer translated. "Awful."

Whether Parcevaux thought André's case looked awful or he considered the prosecution's inquest awfully clever he didn't say, but to properly prepare the case he would need more money.

There was a knock on the door. Before Clara and André could say anything, Xa stuck his grinning head in. Clara forced herself to be cheerful. "I was afraid I wouldn't get a flower today."

Xa had a fresh orchid with him, but he had more than that. He also carried something heavy in a hatbox. Ceremoniously he put the orchid in the vase and heaved the package up on the bed.

"For you—bon voyage," he said with a mysterious grin and invited Clara to open the hat box.

She took the lid off. The object was too heavy for her. André did the honors and lifted a magnificent Khmer head of an apsara out of the hat box.

Xa beamed with pride. André was dumfounded.

"Put it back in the box, Xa," Clara said.

But André wanted to see and admire it.

Xa preened and said "For you."

Clara was the first to recover her senses. She told André to put it back and Xa to hide the hatbox among her luggage going to the dock.

The night before her departure, the hospital let her and André take a solitary bath together, a moment they imagined was meant to allow them to accomplish their conjugal duties one last time. André lingered in the tub longer than Clara, and after she stepped naked on the bathroom scale and saw she weighed thirty-six kilos—seventy-nine pounds—she caught sight of herself, for the first time in weeks, in a full-sized mirror. She thought she looked pitiful. Thirty-six kilos stretching over her five-foot frame didn't leave much fat for feminine forms.

Seeing her husband getting out of the tub, she also realized the physical toll these last months had taken on him. Already gaunt when they met, he not only looked haggard; malaria attacks had also given him a mustard-colored complexion.

They held each other's gaze, almost afraid of letting their eyes wander. What she would remember of their embrace was not how their bodies looked but that they were parting at a time when they needed each other more than ever.

The rain stopped that night. Orderlies carried Clara to the litter, rigged together between two rickshaws, that took her to the riverboat. Louis, Xa, and Tuit were there. Tuit would accompany Clara to the ship in Saigon. André walked next to the litter. Now and then a spasm of dengue aftereffects shook her body.

The riverboat was the same one they had boarded with their loot in Siem Reap six months ago, only to be arrested Christmas Eve. Everybody tried to be brave, especially Clara.

The procession reached the gangplank. André busied himself with the tickets. Xa and a pair of dockhands did the luggage. Louis stood with Clara, telling her that the open sea would be bracing and chase away the last remains of the fever.

Clara didn't listen. She watched André in his limp tropical suit, his eyes brimming with tears. Men carried her on board. André ran after her up the gangplank. Tuit followed.

The whistle blew. André leaned down and kissed her. She burst into tears, held on to him, wouldn't let him go.

"You have the money, passport, my father's address and phone number," he said mechanically.

Clara let tears flow. All she could manage was "Take care of yourself!"

The boat's siren gave three blasts, very strident and terribly long. The aft hawser was hauled on board.

"I'll be sailing from Saigon before you reach Marseille."

Tuit held on to Clara as André tore himself from her and dashed down the gangplank a second before it was lowered to the wharf. The steamer slipped from quayside.

"Help me get up," she cried to Tuit. With desperate strength, Clara clung to the nurse so she could see over the railing.

André stood there watching, a little apart from the others.

Orphaned, Clara thought.

In Saigon Tuit took Clara directly from the riverboat to the departing ship. André had bought Clara a first-class ticket so she could have her own cabin; it was white like a hospital room and had a ceiling fan. She wished she'd never see another white room, never hear another ceiling fan.

She went up on deck with Tuit to say goodbye. At the stern a chain of Vietnamese women was fueling the ship, carrying sacks of coal on their heads up one slanting plank, dumping them into a bunker, and going back down another plank. The same women reappeared a few minutes later with a new load, but always with the narrow stride that the sarong required. When they were ready to sail, the ship's horn gave three blasts, like the riverboat's in Pnompenh. The wails were so terribly sad that tears welled up in Clara's eyes as she thought of André and their humiliation.

She spent the first days in bed, feeling lonely, confused, and brooding over what to expect upon reaching her destination. A glance in the full-sized mirror filled her with self-pity. She sensed the steward's exasperation when, worried because he didn't see her on deck, he knocked on her door and brought her cold broth. She didn't even have the excuse of being seasick.

She ventured up on deck the second week. The sea breeze and fellow passengers' solicitude brought her back among the living. She spent her days in a deck chair—petite, frail and wrapped in blankets, trying to be positive. For the first time as a married woman, the initiative was hers.

After Singapore she took short strolls on the deck, soon in the company of a one-armed man whom she was to identify in her memoirs as Charles G., a war veteran and an official responsible for French colleges in China. He had spent five years in the country. He spoke Chinese, knew a good number of Chinese characters, and had traveled as much as the civil disturbances allowed. Listening to him, Clara was surprised to find herself interested in someone else's venture.

"You are still fatigued by the climate of Indochina," he said. "I know. It's murderous. Even Shanghai is better than Saigon. As for Peking, the spring and fall seasons are delightful."

Finally she was able to put on her Poiret dress and, holding onto the rail, go to the dining room. She smiled to herself. She could barely expect to be invited to the captain's table this time; she had only one pair of shoes. The people at her table included an English couple from Hong Kong, the children of the court clerk in Pnompenh, and a Portuguese trader from Macao, who at one sitting whispered to her that it wasn't true that all Portuguese men in the colony had syphilis. The high point of the lunch conversation was the devaluation of the franc. André and she had experienced the free fall of the deutschemark the year before.

"Now it's our turn," Charles G. told her in the smoking salon.

At noon one day when the dining room was almost empty, Charles asked if she knew where her table companions were.

"Aren't they checking to see who's the winner of the sailing-speed game?" The radio bulletins and game notices were posted at noon every day at the aft gangway.

"They're checking the currency listings," Charles said. "The devaluation may create chaos in France, but they're delighted. They want to see how much richer they've become since yesterday. You seemed surprised."

"Yes, I guess I am."

"For someone with your experience, perhaps you're a little naive."

Her face showed her amazement. "You know my story?"

"Pious souls have taken it upon themselves to inform me. I've found it all rather interesting."

"And it hasn't. . . "

"On the contrary. But if it makes you feel any better, I had already decided to make your acquaintance. Yes, the moment I saw you, I thought, 'Who is this charming little waif?' "

She told him everything, except her uncertainties. She underlined André's qualities, "his marvelous intelligence; the fervor with which he thinks, decides, and sees things; the ardor with which he revels in life's joys." The more she talked the more she found certain of her husband's traits striking—the wealth and originality of his ideas, his generosity when others exploited his brainstorms. "I've got ideas coming out of my ears," he'd say; "stealing a few can't hurt me."

Her listener was a tactful man who now and then smiled, asked the right questions, and at the end gave a sober evaluation. He made her realize that the return to France was perhaps as badly prepared as their departure for Indochina eight months earlier and that she had ignored such crucial elements of the equation as the families' attitude, work possibilities, and—despite her husband's optimism—the probable outcome of the trial.

The next day, a radiogram from André both reassured and worried her. EVERYTHING WENT WELL. SEE YOU SOON. Why didn't he say WE WON? Shore-to-ship communications were terribly expensive, but couldn't he have said where he was? Was he in Pnompenh, or were he and Louis in Saigon, free to leave and just waiting for the next boat to Marseille? And how would he pay for his passage? He had said he'd ask his father. But was he sure Fernand Malraux could come up with still more money?

When they strolled the deck together, she told Charles G. of her concerns. One day he pointed to a slim man with blue eyes and saffron complexion. "You know this man?" her companion asked. "You should; he's Paul Monin."

"I know the name. A friend of ours in Pnompenh has talked about him. He's the lawyer L'Impartial thrashes all the time and calls a traitor?"

"He challenged the owner of that estimable newspaper to a duel."

Djibouti and its harbor prostitutes reminded her of the cliff-dwell-

ing girls who had danced naked for André and her. No telegram was
waiting at the shipping office. She went to the post office intending
to send a wire to her father-in-law to ask him to meet her at Marseille, but when she saw how much it cost she decided to wait till the
ship was closer to Europe.

Anxious for reassurances and a sense of how André might have
fared in court, she planted herself in Monin's deck chair. A long cigarette holder preceded his face as he bent down and said, "Excuse
me, Madame, but I believe you're in my chair."

"I did it purposely," she said.

Before he could take her for a madwoman, she said she needed to
talk to him. She knew he belonged in the select ranks of the enlightened opposition, that his progressive views did not sit well with the
colonial establishment, that because he had defended the Vietnamese
in several cases, Lachevrotière's newspaper had called him a sellout
to the natives. "I'll move over into my seat, but I must talk to you."

He smiled and listened attentively while she told her story. There
was not much he could do. While they were sailing toward the entrance to the Red Sea, the trial was supposed to be under way in
Pnompenh, or, judging by her husband's somewhat cryptic radiogram, it was already over.

Monin, she sensed, was a man's man, someone who was more
comfortable with other men than with women. He was very dark and
very handsome, a wealthy man of action who admitted he hated the
lies Frenchmen of his ilk invented to justify the subjugation of colonial people. He was from an old Lyon family—a Creole grandmother
on his mother's side explained his dark complexion—and after marrying a distant cousin and becoming the father of a now-six-year-old
boy, he had settled in Saigon. Mme. Monin had remained infirm after childbirth and had not been able to adjust to Saigon's climate. She
had been forced to return to France for a prolonged convalescence.
He was on his way to visit her and his son but would soon return to
his practice.

Going back to her cabin with his Saigon business card and his
promise that she could call on him during his short stay in Paris,
Clara told herself she now had two friends.

Off Aden, Charles G. became her lover. "It was bound to happen," she was to write. "I accept it without remorse. Of few men do

I keep such a clear memory; he knew how to be a lover without ceasing to be a friend."

From Port Said she wired her father-in-law, giving him the estimated time of arrival in Marseille. The last days on board were spent in brief-encounter introspection. "If we weren't both married," Charles sighed. "If we weren't who we are," she answered, "things wouldn't be what they are and *that* wouldn't change anything." She pressed her hand in his.

Before disembarking, Monin gave her his address in Paris, saying he would expect to hear from her in a few days.

Fernand Malraux was not at quayside, but a steward brought her a telegram. YOUR WIRE ARRIVED TOO LATE. CALL ME IN ORLEANS. AFFECTIONATELY. FATHER. With money Charles G. thrust into her purse in a gesture he tried to make casual, she took the first train to Paris.

Fearful of her brother Maurice and what her mother's continued silence might mean, Clara avoided the big house in the Avenue des Châlets and instead stood with her suitcase in her one pair of rain-soaked shoes ringing the bell of Jeanne, a former maid of the Goldschmidts now married and running a Montmartre hotel of dubious repute.

"God, Mademoiselle Clara!" the former domestic exclaimed, barely recognizing her.

"Yes, it's me."

"What a mess you've put us all in," Jeanne sighed, letting her in.

"Oh, it's nothing."

"Nothing? The papers are full of stories about his conviction."

"L'Affaire d'Angkor" had indeed caused a stir in the volatile Parisian press. While news dispatches—mostly wire-service rewrites of *L'Impartial's* courtroom coverage—simply milked the caper for its color, depicting one Georges André Malraux as being apprehended hammer and chisel in hand on top of the Angkor Wat, columnists had a field day condemning the audacity of the young temple-robber.

The trial had lasted two days. It had started on schedule July 16 before a Judge Jodin, a picturesque and far-from-straitlaced magistrate who had recently come to Pnompenh with his mulatto mistress and was something of a social outcast for presenting his paramour to the governor-general as his daughter.

Judge Jodin's habitual attire on the bench was a caricature of colonial dress—pith helmet, frayed tropical suit, and dark glasses. André felt the presiding judge might be understanding and perhaps view the misdeed, if not as a youthful prank, at least as nothing more than an overzealous outburst of archeological ardor. The district attorney was Maître Giordani, a quiet, outwardly gentle man. André's lawyer was Maître Parcevaux, while Louis was defended by Maître Dufond. As André sat down he was not unduly pessimistic. The star witness for the defense was to be none other than Henri Parmentier, chief of archeology at L'École Français d'Extrême-Orient.

L'Impartial had a correspondent in the press box. Today it is impossible to say whether is was Victor Golubev; the coverage carried no byline. However, the sympathy and eloquence with which the anonymous court reporter described the principal defendant points to the multi-hatted friend:

> Malraux is a tall, thin, clean-shaven young
> man whose features are illuminated by two extremely
> penetrating eyes. He is very facile in his speech
> and defends himself with a sharpness that reveals in
> him unquestionable qualities of energy and tenacity.
> In addition, he appears to possess considerable culture.[1]

The reporter was also struck by the contrasts between the two young men on the dock. Sturdy, self-controlled Louis Chevasson sat quietly in the dock and admitted everything while the fiery, wiry Malraux sprang up, protesting his innocence.

This tactic of opposites, if strategy it was, was their first error. Louis gave himself the role of sole author of the alleged crime. He insisted he alone was responsible, admitting all the evidence, including the camphorwood chests labeled *Chemical Products* and addressed to the Saigon forwarders. André's defense was that he had never seen Chevasson until they met at Banteai Srey. Unhappily, the dossier forwarded by the Paris police—and not communicated to the defense—showed that Chevasson and Malraux had gone to the same grammar school.

---

[1] *L'Impartial*, July 24, 1924.

Besides a description of André as an associate of anarchists and Bolsheviks, collaborator of *L'Action,* which was nearly seized for a satirical defense of mass-murderer Landru, and married to a naturalized German Jew, the dossier included such proof of moral turpitude as a letter written by Clara to her mother describing the dancing cave dwellers of Djibouti. Neither Clara nor André would ever find out how the letter got into the prosecutor's file. Intercepted by postal inspectors? Turned over to inquiring detectives by Margrete Goldschmidt?

The long afternoon session was given over to testimony by witnesses. The most damaging evidence was by police sergeant Cremazy, recently promoted to an administrative post in Pnompenh. Cremazy told the court how Clara and André Malraux and Louis Chevasson had been shadowed by informer Svai from the moment they rode out of Siem Reap.

Parcevaux, André's counsel, elicited from Professor Parmentier the admission that the two "amateur archeologists" had removed the sculptured surfaces with great care. Still fond of André, Parmentier concluded his testimony with words of praise for the defendant's flair and scholarship. The old professor spoke with an authority that no one else in the courtroom possessed, but when Judge Jodin recessed until the next morning André was frustrated and angry.

In *The Conquerors,* André's staccato novel about revolutionaries in China during the 1925 Canton uprising, his hero is stupefied when charged with helping poor women obtain abortions. The account of Pierre Garin's trial is largely autobiographical:

> It was not that he didn't know that what he had done was unlawful, it was the absurdity of the trial that left him in agony. . . The entire trial felt like a surreal performance, not exactly like a dream but like a strange comedy, a bit contemptible and completely extravagant.
>
> Only the theater has the same sense of protocol: the jury's swearing-in text, read aloud in a school-mastery voice, the effect on the twelve unruffled tradespeople, suddenly moved and visibly anxious to be just, not to make a mistake and to commit themselves. The idea that they might not understand the facts they would have to judge didn't bother them for a second. The confidence of some witnesses, the hesitation of others, the judge's attitude (the attitude of an expert

at a gathering of illiterates), his hostility toward some defense witnesses, all showed Pierre how the facts and this ritual had nothing
to do one with the other. In the beginning, he was very involved—
the defense strategy fascinated him.

But he got tired, and toward the end of the depositions, told
himself with a smile, "To judge obviously means not understanding, because to understand means you can't judge."[2]

André thought himself a bit player in the court drama and couldn't
wait for the third act. Closing arguments were heard the following
morning. Prosecutor Giordani demanded a penalty so severe that
others would think twice before embarking on similar plunders.
Louis' lawyer respectfully asked the court to take into consideration
the sober and blameless life of his client. André's counsel took a different tack. Parcevaux maintained that no crime had been committed
because the Banteai Srey ruins had not been officially classified as a
historic monument. How could anyone be prosecuted for entering
an abandoned site and making off with a few blocks of stone? And
even if the site *were* classified, who had the authority to carry out
such classification in the protectorate of Cambodia? The governor-
general, the king of Cambodia, or the Far-Eastern French School,
the nominal custodian of Indochinese archeology?

Judge Jodin refused to entertain arguments that would raise jurisdictional questions and, the following Monday, July 21, handed
down his sentence—Georges André Malraux, three years' imprisonment and five years' banishment from residence in Indochina; Louis
Chevasson, eighteen months' imprisonment. As for the sculptures,
Jodin ruled they belonged to the French government.

Although for different reasons, both prosecution and defense
wished to appeal the jurisdictional point that Parcevaux had raised,
and both immediately petitioned for a hearing before the Correc-
tional Appeals Court in Saigon. Pending the appeal, the two appel-
lants were released on their own cognizance but forbidden to leave
Indochina. September 23 was set for the appeal hearing.

---

[2] André Malraux, *Les Conquérants* (Paris: Grasset, 1928); *The Conquerors*, translated
by Winifred Stephens Whale (New York: Random House, 1929).

"You have no right to keep me here," she repeated.

"Believe me, Madame, it is for your own good."

"You have no right."

"To submit to treatment is the best thing you can do."

The walls were white; the three doctors' smocks were white. A nurse sat with her arms crossed, pretending not to hear what was going on.

"What you have been through would unsettle anyone," said the gray-haired doctor in the middle.

"We're supposed to be talking about my mother," she retorted.

The goateed doctor on the left reminded her of her illness in Pnompenh. Clara told herself, God, they know everything. She had tried to conceal the dengue attack from her family, but somebody had alerted them. André? The Cambodian doctor?

"A few weeks here and you'll have a much better perspective on the events of these last months," said the doctor on the right. A silly little smile never left his sensuous lips.

"I'm not sick," she repeated.

When they hinted that they had the power to certify her, she flung herself from the room and raced down the corridor. She heard male shouts and heavy footsteps behind her. She ran out into the garden and down the long driveway toward the entrance. Maurice was at the gate with the family chauffeur. Together they caught her. Triumphantly Maurice brought her back, assuring her she was mad.

Two hefty male nurses stood at the door when the interview resumed.

"You need rest," the gray-haired doctor repeated.

Fear sharpened her wits. "You think you should keep me here because of the state I'm in."

The smiling one smiled, the goateed one whispered to the gray-haired one, who nodded.

"In that case, I'll have to notify my father-in-law."

They told her to write out a telegram that would be taken to the post office. At this point her handwriting would be such as to justify internment.

She had started reading the newspapers at Jeanne's the night before. One paper described her husband as a dandy, author of one failed book, living at 10 Avenue des Châlets in a townhouse rented by his mother-in-law for ten thousand francs a month and filled with delirious modern art. "It was no doubt inevitable that Negro art and other expressions of barbarian and mysterious art should be mixed with the art of the cube. Evocative statues of Khmer art were to be found at Avenue des Châlets, but they were reproductions. 'Ah, if you had the originals,' certain amateurs said, 'What a fortune you'd have! They'd pay any price for them in New York and Boston.' "[1]

She had not been able to sleep that night. In the morning she had confronted the family. The return of the prodigal daughter, she thought as she rang the bell at 10 Avenue des Châlets, still wearing her only pair of shoes. The chambermaid who had replaced Jeanne took her into the library.

"Mother is suffering from a nervous breakdown," Maurice said when he came into the room.

---

[1] Quoted in Clara Malraux, *Nos Vingt Ans*.

"Where is she?"

He gave her a formal peck on the chin and for a second seemed disarmed by the sight of his emaciated sister. Quickly, however, he stiffened.

"Where's mother?" she repeated.

"She's coming."

Her mother came in on Paul's arm. She was completely gray-haired and looked pale and fragile. Only she sat down.

"You're not going to stay married to that convicted felon," Maurice thundered.

"More than ever!"

Shrieking retorts followed wounding accusations. At one point she crossed to the secretary and, seeing three letters addressed to her, went for them. "Don't you touch anything in this house!" Maurice shouted, following with a slap across the face that sent her reeling. She hit back, knowing she couldn't win. Their mother's voice demanded that they stop. While her mother upbraided her son, Clara slipped the letters into her purse.

The explanations continued, in a somewhat calmer atmosphere, with new demands that Clara start divorce proceedings and her assurances that things would clear themselves up. Her mother cried.

Through the brothers' reproaches and insinuations Clara thought she could hear echoes of a police inquiry, or perhaps police irritation at not uncovering a more serious crime. A detective had asked if the Goldschmidts had interests in Middle-East oil. Could the young couple be spying for a foreign power? A hint of anti-German sentiments, she wondered, of anti-Semitism? Maurice had fought the war in a French uniform and was indignant when he felt his French identity questioned.

"He was always a liar," Maurice scoffed.

"His father isn't the director of anything," Paul said.

"You must ask for a divorce, and you must ask for it *now*," Maurice said with finality.

Mother chimed in. "You cannot stay married to that boy." Clara tried to make them understand that to sue for divorce now would only aggravate the situation.

Paul knew how to hurt her. "Mother doesn't dare see her friends any more," he snapped.

Their mother stood up and with indignant composure walked to the door. "This is all too trying for me," she sighed, leaving the room.

Clara imagined their mother trying to slip past the snickering concierge, the scornful glance of the next-door carpenter, the pitying glances of the baker. Clara had no right to cause her mother such humiliations.

The litany of reproaches continued. André was lazy; he had never worked. When Paul said André had never graduated, Clara snapped back that nor had he. The doorbell rang and the brothers left the room.

Left alone in the study, Clara opened her letters. One was a nice little note from Florent Fels. The second letter was from André Breton, the surrealist leader, offering his help if she needed it. Neither she nor André really knew the surrealists. The third letter was from Jean, her onetime fiancé, urging her to divorce André and marry him.

Maurice came back to announce that Mother's doctor had arrived and wanted to talk to her about Mother. Clara went into the parlor and met a physician she knew was the son-in-law of one of her mother's friends.

"The recent events have been an ordeal for Madame Goldschmidt," the doctor said gravely.

Clara could only bite her lip. "It's all my fault."

Under the circumstances, the physician continued, it was perhaps advisable that Mme. Goldschmidt spend some time in a rest home. In fact, he knew a very good one in suburban St.-Cloud. "I was wondering if I could ask you to stay there with her for a few days," he added.

"Of course," she replied. "As long as I can get into Paris whenever I need to."

She never suspected the trap.

For two hours she stood leaning against the white wall. To the three doctors' coaxing and arguments she had only one answer, repeated over and over again through her tears: "You have no right to keep me here."

Finally they gave up. Maurice allowed the family chauffeur to take her back to town.

After the driver dropped her off at Jeanne's, Clara realized this was another mistake—the family now knew where she was. After a sleepless night, she sneaked out into the gray dawn and hailed a taxi to take her to the Rue Fontaine, the sender's address on André Breton's letter. When the meter read three francs, she asked the cab driver to stop and let her out. Carrying her suitcase, she walked the rest of the way.

At her tenth ring, Simone Breton stuck a sleepy head out.

"I'm Clara Malraux."

The premier surrealist couple were used to unconventional, even bizarre rituals, but seldom at six o'clock in the morning. Once they had filled themselves and Clara with coffee and Simone had given their guest a pair of shoes, the poet began organizing the Malraux defense.

André Breton was a natural if sometimes touchy clan leader. He inspired a doglike devotion, largely because he was very inventive, very perceptive, quick and definite in approval and scorn, gifted when it came to polemics. An army psychiatrist who dealt with traumatized, shell-shocked victims of trench warfare during the war, he had become interested in the ideas of Freud.

At the end of the conflict, he, like so many young survivors of the trenches, turned violently against the generation that had demanded the colossal losses. If the fathers were patriotic and nationalistic believers in the myth of the sacrifice, the sons were pacifists and internationalists. Dadaism, which had started in a café in Zurich as a revolt against the war, stood for nihilism, freedom to experiment, and parody. When Tristan Tzara brought dada to Paris in 1919, Breton took charge. Renamed surrealism and given a more positive angle, the movement sought to explore the frontiers of experience and to broaden the local and matter-of-fact view of reality by fusing it with the instinctual, subconscious, and dream experience. The circle of friends who gathered around Breton all shared a belief in the supremacy of poetry and a loathing of the parental generation whose values had led to the senseless slaughter.

As Clara explained and filled out her story and Simone made more coffee, on the phone Breton dictated telegrams alerting Fernand Malraux and Marcel Arland, André's editor friend at the Gallimard publishing house. Clara called Paul Monin at the address he had scribbled before disembarking in Marseille. By midafternoon, a tentative plan of action was beginning to take form.

Clara and Simone were exactly the same size, and Clara happily slipped into the first clothes that hadn't been to Indochina with her.

Fernand Malraux showed up at nine the next morning, looking dignified and distressed. He hugged his daughter-in-law, slipped money into her purse, and came up with sensible suggestions. Unlike the Goldschmidts, he had not been bothered by detectives or journalists. Next, Paul Monin joined the strategy sessions and gave the political perspective of colonial Saigon. Compared with all other Frenchmen busily exploiting Indochina, Clara and André, he said, were "spotless souls."

Three days after Clara had arrived, moral support was being organized. *L'Eclair* printed an open letter from La Connaissance bookstore owner René-Louis Doyon. Exasperated by the sniping attacks on his former ragpicker, Doyon wrote a reasoned plea for Malraux and pinpointed some of the more malicious inaccuracies in the big-circulation accounts. Still, fanciful accounts of "L'Affaire Angkor" were picked up by foreign press services. On September 21, 1924, *The New York Times* carried this Associated Press dispatch: FRENCH SLEUTH TRAILS MAN TO ANNAM JUNGLE, DROPS HIS DISGUISE AND ARRESTS ROBBER OF PARIS MUSEUMS AND NATIVE TEMPLES.

PARIS, Aug. 25 (AP)—This is the story of a Paris detective who traveled half the way around the world for his quarry, and finally, in the dense jungle of Annam, threw aside his disguise and arrested his man, who is now doing three years in jail.

An antiquary named Malraux was under the observance of the Paris police, suspected of being responsible for thefts from French museums. It was thought he had designs on collections of antiques in one of the the French provinces and as a matter of routine a detective was assigned to trail Malraux and a companion, wherever he might go.

The pair went to a seaport and there took passage on a steamer for Saigon, French Indo-China, and the detective went along in the same vessel. He did not even have time to buy a change of clothing, but made friends among the cre.v and borrowed what he needed.

At Saigon Malraux and his friend posed as rich travelers, anxious to see the country, while the detective kept in the background. He had, however, made known his mission to the local French authorities, and when Malraux asked for guides to the remote district of Annam, the detective was among the natives assigned, but cleverly disguised.

The party scoured the region of Angkor, rich in holy relics and specimens of old Chinese art, and Malraux and his friend bought freely. Also they did not hesitate, conditions being favorable, to rob Annamite temples of particularly fine specimens.

The border of Siam was not far away, and the collectors, having decided to leave the country by that route, called up the native guides and dismissed them.

Then the Parisian detective had his day. The humble disguise was cast aside, the French policeman stepped out and Malraux and his friend were placed under arrest.

Doyon's open letter in *L'Eclair* drew responses from Florent Fels and Max Jacob, both congratulating Doyon on setting the record straight. Somewhat cautiously, Jacob put himself at the disposal of what he called the "Malraux clan."

To thank Doyon, Clara went to La Connaissance and immediately fell in love with the bookstore couple. René-Louis was a puckish erudite and Marcelle a woman who quickly became a friend. Together, they told Clara what André had never admitted to her: that he had worked as a *chineur* for the Doyons.

Clara and her family were now completely alienated. She asked Doyon and Breton to go to the Goldschmidts' to pick up her and André's personal belongings and to help her sell the Picasso and whatever else they thought had any monetary value. A letter from André told her not to worry about the immediate payment of the hotel bill that Manolis demanded, but a telegram from André informed her of the imminent due date of a check he had written on their joint Paris account. To cover it, she sold, for next to nothing, her strand of pearls and a diamond inherited from her grandmother.

Breton was the first of the big guns to sound off, with an article in

Les Nouvelles Litteraires.[2] Monin delayed his return to Saigon to be helpful. As he explained to Clara, what might impress the appeals court in Saigon was testimony—character witnesses, depositions, affidavits—showing André in the best possible light. As she listened, she got an idea. Since everybody in Pnompenh and Saigon took her husband for an unknown fake, a cheap little con artist without friends and connections, she would ask the most illustrious literary figures to offer themselves, if not exactly as André's guarantors, at least as intellectual celebrities who had confidence in his talent, men of consequence who believed that although André was not yet a known writer, he did show innate promise.

Marcel Arland knew exactly where to go with such a proposition.

If Gaston and Raymond Gallimard's publishing house was the most dynamic commercial presence in French letters in the 1920s, Arland was its young star editor, whose unerring flair for discovering writing talent made him pick practically every author of note over the next twenty years. Only two years older than André, this bespectacled bookworm had, after a flirt with the surrealists, settled down as the editor of Gallimard's literary monthly, *Nouvelle Revue Française,* better known by its acronym *NRF.* If anyone knew everybody in the literary world, it was Arland.

André and Marcel had met in 1920 when Arland was looking for authors for an avant-garde magazine and invited Malraux to join such bylines as Max Jacob, Tzara, and the poet Paul Eluard. The two young men had talked painting then, not literature. Their heroes were Picasso and Derain, and if André had one ambition, he confided to Marcel, it was to write a grand art history.

Every August, the philosopher Paul Desjardins organized a summer symposium at a former cloister in Pontigny, a hundred miles southwest of Paris. The encounters were dominated by Gallimard's star authors—André Gide and Paul Valery—but numerous French and European intellectuals usually attended. The tone was "serious," all-masculine, with a penetrating odor of Thomist Catholicism and a whiff of homosexuality. If Clara would draw up some kind of peti-

[2] André Breton, "Pour André Malraux," *Les Nouvelles Litteraires,* August 16, 1924.

tion, Arland would take it to Pontigny and urge everybody to sign it.

The *NRF* published the slightly modified petition and the names of its signatories in its September 6 issue:

> We, the undersigned, touched by the condemnation which has hit André Malraux, express our confidence in the esteem with which justice usually deals with those who contribute to improve our country's intellectual patrimony. We want to act as guarantors of the intelligence and true literary value of this personality whose youth and already-accomplished work authorize the highest hopes. We vigorously deplore the loss that results from the administering of a penalty which will prevent André Malraux from accomplishing the things we have the right to expect from him.

The roster of signatories was as brilliant as anyone could produce in 1924, running from the Gallimard brothers and the Catholic François Mauriac to the stars of the noisy surrealist movement. The friends who joined Arland and his fellow Gallimard editor Jean Paulhan in signing were Florent Fels, Max Jacob, André Breton, and Pascal Pia. André Gide and his longtime friend, the wealthy essayist Charles du Bos, headed the list of maturer authors: Mauriac, Edmond Jaloux, Pierre Mac Orlan, Roger Martin du Gard, André Maurois, and Jacques Rivière. Surrealists who signed included Louis Aragon and Philippe Soupault. Joseph Kessel and Guy de Pourtales represented the international set.

Half the signatories had never met André Malraux. Some, like Rivière, wanted to be sure the Banteai Srey adventure had no commercial motives, something Arland assured everyone of.

Clara could congratulate herself. She had opened an unsuspected reservoir of sympathy for her husband.

Paul Monin came to say goodbye. He was returning to Saigon. Clara had become used to the concern and advice of this overseas Frenchman who, in Paris, looked out of his element. He said little about his private life, but she divined that Indochina was an escape for him, that the confidence and affection that Saigon's Chinese minority and its Annamese majority had in him compensated for a disappointing marriage.

"All I can do," she told him, "is to entrust my husband to you.

You'll see he's amazing. Everything makes sense when he talks. You two will understand each other."

In order not to be totally without lawyerly advice, a friend of a friend introduced her to an attorney couple. Madeleine and Leo Lagrange had met in law school and were each other's first love. They sympathized with Clara and put themselves at her disposal.

Letters took four weeks between Paris and Pnompenh, but Clara and André wrote each other every day. Her dispatches detailed her initiatives; his missives talked of Chinese theater, art dealers, and his meeting with various cats—all, he assured her, possessed of beneficent powers.

In a quiet moment she decided to write a few appropriate words to André's mother, to say she was at her disposal should Berthe Malraux want to see her. A few days later, a tall handsome woman with a young girl's voice showed up at Simone and André Breton's apartment and asked for Clara. "I'm André's mother," she said. Clara gave her all the good news. Berthe, in turn, told her daughter-in-law that the grocery store in Bondy had finally been sold. Together with her mother and her sister, she would be looking for a decent apartment in Paris. Perhaps Clara would come and live with them, at least until André's return.

"I'm sorry I was opposed to your marriage," Berthe said after a silence.

Clara couldn't find it in herself to despise this woman who admitted she had not been able to tolerate the idea of her son marrying a Jew. "From that moment, I loved her," Clara would write. "A little later I met her sister and mother. Grandmother Adriana Romania impressed me; tall, straight like a queen mother in a Frans Hals painting, she treated neither the divorced Berthe nor her single daughter with harshness or asperity."[3]

---

[3] Clara Malraux, *Nos Vingt Ans.*

11. KNOWING THEIR PLACES

Deep in the history of Vietnam are not one Joan of Arc but four woman warriors.

For a millennium a Mongolian people had settled northern Vietnam and built a Bronze Age civilization, but in 111 B.C. the Han dynasty of China overran the country and named it Annam, "pacified country," a name the conquered people resented. The Chinese created administrative districts under military governors while civilian advisers imported Confucian concepts stressing respect for authority. They levied troops and taxes and taught the population Chinese, but failed to assimilate them. Over the centuries the Vietnamese repeatedly challenged the Chinese, and hostility to foreign domination was to be a part of the national psyche.

In contrast to women elsewhere in Asia and Europe, Vietnamese women could inherit land, serve as trustees of ancestral cults, and share their husbands' property. To avenge the murder of her dissident husband by a Chinese commander, Trung Trac, a titled lady, and her sister Trung Nhi mustered other restive nobles to drive out the Chinese. The Trung sisters were joined by a third woman, Phung Thi Chinh, who in the middle of the battle is said to have given birth and, after strapping the newborn to her back, continued to fight. Their victory was short-lived. Two years later, in A.D. 42, the Chinese crushed the Trung sisters' independent state and the sisters committed suicide by throwing themselves into a river.

The Chinese model, often imposed with cruel harshness, shaped the Vietnamese people. Ancestor worship and its attendant family structure rooted itself in the popular consciousness together with the solid village structure, the Chinese alphabet, and the begrudging dominion of Mandarins—a caste of nine ranks of public officials, each distinguished by a particular kind of button on the cap—that effectively governed the Middle Kingdom.

Three hundred years after the Trung sisters, another woman launched a revolt against the Chinese. Trieu Au wore golden armor and led a thousand men into battle riding an elephant. Like the Trung sisters and Phung, she was remembered by a temple and, in the late twentieth century, became a national heroine for her words of defiance: "I want to rail against the wind and the tide, kill the whales in the sea, sweep the whole land to save the people from slavery, and I refuse to be abused."

Seven hundred years after the Han invasion, the Annamese succeeded in throwing off direct Chinese rule. After a brief reoccupation by the Chinese Ming dynasty, the Annamese themselves became imperialists and declared war on their neighbors. They defeated the Khmers in the south and extended Annam south to Danang. Although nominally independent, Vietnam remained a tributary state to the Ming dynasty. The Chinese forced Annamese peasants to mine for gold, confiscated Vietnamese literature, compelled schools to teach in Chinese, and issued identity cards to families to control them and to facilitate tax collection.

The next rebel leader was Le Loi. Legend has it that he was a simple fisherman who one day cast his net into a lake only to bring up a sword that made him superhuman. Like the women warriors in their misty past, the Vietnamese would never forget Le Loi. They would compose folksongs and poems in his honor and in future struggles recall his Arthurian legend.

In reality, Le Loi was a wealthy landowner who had served the Chinese before starting his uprising. "Every man on earth," he said, "should accomplish some great enterprise so that he leaves the sweet scent of his name to later generations."

Proclaiming himself the prince of pacification, he withdrew to the mountains near his home and rallied relatives, friends, villagers, and even local outlaws, teaching them guerrilla tactics to harass the enemy.

Like the French and the Americans five centuries later, the Chinese occupiers became increasingly insecure as Le Loi's insurrection spread. They clung to towns, building fixed fortifications and venturing out by day only, their big battalions hugging roads and avoiding the bush. Like their Vietcong descendants, the insurgents knew when to strike and when to fade into the jungle, and how to subordinate military action to winning the hearts and minds of the people. Nguyen Trai, a poet who was Le Loi's adviser, wrote "Better to conquer hearts than citadels."

The revolt Le Loi started in 1418 ended in victory ten years later when the Vietnamese, fighting in rain and mud, routed the Chinese in a field near Hanoi. Le Loi established his capital in Hanoi, which he called Dong Kinh and which the Portuguese, when they arrived in search of trade, spelled Tonkin. He distributed land to the poor, rewarded loyal nobles, and set up departments to build dams and irrigation systems to increase the growth of food. Trai sang his praise:

> Peace follows war as day follows night.
> We have purged our shame for a thousand centuries.
> We have regained tranquillity for ten thousand generations.

In 1558, a hundred years after Le Loi had started a golden age, the Le dynasty splintered and two families, the Trinh and the Nguyen, effectively divided the country and fought each other for centuries. The Portuguese, the first Europeans to visit Vietnam, were followed by the Dutch, French, and English during the seventeenth century. In the late eighteenth century, a Nguyen leader turned to France to bolster his cause, setting the scene for French intervention.

While Indochina—and to a large and humiliating extent China—became colonized, Japan was not. After the jolt of Commodore Matthew Perry's 1853 visit, Japan was fortunate enough to have an emperor, Mutsuhito, and a ruling class that realized the country needed to modernize in order to escape creeping colonization. The result was the sweeping social and political reforms of the Meiji ("enlightened rule") period that started in 1868.

The attitude of Vietnam's emperor Tu Doc and his Mandarin court in Hanoi, on the other hand, was exactly the opposite: resist the intruder by locking the country into its past and into ultra conservatism. Two years after the French captured Saigon in 1859, Tu Doc ceded to France the three provinces adjacent to Saigon.

It took the French another twenty years to "pacify" the country, but by 1880 the French controlled not only Cochin China but also Annam (as they named the central part of Vietnam) and Tonkin, the name given to the region around Hanoi. By 1887 France had established the Federation of Indochina, comprising Vietnam, Cambodia, and, after 1893, Laos.

Resistance continued. Phan Boi Chou, a radical monarchist, believed that with Chinese and Japanese help a powerful Vietnamese emperor could prevail over the French. His deputy Phan Chu Trinh, on the other hand, was for a Vietnamese Meiji. To have any future at all, Trinh maintained, Vietnam would have to cooperate with the progressive elements in the colonial power structure as well as with enlightened governments in Paris.

Colonialism never quite had the bracing effect on public opinion in France it did in Britain. No Cecil Rhodes dreamed of making half of Africa part of the empire—and of recovering the United States for the crown—and no Rudyard Kipling sang the glories of the "white man's burden." Still, to salve France's humiliation by Germany in the 1870 Franco-Prussian war that resulted in the loss of Alsace and Lorraine, compensatory attention was focused on overseas enterprises. Commercial interests were captivated by the prospect of new markets abroad and cheap raw materials and maintained that such goals were commensurate with the ideals of the French republic.

There was resistance to overseas expansion at both ends of the political spectrum. Conservatives condemned colonialism as adventurous, costly, and essentially futile, while liberals denounced imperialism as contrary to the first credo of the French revolution—peoples' rights of self-determination. When left-of-center politicians managed to accommodate colonialism as an export of higher ideals, they liked to stress the temporary nature of such undertakings.

Governor-General Paul Bert died in Hanoi in 1886, but during his short tenure he organized France's "civilizing mission" in the new colonies with a policy of association and the creation of a school system that tried to fuse science and Western values with ancestral learning. By making the French penal code the law of the land, Paul Beau, Bert's successor, humanized a justice system that required thieves to be beheaded and adulterous women trampled to death by elephants and that people prostrate themselves before dignitaries.

The conquest of Indochina was expensive, and by the time Paul Doumer became governor-general in 1897 the Paris government had decided to make the Federation of Indochina pay for itself. Doumer's tenure lasted only five years, but it changed everything.

Doumer was a self-made man, a onetime newspaper editor, cabinet secretary, finance minister, and author of a tax reform that had aroused heated arguments. His nomination was partly due to the desire of his enemies to remove him from the political scene in Paris. Not yet forty when he became govenor-general, he centralized the colonial power in his own office and created a vast administration, financed through tariffs and state monopolies on alcohol, salt, and opium, or (as Stanley Karnow would write eighty years later) by essentially transferring "the burden from the French taxpayer to the Vietnamese people, not only saddling them with the cost of supporting their own dominion but also exploiting them in order to gain a fat yield on the colonial investment."[1]

The tax levies provoked sporadic violence. When in 1899 a member of the French Geographical Society asked a courtier at the Hue palace whether one should call Annamese who had attacked a French military outpost pirates, political insurgents, or vulgar Mandarins, the caustic answer was "They are taxpayers."

Traditionally only the Chinese residents of Vietnam had smoked opium, but Doumer built a refinery in Saigon which concocted a

---

[1] Stanley Karnow, *Vietnam: A History* (New York: Viking, 1983).

blend that burned quickly and encouraged consumption. Vietnamese addiction rose so sharply that opium accounted for one third of the colonial administration's income. Doumer's other economic reforms were just as calamitous. Rice was such a lucrative commodity that it spurred land seizures. French speculators and prominent Vietnamese families were so voracious that within twenty years a majority of the country's peasants were tenants or farmed uneconomical small plots. Landless farmers were employed as cheap labor in rubber—after rice, the second largest export—mining, construction, and other industries.

The political establishment in Paris never stood up to colonial interests, and various Paris governments' attempts to impose reforms were effectively killed. "Doumer's economic stewardship brought about powerful and oppressive financial interests, headed by the Banque de l'Indochine, with its triple role of commercial bank, saving and loan institution and issuer of the currency," French historian André Teulières would write. "Only Paris could counteract this by imposing a representative or democratic body, but it didn't. As is so often the case, the colonial lobby ended up believing it ruled by divine right. It curbed, when it didn't outright sabotage, all changes that challenged this pseudo-divine right."[2]

The event that buoyed Vietnamese nationalists was Japan's victory over czarist Russia in the 1905 Russo-Japanese war. It was the first-time an Asian nation had defeated a European power, and Phan Boi Chou immediately traveled to Tokyo to meet Japanese political figures and Sun Yat-sen, the American-educated Chinese leader who in 1911 founded the Chinese Republic. In Japan, Phan Boi Chou formed a political organization to agitate among merchants, students, and other middle-class Vietnamese at home and abroad, and helped create an East Asia United League composed of Chinese, Korean, Indian, and Philippine nationalists. His deputy Phan Chu Trinh broke with him over the reliance on Japan. A Mandarin scholar and essentially a moderate, Trinh—of whom André Malraux had first heard

---

[2] André Teulières, *L'Indochine: Guerre et Paix* (Paris: Charles Lavauzelle, 1985).

when he was interviewed by Victor Golubev—returned to Vietnam and, trusting the instincts of progressive politicians in power in Paris, boldly addressed an open letter to the French government, warning that unless the Vietnamese people could express themselves politically, economically, and socially, upheaval would follow. The abuses of the colonial system, he said, not only humiliated the hearts and minds of the people France was trying to attract; they violated the very ideals France stood for.

This scurrilous epistle, plus Trinh's backing of a revolt in the central highlands and his decision to open a modern school in Hanoi, had ended with imprisonment and a death sentence. After a few years at the infamous Poulo-Condore penal colony in the South China Sea, Trinh had been exiled to France. To earn a living, he became a photographer in Paris.

More than ninety thousand Indochinese served in the French armed forces or as guest workers in France during World War I (flying ace Georges Guynemer's copilot was Captain Do Hun Vi). When they returned, they carried with them a new consciousness of the Western world, its positive side and such negatives as the fact that white men could cheerfully murder each other in war.

Some of them also brought back a rudimentary précis of a new driving force: communism. One who stayed was Nguyen That Thanh, a twenty-nine-year-old who, as a seaman, had been dazzled by the sights of New York, and as a cook had worked in London for the renowned chef Georges Auguste Escoffier and met Irish nationalists, Fabian socialists, and Chinese and Indian workers. In Paris, he worked a while as a retouch artist in Trinh's photo lab. When Woodrow Wilson arrived in Paris in 1919 for the signing of the Versailles Treaty, Nguyen appealed to the American president to support constitutional government, democratic freedoms, and other reforms for Vietnam.

Nguyen never met Wilson.

Several French socialists, including the future prime minister Léon Blum, however, were impressed by the intense Nguyen. They had him address their convention in Tours in 1920 and applauded when he asked for their help.

His acerbic wit and gift for polemics turned him into a pamphleteer and a writer in *L'Humanité,* the new French Communist party newspaper, and *Le Paria,* a journal put out by a group of Asian and African nationalists. "Taxes, forced labor, exploitation; that is the sum total of your civilization," he wrote. French police became interested in him. One inspector suggested that Albert Sarrault, the former governor-general of Indochina and now minister of colonies, meet him. Sarrault refused, saying Nguyen was merely an alias for Trinh.

A decade later, Nguyen changed his name to Ho Chi Minh.

The atmosphere in Saigon in 1924, when André, Louis, and the ever-faithful Xa arrived from Pnompenh to await the appeal, was a mixture of satisfied languor and, for the Vietnamese majority, creeping anger. The royal houses of Annam, Cambodia, and Laos were left with only a figleaf of authority. Any idea of training the indigenous population for ultimate autonomy was utterly repellant.

Indochina was the most profitable of all French overseas possessions. Enterprising white settlers enjoyed the good life, as did that overwhelming majority of French people—the members of the civil service. Until the world slump in rubber prices, business was healthy and fortunes were quietly being made under the often competent rule of successive governors-general who had really only one iron dictate—that no one rock the boat.

The current governor-general, Martial-Henri Merlin, a former governor in French Africa, was a hardliner who cracked down on any form of native protest following an attempt on his life in Canton. Not that anyone saw the assassination attempt as the writing on the wall.

Indochina was a police state attenuated by tropical torpor, a multiracial society that operated more by explicit permission than implicit consent and contained an amorphous gray area of activities that were never officially approved. As Victor Golubev had told André, the prosperity was, to a large extent, based on the meticulous exploitation of eminently proud and sensible people. More than Cambodians and Laotians, the inhabitants of Vietnam's lush southern delta were victims of continued land confiscation, but all three ethnic groups were deprived of practically all liberties. Only one native in a thousand, and only in Cochin China, had the right to vote. They were excluded from most economic sectors except in the most menial jobs. Only about one thousand of the seventeen million Indochinese could ever hope for higher education. The University of Hanoi, the only institute of higher learning in Indochina, accepted only one thousand graduate Annamese students a year. A press law enacted under Doumer required preliminary authorization for anything published in quoc-ngu or Chinese. Pesky interference, intimidation, direct and indirect pressures, plus the governor-general's pleasure effectively muffled the mild French-language dissent.

Education was a prickly issue. The best French minds, often generous and unselfish, espoused the sonorous idea of their country's *mission civilisatrice*, while cynics, especially in the higher echelon of colonial administrations, tended to believe that to educate anyone was to create a potential revolutionary.

If a majority of settlers agreed that a strong injection of French culture was probably the best way to prevent native restlessness, it was still surprisingly difficult for an Annamese actually to *get* an education. Grades from the University of Hanoi were not transferable to schools in France. Annamese who graduated from the Hanoi medical school were not doctors but "health officers." The departure of Annamese graduates who nevertheless wished to pursue their studies in France (and whose parents could afford to send them) depended on the colonial administration approving their dossiers. And the deciding paper in any young Vietnamese person's dossier was a police affidavit.

The French civil service had more power than the Mandarins ever had. The requirement that Frenchmen learn Vietnamese as a prerequisite for civil service had proved a failure. A 1910 government survey had revealed that in all of Annam only three Frenchmen were sufficiently fluent in Vietnamese to carry on the complex business of administration. Ironically, while so few French officials spoke the language or could appreciate the outlook of the people they ruled, French Oriental scholars at L'Ècole Française d'Extrême-Orient, established in Hanoi in 1899, carried out the most remarkable research into the Indochinese languages, customs, history, and—as Clara and André had found out—archeology.

To overcome the language barrier, a new native profession had sprung up—the Vietnamese interpreter. Chauffeurs, houseboys, and others who had learned enough French in their work to communicate took up interpreting. Most French administrators felt comfortable with these Vietnamese who "knew their place." Essential middlemen with shrewd knowledge of the colonial system and its fuzzy edges, these interpreters manipulated the process at the expense of their fellow Vietnamese. They got away with anything. If one of their victims did try to complain to the authorities, how could he or she do it except through the interpreter?

The end of World War I had increased France's overseas territories in Africa and in the Near East, land taken from Germany and Turkey and administered under a League of Nations trusteeship. Sprawling over four and a half million square miles of territory in Africa, Asia, the Caribbean, and the South Seas, the French empire had a population of one hundred million, more than twice the number of people in metropolitan France. By the mid-1920s the colonies were providing prestige and economic benefits. They supplied raw materials and, in a world economy sliding toward protectionism at the end of the decade, provided a profitable outlet for capital and for expanding markets.

From his exile in Canton, where he went to avoid French police, Phan Boi Chou might call on the Vietnamese people to revolt. In Saigon, Paul Monin might channel Saigon dockworkers' discontent into a strike and Trinh (who had been allowed to return from exile in Paris) might call for a national awareness, but the anticolonial resentment was still subterranean.

As *Le Paria* was being smuggled into the country and read furtively behind closed shutters, so the new ideas were being secretly circulated.

12. IF YOU HADN'T SAVED MY LIFE

None of the correspondence between Clara in Paris and André in Pnompenh and Saigon was to reach posterity. A letter from Fernand, dated August 12, 1924, however, survived among Clara's papers. After explaining how and why he had not been able to meet Clara at dockside in Marseille, the forty-eight-year-old father wrote to his son:

> I met Clara in Paris at 9 this morning. Just in time; badly received by her family, the poor thing was at wit's end and our affectionate meeting was a great comfort. As I write, she is resting in a room near mine, calm and collected, surrounded by the warm tenderness she so much needed.
>
> Because we're in Paris, doing what we have to do to redress the situation. Newspaper stories—have a look at the dates—will show you that you're no longer alone and that the struggle will henceforth be less arduous, because you'll no longer be the only one to carry on the fight.
>
> After a moment of panic when your flabbergasted comrades saw the grotesque revelations in the papers, Clara, let me tell you, en-

lightened your friends and aroused them from their torpor. Articles, destined for the literary press to begin with, will show 1) that you are not the alleged adventurer, 2) that you are a real author, recognized as a member of the young literary set, 3) that you are appreciated and liked, and 4) that after what you have been through, even your bookish enemies join forces with older writers to testify to your worth and to protest, via a petition, against your conviction.

Clara is some little woman. Feeling confident now, she's like an alert bee, buzzing all over the place with an intelligence and judgment that I find astonishing although, of course, I admire it. No step is too much for her. She charms me with her analysis of the situation, her perfect common sense, her unquestionable knack for saying and doing the right thing, when, with your friends, she outlines the main points of stories that others then write practically as she dictates them.

You sure did the right thing when you sent her to France.

Louis Chevasson had a new lawyer, a Maître Gallois, who obtained a two-week postponement, but on October 8, André and Louis faced their new judges, confident the Pnompenh conviction would be squashed. André, too, had retained new counsel, a Maître Béziat.

The three-judge appellate court was presided over by Superior Court Justice Edmond Gaudin, a magistrate with a reputation for integrity. With only minor objections by Béziat and Gallois, Justice Gaudin used the brief morning session to sum up the known facts of the case. During the afternoon the court heard the prosecution's long and detailed indictment: the crime was premeditated and André Malraux was a vainglorious liar and not at all the scholar he claimed to be. The prosecution demanded that the three-year conviction be upheld and that the defendants be deprived of their civil rights.

Béziat was a strapping man with striking features and a booming voice. Rising to defend his client, he immediately zeroed in on the central point of law. The question was not whether a crime had been committed, he said, but *which* law allegedly had been transgressed.

"Cambodian law?" he began. "The edifice we're concerned with is situated in a territory that wasn't even part of Cambodia until so declared by a standing order issued by the governor-general of Indochina, a standing order that, incidentally, was only confirmed by presidential decree eight years later. Now, if we go by French law, there is no crime. Why? Because French jurisprudence can only consider these mounds of stones as belonging to no one, the *res nullius* of Roman law.

"How can you talk of classified monuments?" he thundered in the direction of the prosecutor. "After Professor Parmentier visited the site in 1916, he started an inventory of, and I quote, 'fragments.' Why didn't he start the process of classifying a monument? Because the ruins were in a lamentable state, because what he found was no more an edifice than construction materials that someone has stacked while awaiting a building permit?"

The lawyer cited a number of precedents that established the government's obligation to issue a decree specifically naming a monument or national treasure before it could be classified and finally undertook to discredit the prosecution's argument that his client was simply a rapacious adventurer and a liar. From his bulging briefcase he pulled the petition signed by twenty-four literary figures attesting to André Malraux's literary and intellectual gifts.

When Gallois rose to speak he was brief but stinging. Since his colleague had made the major points, he merely described Louis as a sober, hard-working young man. Neither defendant, he maintained, deserved the label "common criminal." Moreover, he reasoned in a calculated crescendo, if these young men were to be imprisoned for taking carved stone from Banteai Srey, should not the same penalty be meted out to various governors, high commissioners, and administrators who had done the same thing? "Khmer art!" he growled. "Khmer art, everybody has the mouth full of Khmer art since the misfortune of these two young men." Instead of having them ordered shadowed, wouldn't it have been more generous for Police Commissioner Cremazy and other officials to have *warned* them?

The documentation and the eloquence of the defense had some influence on Justice Gaudin and the two other magistrates. On October 28 the court reduced André's punishment to one year, Louis' to eight months, and granted both right to petition for a suspended sentence. The verdict meant they would never serve the terms but that the convictions became part of their permanent judicial record.

ONE YEAR SUSPENDED SENTENCE was the extent of André's message to Clara. He was furious but couldn't afford to tell it all in a telegram. He met Monin and was convinced that, like the Annamese, the Cambodians, and the resident Chinese who were Monin's friends, he too was a victim of the people who exploited the colony. And he wanted his devatas.

Six years later André would claim the bas-reliefs were "sequestered at the museum in Pnompenh, that all I'm waiting for is the final judgment." As things stood he was never to obtain a conclusive decision. The Cour de Cassation in Paris ordered a technical retrial before three different judges of the Saigon Appeals Court in 1930. By then, however, André was in no mood to travel to Saigon for a third trial.

Two days before André's twenty-third birthday, he and Louis boarded a freighter for Marseille. The estimated date of arrival of the *Chantilly* was November 24, 1924, twenty-four days after departure.

In Paris, Clara was still selling books and knickknacks and trying to find a publisher for her translation of Friedrich Hölderlin's 1797 novel *Hyperion*. André and Simone Breton continued to feel responsible for her. They had her come with them to the Cyrano café on Place Blanche where the surrealists met every day.

Simone took Clara to the Shakespeare and Company bookstore to see if Anglo-American names could be added to the still-growing list of signatories on the André Malraux petition. Sylvia Beach wasn't in, and Adrienne Monnier, the other half of the lesbian owner-duo, barely had time for them. Jean Painlevé, son of the Sorbonne University mathematician and wartime prime minister Paul Painlevé, added his name to the petition. For a while the eighty-eight-year-old Anatole France was rumored also to be ready to sign. He died before he could accomplish the gesture, however, and the surrealists scandalized the mourning world of letters by calling him "an exquisite cadaver."

François Mauriac, the sensitive and self-conscious poet, novelist, playwright, and biographer, wrote Clara a moving letter that, with his permission, she had published.

Besides managing the Connaissance bookstore when her husband was busy as a publisher, Marcelle Doyon was an expert seamstress. She stitched together a modest new wardrobe for Clara.

Clara stayed for a while with Claire and Ivan Goll. When André's mother, grandmother, and aunt found an apartment near the Gare Montparnasse, Clara stayed there. The concern that her in-laws showed made Clara think of her own mother and the third floor of the townhouse now void of her and André's presence. A cousin visiting from Germany told Clara he thought the way her brothers had treated her was sad.

On Sundays she sometimes visited André's father and his young wife and two young sons in Orléans. On weekdays when Fernand came to Paris to tend to his stock market affairs, Clara and he sometimes lunched together. If she went with him to Orléans on a Friday afternoon, they relaxed and laughed in the restaurant car until a few kilometers before the train reached its destination. As the train pulled into the station, his face took on the restrained mien of a family man.

One day he told her "A woman should never tell the whole truth to her husband. My son is like other men. Don't idealize him."

She laughed. "I know him better than you do. I'll never keep any secrets from him."

In the hindsight of her memoirs, Clara never commented on the irony of the way the families treated her. When André was a child, he couldn't wait to grow up and get away—and, once out of the skirts of the three women, to feel ashamed of them. But it was now these women and André's divorced father who came to her rescue and comfort. Her own childhood had been coddled, yet with the mistake of her marriage and the humiliation of André's conviction, all her beloved mother and brothers could think of was family appearances and locking her out of the way.

Clara was in Marseille to greet André. Her eyes sought her husband among the passengers in the stern of the *Chantilly*. She couldn't find him.

Instead of docking, tugboats turned the ship around. It seemed to take an eternity. When the gangplank was hoisted into place, she saw him—tall, emaciated, ridiculous in his tropical suit, running down toward her in the December rain. They flew into each other's arms, and before she could ask him how he was, he told her they would be returning to Saigon.

He slipped out of her arms for a second to say goodbye to a Vietnamese who was wrapping himself in furs as if he had debarked on the North Pole. "This guy was at a banquet they gave me just before I left," André said when the man left.

"What banquet?" She had forgotten his intuitive impatience and half-finished sentences.

"The Vietnamese need a free newspaper and Monin and I will publish one," he said, offering her a package of Indian hemp—which, he said, provoked marvelous music and colored images.

"So you and Monin met?"

"You're right, he's great."

They couldn't wait to be alone together and took a room near the Gare St.-Charles. On the way upstairs he told her he had met Monin every day, sometimes alone, sometimes with politically aware Chinese and Annamese. "You and I are leaving in a month or six weeks."

After they had made love, she tried the marijuana. "You chew it, and when you're down to the ligneous part you spit it out," he said.

"Like coco leaves?"

"You can direct your inner show and I'll keep you company by reading poetry."

He had tried it three or four times, he said. What was nice about Indian hemp was that it was not habit-forming. As she chewed, she asked him if he had had other adventures during the four months they had been separated. He had not.

It would be easier to tell him about her brief intimacy with Charles G. had André spent a night with Tuit, with Bah, or someone else. Lying on the bed, wrapped in sheets, she began to feel the effect of the drug. No marvelous music assailed her—if anything, she heard the all-too-real whistles of shunting locomotives. She told him about the shipboard affair.

After a while she became aware of him sitting at the foot of the bed in silent tears. Later he stood by the window curtain and, when she called to him, quietly said, "If you hadn't saved my life, I would leave you."

Still later, she said, "I don't want you to stay because I've saved your life, because you feel you owe me something." She wanted him to stay for deeper reasons. She told herself that if his next words were that he'd somehow find it in himself to forgive her, she would leave.

"Why did you do it?" he said.

She sensed that he loved her, but wished his question had been asked with more tenderness.

A nearly empty apartment became available next to that of André's mother, and André and Clara moved in. Clara wished the two of them would have it out, that they would be naked in the bare apartment when they confronted each other. But it was when they crossed a city park that they suddenly squared off.

One more time he asked: "Why did you do it?"

For a while they walked. She wanted it to come out right.

"With that hopeless ass."

She got angry and told him Charles G. was not an ass. He grabbed her wrist and said, "It's better if you don't defend him."

"Why?"

He let go. She felt he was stupid and unjust.

"To think that this guy can despise you now," he sighed.

"I know he doesn't despise me."

"I know what a man thinks of a woman he's had."

She didn't know whether she should comfort her husband or stand up to him. Instead, she said, "I'm not an object whose worth is restricted to the personality of its buyer."[1]

The word *forgiveness* lurked under their dispute but was never pronounced. He was deeply hurt, but he didn't say he could forgive her; she didn't think of saying she was sorry.

---

[1] Clara Malraux, *Nos Vingt Ans*.

Their love was total, they had always said.

Total love meant both total devotion and total freedom. That marriage could take on conventional forms was something new. Still, how could either of them—he, now; she perhaps some day—question their commitment? Seeing how deeply in pain he was, she almost wished—but how?—that he could be spared the grief.

OPPOSITE: *The object of their lust: Classic stone relief of heavenly concubines similar to those "lifted" by Louis Chevasson and the Malrauxs. These are from the Angkor Wat temple in Siem Riep, Cambodia. (Library of Congress)*

TOP LEFT: *Amateur archeologist Lunet de la Jonquière (center) looking for lost temples during his 1901 expedition into the Cambodian jungle. His writings added fuel to the fire of André's scheme. (Library of Congress)* BOTTOM LEFT: *The Louis Finot Museum at L'École Française d'Extrême-Orient in Hanoi, where André and Clara met Henri Parmentier, the chief of archeology. The Far-Eastern French School was the Paris government's appointed custodian of Vietnamese, Cambodian, and Laotian art treasures. (Library of Congress)* ABOVE: *A coddled German-Jewish childhood: Clara Goldschmidt with her brothers Paul and Maurice about 1905. (Florence Malraux Archives)*

ABOVE: *André and his father at the end of the Great War. Fernand Malraux was an inventor of better mousetraps, a stock market habitué, and a ladies' man with few principles but a big heart. (André Malraux Archives)* OPPOSITE: *Clara as a teenager with her mother, Margrete Goldschmidt, and her brother, Paul. (André Malraux Archives)*

ABOVE: *A pale and intense André Malraux at twenty-one, about the time he and Clara met. (André Malraux Archives)* TOP RIGHT: *Clara Malraux in 1926, just back from the colonies. (Roger Viollet Archives)* BOTTOM RIGHT: *The market at Pnompenh in 1923. Europeans always wore white suits and cork helmets. (Library of Congress)*

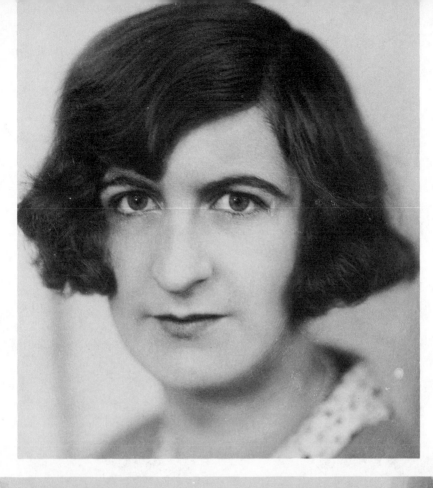

TOP LEFT: *The famous Khmer smile of the aspara, Angkor Wat, thirteenth century. (Musée Guimet)* BOTTOM LEFT: *The ruins of Banteai Srey. "There were lengths of wall in slabs of purple sandstone, some carved and others plain, all overgrown with hanging ferns," André wrote. Clara remembered the stateliness, the beauty of the ruins, and the glimpse of an emerald snake. (Library of Congress)* ABOVE: *Convicted grave-robbers André Malraux (left) and Louis Chevasson at the time of their July 1924 trial in Pnompenh. (André Malraux Archives)*

ABOVE: *André at the Manolis Hotel. On Wednesdays the hotel set up a gramophone in a large upstairs room, and settlers and their ladies from surrounding plantations came in for an evening of socializing. (Axel Madsen)* TOP RIGHT: *"Tourists demanding comfort and good food stay at the Grand Hotel," says Aristotle Manolis' advertising. Clara and André stayed there in early 1924 while awaiting a trial date. (Library of Congress)* BOTTOM RIGHT: *Pnompenh Hospital's indigent women's ward. While Clara was hospitalized here with dengue fever, her destitute husband was allowd to share her hospital room. (Library of Congress)*

ABOVE: *The colonial serenity of the hotel and restaurant at Do Son, Vietnam. Cambodia, Laos, and Vietnam had been French colonies for over a hundred years; life was sweet if one was French. (Library of Congress)* OPPOSITE: *Last hurrah. After their first paper,* L'Indochine, *was abruptly shut down, Paul Monin and the Malrauxs published* L'Indochine Enchainée *with hand-set type brought from Hong Kong. More flysheet than newspaper,* L'Indochine Enchainée *continued to attack the colonial regime. The front-page editorial above appealed to the new governor-general, Alexandre Varenne, to give Vietnam meaningful reforms. (Axel Madsen)*

L'Indochine enchaînée

Sommaire

EDITION PROVISOIRE DE L'INDOCHINE
PARAISSANT DEUX FOIS PAR SEMAINE,
LE MERCREDI ET LE SEMEDI, EN ATTEN-
DANT QUE L'ADMINISTRATION NOUS
RENDE OU SE DECIDE A METTRE EN
VENTE, LES CARACTERES D'IMPRIMERIE
QUI NOUS APPARTIENNENT ET QU'ELLE
A CONFISQUES AU MEPRIS DE TOUTE LOI
ET DE TOUT USAGE.

DIRECTEURS :
ANDRE MALRAUX ET PAUL MONIN

DIRECTION : 12, RUE TABERD
LE NUMERO : 20 CENTS.

Editorial

LETTRE OUVERTE A MONSIEUR
ALEXANDRE VARENNE
GOUVERNEUR GENERAL,

Monsieur le Gouverneur Général,

La dépêche annonçant votre nomination au
poste que vous allez occuper était à peine parve-
nue en Cochinchine, que le Gouverneur se mettait
à l'œuvre pour vous donner en spectacle, lors de
votre arrivée, la Comédie qu'on appelle votre
Réception

Vous n'êtes pas sans avoir entendu parler du
mécontentement qui, de jour en jour, grandit en
Cochinchine. Vous l'avez marqué dans vos discours, où vous avez parlé, à plusieurs reprises,
de réformes nécessaires. Or, il va de soi que lorsque les institutions sont bonnes, il n'est point
nécessaire de les réformer ; lorsque les hommes
qui les appliquent sont justes, il n'est point nécessaire de les mettre à la retraite.

Donc, vous ne croyez point que tout allât pour le
mieux en Cochinchine. Cette pensée qui annon-
çait des demandes d'explications, voire même
d'enquêtes, ne pouvait être admise. Il convenait
de vous préparer une Cochinchine toute en or,
avec de beaux discours dans lesquels l'émotion
voilât l'indigence de la langue française ; de vous
faire savoir que le Gouverneur Cognacq est aimé
de ses administrés ; de former un bloc impres-
sionnant et de vous amener, enfin, à vous péné-
trer de cette idée que la politique antillaire des
pourboires ingénieusement distribués est la plus
précieuse acquisition de l'esprit français et la
base de toute action coloniale.

Maintenant, Monsieur le Gouverneur général,
que les diverses fanfares vous laissent en paix,
nous voudrions vous demander un effort : celui de
lire cette lettre, dans laquelle nous avons l'intention d'établir ceci :

BELOW: *The Continental Hotel and Saigon municipal theater in the stillness of noonday heat, 1925. (Library of Congress)* OPPOSITE: *Governor-General Alexandre Varenne, who gave the people of Vietnam, Cambodia and Laos their first real reforms under French rule. (National Archives)*

TOP LEFT: *Lenin's man in China, Mikhail Borodin. André was fascinated by this former schoolteacher who masterminded a revolution in Asia. Borodin would later figure prominently in André Malraux's fiction.* (National Archives) BOTTOM LEFT: *Colonial splendor. An aerial view of the governor-general's palace in Saigon.* (National Archives) ABOVE: *Treasure of the Silk Road. If the* devatas *of Cambodia eluded Clara and André in 1924, they managed to get their hands on Greco-Buddhist art seven years later while traveling in Afghanistan along the ancient Silk Road between China and Europe. This "hybrid" carving of Buddha shows Western—even Christian—influence in its bowed head.* (Roger Viollet Archives)

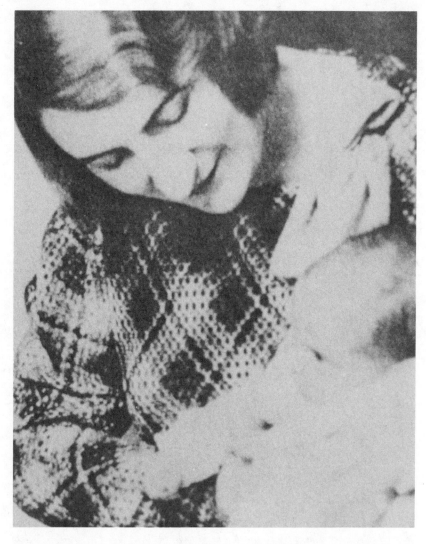

ABOVE: *Clara with Florence a few months after the Malrauxs' only child was born in March 1933. In October of that year,* Man's Fate *was published and André became world-famous. (André Malraux Archives)* OPPOSITE: *Throughout her full, turbulent life, Clara Malraux struggled to find herself. She never remarried. Here is Clara in 1982, going on 85. (Florence Malraux)* FOLLOWING PAGE: *André Malraux (left) and author Axel Madsen in 1975 at Verrières outside Paris, where Malraux spent his last years. (Paula Porter)*

PART TWO

13. THE CHALLENGE

Clara and André left for Saigon in January 1925. They were in third class this time, segregated by sex—six women passengers in one cabin, six men to another. Moments of intimacy were snatched under the stars by crawling into one of the lifeboats. When they were alone they talked about the journalistic enterprise lying ahead and the three books André was to write—books sure to be set in the Asia they both loved and feared.

The women in Clara's cabin were the wives of noncommissioned officers returning to garrisons they already knew and preferred to any town in France. When they talked about the Annamese, the running theme was make sure they do what you tell them. Several of the women had small children, who woke each other up crying in the clammy night. If André resented anything besides the proximity of sweating and snoring males, it was the way the crew made them know they were in third class.

Maurice Sainte-Rose was a fellow passenger who became a friend. When Andre spent long hours reading in a deck chair, Clara often strolled the deck with the soft-voiced young man whose father was French and mother Vietnamese. As they talked, she sensed how deeply the humiliations of being Eurasian had scarred him. It was perhaps more difficult to be of mixed race than to be Jewish. Maurice's family was wealthy, and Clara believed him when he said he had lost or spent all his money in France. "My mother must not find out that I travel third class," he told her. "Before Saigon I'll change to first class." Clara didn't tell him that André and she planned to do the same thing, that they, too, wanted to blur their footprints.

The voyage was long and boring. It was hard even to spend money in third class. In the Strait of Bab el Mandeb they decided to do something positively silly. They would spend the three thousand francs still in their possession on a party for their fellow passengers. They got hold of a gramophone, bought a case of champagne from the steward, and in the third class dining room saw the men take off their jackets and the tight skirted ladies try the black bottom before everybody linked hands and executed an old fashioned farandole.

"We're gonna win," Clara cried, flying past André.

They drank, danced, and sweated. When the music stopped, André climbed on a table to declaim a few verses from a Maurice Magre reader, the only book of poems he had found in the shipboard library. The guests demanded silence. They were curious. The Malrauxs were a funny couple.

André read a poem in which sensuousness and Oriental mysticism blended with symbolist subtlety. The guests seemed fascinated by the rhythm of his voice. When he was through and jumped down, no one started to rewind the gramophone. Some stayed and had another drink, others went to their cabins.

Clara and André went arm in arm out on deck. They were going to make a success of their lives. Almost everything had gone wrong the first time out. This time it would be different. This time they were becoming involved in a cause that was not their own.

The ocean was calm, glittering in the moonlight. On the horizon they could see the sliver of the African coastline. They knew what they were doing this time. The fight ahead was to be a joint struggle, a rallying of dynamic forces, a bridge toward awakening aspirations.

Leaning on the railing, they felt the heat invade them again, clammy and annoying but familiar like well-worn clothes.

The book contract had come only two days before their departure, but it had crowned four successful weeks in Paris. Bernard Grasset was the arch rival of the Gallimard brothers. Solely on the strength of a letter of recommendation of Grasset's star author, Francois Mauriac, the publisher had offered a three novel contract and a three-thousand-franc-advance.*

"Here you go," said Grasset. "And don't take too long writing the first book. Think of the lovely publicity that all those writers just gave you."

André's family had doted on him. His mother, grandmother, and aunt treated him like the Prodigal Son, and his father and stepmother listened with fascination to the upcoming newspaper venture, which André described as sweet revenge. Together, Clara and André met their friends and supporters. They saw Pascal Pia, Marcel Arland, the Doyons. André thanked all the signatories of the manifesto and made a special trip to Benoit sur Loire to see Max Jacob in his monastery. "You wife has been fabulous," Max told him.

To have to say thank you to André and Simone Breton was more difficult. André didn't like the clannishness, the dogmas and rituals, catechism and excommunications that the surrealists savored. In art he had a lot in common with them, and in literature they laid claim to the same ancestors—the Marquis de Sade, Nerval, and Jarry—but he wasn't too eager to meet the Bretons.

"Why did you go to people who are my enemies?" he asked dramatically.

"Because Simone and André Breton offered their help," Clara answered. "And, anyway, they didn't behave as your enemy or mine."

She made an appointment with the Bretons and managed to drag André up to Montmartre. When they rang the doorbell, however, no one answered.

---

* Approximately $5100 in 1989 currency.

"They're home," André said. "I'm sure I heard them."

"Maybe they forgot."

Clara and André left. The next day they received a message, telling them that since Breton and several others had been in the middle of an automatic writing seance, they had thought visitors could only be an element of disruption.

The next weekend in Orléans, Clara listened, intrigued, while her husband retold their Cambodian adventure with a whole new overlay of political intrigue. André's indictment of the colonial administration was full of precise details she had never heard before, and he expressed with a conviction that was also new the reasons for his impetuous enthusiasm for an oppressed people. Fernand loved it. His son had been the victim of a political frameup.

In Saigon, André explained, Monin was raising the not inconsiderable funds necessary to start a daily newspaper. Clara and André would have to finance their own return to Indochina.

"I can't dwell on a defeat," André said.

Paternal pride swelled Fernand's chest. The stock market, he admitted, was doing all right. "When you get to Singapore," he told Clara and André, "you'll find a check for fifty thousand francs waiting for you. Do whatever you have to do to get there."

As they sat down for lunch, Fernand said, "Everyone can make a mess of things once," making it perfectly clear that they shouldn't come to him a second time.

They sold what they had left of books and jewels and bought two one way tickets to Singapore, where, perhaps after a short side trip up the Malay Peninsula to Bangkok, Fernand's money would allow them to cross the South China Sea in first class and arrive in Saigon in style.

They had taken the time to visit Marc Chagall's new exhibition and to renew their friendship with the painter and his wife, but André's remaining weeks were taken up with preparations for the newspaper venture.

He made Chevasson the Paris correspondent and tried to enlist the political commitment of Jacob, Breton, and others. Despite vocal leftist sympathies for Abd-el-Krim and his guerrilla efforts to resist French advances in Morocco and the Syrians' armed struggle to shake off the French mandate, no one was particularly interested in André's conscience-raising plans for Indochina. Jacob was deep in his religious period, Breton was busy writing the second surrealist manifesto, and the left in general was busy commenting on Stalin's elimination of Leon Trotsky from power, a first intimation of things being less than perfect in the Soviet Union everybody fervently believed in.

André arranged with A. Fayard and Co., publishers of the recently founded magazine *Candide*, for the right to reprint articles, short stories, and news items. From Messagerie des Journaux, a subsidiary of the giant Hachette publishers and distributors, he obtained Asian distribution rights for a number of supplements and bargained them into reprinting a number of articles from the still nonexistent Saigon daily.

Telling Sainte-Rose they would see him in Saigon, they disembarked in Singapore.

The train ride to Kuala Lumpur, capital of British Malaya, with its Taj Mahal railway station, and on up the Malaysian peninsula to Bangkok was long and exhausting. The heat, which entered the open window along with dust, smoke, cinders, and a thousand insects, made them insensitive to the train's vibrations and to their lack of comfort. The car was full of Chinese who all sat on their legs, talking, laughing, eating, drinking, belching, spitting, and blowing their noses without handkerchiefs, and Indians who sat bunched together like royal poinciana flowers, drops of sweat easily visible on their dark faces. At night the Chinese stripped down to their long johns, the Indians to loincloths.

Listening to the rapid-fire Tamil speech, André said, "You'd get the illusion of speaking Tamil if you ran a cane over an iron grate."

Clara was the only woman, André the only white man on the train. Their fellow passengers offered them tea, kebabs of marinated vegetables, and fruits whose stones they energetically spat out. In her window seat, Clara watched the men and the landscape. This was a country where tin and rubber supported a large polyglot population of Malays, Chinese, Indians, Eurasians, Arabs, Christian Brothers, and pale English administrators.

During a stop at a station it started to rain. They wound up the window and, with the rain drumming on the roof, sat slouching in the suffocating heat. Under the awning on the platform, small muscular men in trousers and small women gaped at the apparition of Clara. The rain stopped as the train chugged away. A tall Sikh with a toothy grin lowered the window. Everything smelled of wet grass and trees and earth.

"Toward the end of the afternoon, I opened a book and the whole exciting and aching world disappeared," she would remember. "Instead, I found myself in a French never-never land full of discreet vegetation that somehow became truer than the reality of the Malaysian odors, sticky contacts, and vocal chanting. I surrendered to the predicaments of modest Europeans whose obsessions were not mine, whose lies were not ours, whose concerns we couldn't understand. Spread out to my right was a rediscovered Asia, the same and yet different from the Asia I knew. In the book I saw an almost mythical France, foreign and familiar. Both were close and each overlapped the other. In Pnompenh, the absence of food had made me delirious. Here again, I felt I was the focal point of things that were both possible and temporary. The only permanence in this gelid world was the man next to me whose presence I wanted to be lasting."[1]

The train arrived in Bangkok at dawn. Clara and André weren't sure they should allow themselves to be pulled in rickshaws, but the coolies outside the railway station were so insistent they finally climbed into a pair of wicker seats and had their luggage loaded into a third.

Rickshaw drivers swerved and sidled with their human burdens all around them. Music blared from coffee shops full of signs in squiggles and curlicues. Riding through town, they thought it was the most radiant and light-hearted city they had ever visited.

They spent six days in a modest hotel owned by a fat and wheezy widower of dubious origin and his two blonde daughters. Clara and André thought the father was someone right out of a Joseph Conrad

---

[1] Clara Malraux, *Les Combats et les Jeux.*

novel. The literary allusion would have been complete, they decided, had the nubile daughters, who entertained sailors but never took them up to their rooms, been half-bloods.

Bangkok enchanted Clara and André. They saw the houseboats and the floating market on the Menam River, the marble courtyards of pagodas where adolescent priests in saffron robes smiled at cripples, and the children, the only beggars in the city. They saw dressed-up dancing monkeys, squid hanging in the entrances to shops next to flattened chicken and pinkish litchis. They felt happiness radiate from the small, vivacious people, the men dusky and animated, the women in surprisingly short haircuts, and the children, little boys naked, little girls with a tiny metal heart covering the pubis and held in place with strings around their waists.

Clara and André didn't know anybody in Bangkok and spent mornings having themselves paddled around in a gondolalike sampan. Here were people, André marveled, who had known oppression but never colonialism, people who had never had values imposed on them from the outside. In the eleventh century Thailand might have been a viceroyalty under the Khmer empire, but the people had nevertheless gained control by absorbing the Khmers. Only once in five hundred years was the capital of Ayutthia sacked and burned by invaders from Burma.

Before Clara and André boarded a Chinese steamship for Saigon, they bought a bronze head, greenish with patina on the outside and blackened with soot on the inside. The carbonized inside was proof, they were told, that it had survived the burning of Ayutthia. They were willing to believe the story, because the head was a consolation for their confiscated Khmer devatas.

Paul Monin greeted them at the bottom of the first class gangplank. Saigon felt tame and drab after fairyland Bangkok, but André was anxious to plunge into the newspaper project.

Paul installed Clara and André at Saigon's Continental Hotel, with its Paris style ground-floor terrace, wicker chairs, noisy ceiling fans, and silent Vietnamese waiters. The three-story hotel was on the corner of the Rue Catinat and the Boulevard Bonnard in the heart of the European district, close to the Monin law office and to the space he had rented in the Rue Taberd for the newspaper. The French elite met between the potted palms on the narrow terrace.

Clara and André's room was big. If they stepped out onto their tiny balcony they could look across at the saffron-colored Municipal Theater and up the Rue Catinat toward the cathedral. With its arcades, Rue Catinat was a replica of the Rue de Rivoli in Paris; the Quai de Commerce was the Quai d'Orsay. In the evening, the cafe *terrasses* were as thick with people as the *grands boulevards* at home. Maurice Sainte-Rose came for lunch one day and told Clara that Vietnamese not accompanied by whites were not allowed on the Continental terrace. Her indignation surprised him. "You must take life as it is," he said, "even if you have to cheat a little."

One night when Clara and André were Paul's guests on the terrace, the lawyer pointed discreetly toward a bald man with pince-nez and a luxuriant, old fashioned mustache. "Colonel Darles," he whispered. Everybody knew the colonel was the governor-general's henchman, but there were stories that Darles was the real power, that Martial-Henri Merlin was in *his* pocket. Clara stared. It was the first time she had seen the chilling personage, notorious for having ordered native ringleaders of a prison uprising buried to their neck in sand until red ants devoured their faces. Men in tropical white and ladies in pastel hats nodded and smiled to the monocled colonel.

The attempt on Merlin's life was not the reason he resigned. The Paris government recalled him because he was unable to solve the financial deficit in the colony. His successor had not yet been named and Indochina was going through an interim period that Paul thought gave them an opening.

The last months of the Merlin regime had wiped out all opposition outlets. Since newsprint in quoc ngu demanded prior approval by the governor general's office, only a pair of French language opposition papers, published by Vietnamese intellectuals, had managed short lived existences. Bui Quang Chieu was a heavy set engineer who had been editor of *La Tribune Indigène* and leader of a timid reform movement, both shut down by the government. The satirist Nguyen An Ninh had turned *La Cloche Felée* into a lampooning weekly sufficiently courageous to be subjected to the same fate. Merlin's phrase in ordering the suspension was to remain famous. "If you want to train intellectuals, go to Moscow," he told Ninh, "because the seeds you want to plant in this country will not germinate."

Besides Henry Chavigny de Lachevotière's *L'Impartial,* the big circulation newspaper, and its strident competitor *Le Courrier Saigonnais,* the daily press included the scandal sheet *La Voix Libre* and perhaps Saigon's best paper *L'Echo Annamite.*

As publisher and editor of a new competitor on the newsstands, Monin and Malraux could expect little sympathy from *L'Impartial.* The establishment paper had campaigned against Monin when he ran for office and called him a Communist when he organized the dockworkers' strike. As for André, the paper had not only covered the trial in Pnompenh but also published an aroused editorial against the principal defendant in "L'Affaire d'Angkor." Despite his sonorous name, publisher Lachevrotière was a rather dubious upholder of colonial rectitude. His paper was bankrolled by the Indochina lobby and a word from the governor-general's office made him pen vituperative editorials against designated targets.

L'Echo Annamite was owned by a Vietnamese physician, Dr. Le Quang Trinh. Dr Trinh's medical function was to examine local prostitutes for syphilis. In a whorehouse one day, he had been severely beaten. Rumor had it that the beating had been administered—by Colonel Darles' henchmen?—to make sure that he and his newspaper didn't step out of line. His editor-in-chief was Dejean De la Batie, a newspaper pro, journalist, and Saigon habitué. De la Batie was the son of a French diplomat and a Vietnamese mother. He could pass for French, but, unlike Sainte-Rose, was proud of his mixed blood. Of his Eurasian heritage he said, "Being neither fish nor fowl, I have the appreciable advantage of being both at the same time, although my natural inclination is toward the underdog."

When it came time to hire staff, Paul had decided he would approach De la Batie about coming to work for them. After the first full week of discussions and preliminary planning, André and he were optimistic. If all went according to plan they should have the first issue on the newsstands in less than three months, in early June at the latest.

Paul Monin and André Malraux knew little about newspapering.

Paul was a brilliant lawyer who, as Victor Golubev had said in Pnompenh, believed the solution to colonialism was not so much a matter of ideology and class struggle as of respect for basic human rights. André knew a lot about publishing, was full of ideas and could write biting editorials, but he knew little about deadlines and straight news reporting.

Monin had run for the Colonial Council, lost, and—in a second try in 1922—had been elected with a comfortable margin to a two-year term, the only progressive among this assembly of ruling notables. Instituted in 1880, the Colonial Council had been designed to begin educating the Vietnamese in democracy. By the time Monin was elected, it had twenty-four members. Frenchmen occupied fourteen seats. Six were elected by French residents, eight were appointed by the governor-general and the Chamber of Commerce. The tenVietnamese were elected by twenty-two thousand worthy natives, the only nonwhites with a right to vote.

Monin had been defeated by the establishment candidate in the 1924 elections and was now the rallying point of those minority forces among the colonial French who were progressive and left of center. He believed a different rapport could be established with the Vietnamese, Cambodians, Laotians, and, in Saigon, the sizable Chinese community, to which he felt particularly close. Suspicious of theorizing but a believer in causes and principles, he was more man of action than man of words. He needed a mouthpiece and counted his meeting with Clara and André among his better fortunes.

What lawyer and writer had in common was a contempt for a society built on compromises and the surrender of principles, on conformity and exclusion, racism and idiot bureaucracy. In retrospect, Clara would see the contrast between the two friends as a difference of attitudes toward the people they set out to help.

Monin was no T. E. Lawrence, dreaming of compensating past humiliations by becoming king of some Arabia, she would write. "If he sometimes used the Annamese or the Chinese to raise his own consciousness, he nevertheless saw them as an end in themselves, as people who had not undergone whatever experiences they had endured merely to allow him to sharpen his. Did he know that their values were not his, that it was precisely the lack of western values that had allowed western domination? I doubt it. On the other hand, my companion realized already then that Asians and Africans would have to destroy their own world view, their own convictions, if they were to build a world of their own."[2]

André wondered whether the colonial system could accommodate the inevitable demands for reform and whether France wasn't backing the wrong side. Since only very few young Annamese were allowed to pursue an education in France, they might rise in revolt.

"The crime is not that the French are colonizers, but that they fail to recognize their logical allies—the young Annamese who possess the energy and among whom are students so determined to acquire an education that they stow away on ships to China, England and America, preparing themselves for a time when Indochina will be free."[3]

Late in life he would remember Monin with a touch of condescension while underlining the lawyer's sense of justice, his unselfishness and courage. In 1933 André would predict the colonial empires would not survive a second European war. In 1945 he would tell Charles de Gaulle that France should not try to keep Indochina because it couldn't be done. Toward the end of his life he said people have a tendency to take their problems for examples, that the question of one people ruling another was not one of morality but of destiny.[4]

To introduce André and Clara to the physical dimension of the challenge they were facing, Paul took them on a trip to Phant-Thiet, a fishing town northeast of Saigon famous for its *nuoc mam*, the national fish spice sauce. Paul had friends here, a mixed couple. Thi Sao, the woman, wanted Clara to tell how a Western man and woman expected each other to behave. Through her questions Clara divined the severity of Vietnamese etiquette, a rigidity that the young woman expected European society to match. Their arrival in the town, where fifteen years earlier Ho Chi Minh had taught school,

---

[2] Clara Malraux, *Les Combats et les Jeux*.

[3] André Malraux, "Selection d'energie" in *L'Indochine*, August 14, 1925.

[4] In conversation with the author, November 1975.

coincided with an outbreak of pestilence. The epidemic forced them to leave for Langbian in the Dalat highlands. Thi Sao came with them.

On the road, the foursome ran into coolies fleeing rubber plantation "recruiters" and saw one emaciated man die on a straw mat. In Langbian, local elders came to tell Paul and André that plantation laborers were contracted for three years, encouraged to run up debt in company stores, and kept on subsistence wages. When recruiters came to outlying villages, able-bodied men fled into the jungle. In Cambodia things were worse. Villagers were taxed according to a census that no longer corresponded to reality. To maintain the tax yield, dead souls counted for live people, as in Gogol's Russia. So did the men hiding from plantation recruiters in the bush.

To the east of them was the country of the M'ongs, a matriarchal people. All property belonged to the aged and powerful mothers-in-law. The country was overrun by tigers and all of the M'ongs' stories were about tigers. Local wizards were reputed to specialize in tiger-taming and obtained their hold on the villagers by allowing themselves to be seen riding a muzzled tiger.

Despite an economy based on indentured labor, a repressive tax system, and the occasional excesses of Colonel Darles, conditions in Indochina were no worse than in other Asian colonies. During one month in 1922, British authorities had imprisoned ten thousand Indians for political offenses and, while Mahatma Gandhi's march to the sea to protest the British salt tax (which landed sixty thousand Indians in jail), was still a few years away, Indonesians who had helped Dutchman Hendricus Sneevlier create a political party were sentenced to hard labor and Sneevlier deported back to Holland.

But to seventeen million Vietnamese, Laotians, Cambodians and the ten thousand French bureaucrats and fewer than twenty thousand settlers, events in colonial India, Dutch Indonesia, Portuguese Macao, Japanese Korea, and the American Philippines were minor sideshows compared to the convulsions taking place in China. The huge country to the north had long since lost its coherence. It was a semifeudal country in perpetual civil war being modernized from without by competing expansionist powers: Great Britain and Japan and, to a lesser degree, the United States and the new Soviet Union.

The French administrators looked at the spasms racking China with fear and horror while the Vietnamese, Cambodians, and Laotians looked north with suspended judgment. Rival warlords with private armies controlled entire provinces of China and fought each other with a barbarity that hadn't changed since the Middle Ages. The warlords, sometimes manipulated by one or another foreign interest, sometimes operating as simple bandits, shifted their alliances continually while the Nationalist government, the Kuomintang, tried to impose its will on the four hundred million Chinese, of whom barely five million lived in cities.

The last Manchu ruler, the child emperor P'ui, had been swept from the throne in 1912 and the Republic established by the Kuomintang—the "people's party"—by intellectuals who had studied abroad and somehow represented everything that belonged to the twentieth century in China. Without control of the army, however, the Kuomintang leader Sun Yat-sen, a Christian convert educated in the United States and an early admirer of Japan's Meiji revolution, had soon found himself powerless and driven from Peking by shifting combinations of warlords and petty factions. Since 1921, however, Sun had maintained a government in Canton.

Nationalism and communism were the new forces. Both hoped to be the solution to China's weakness and instability. Frustrated by his inability to attract either Western or Japanese aid and out of sorts with his Canton warlord host, Sun had sought help from the Comintern— the term for the Third International founded in Petrograd in 1919 at the instigation of Leon Trotsky at an international workers' conference chaired by Lenin himself. The Comintern provided militant Communists all over the world with a central organization and, as an intended part of Soviet foreign policy, fomented and supported revolution wherever appropriate.

The Soviet commissar in Canton was a revolutionary André was soon to hear about, an urbane and revolutionary adventurer who radiated both charm and sincerity, a man who before the Russian Revolution had been a teacher in Chicago and who one day would beg André to intercede on his behalf with Joseph Stalin.

Mikhail Borodin was born Mikhail Grusenberg in Vitebsk, the same *shtetl* as Chagall, in 1884. He had joined the Jewish Social Democratic Bund in his teens, switched to the Bolshevik party in 1903 and three years later been arrested and exiled for revolutionary activities. He had emigrated to the United States and, under the name Michael Berg, taught a term at the University of Indiana at Valparaiso before setting up a business school in Chicago. When Lenin's Bolsheviks overthrew the czar, Borodin had returned to Russia to become an agent in Mexico, Scandinavia, and England. In 1923, the Soviet leader had sent the canny Borodin to Canton to become Sun's adviser in a program of reorganizing the Kuomintang into a strong, disciplined, and centralized party strong enough to march northward against Peking and finally create a unified Chinese Republic.

But the aging Sun was reported to be dying.

Cholon, Saigon's huge Chinatown with its own pipeline to events up north, was abuzz with rumors. A workers' demonstration in Canton had turned into a bloodbath when a volunteer brigade sponsored by Cantonese merchants had slaughtered the workers, only to be routed in turn by a "workers' army" organized by the Kuomintang.

In the French colonies the powers that be, from the governor-general's office and the Banque d'Indochine to the plantation owners, had a visceral fear of the Chinese example. Beyond the nightmare of spreading anarchy was the terror of the Chinese republic actually succeeding. Less than three hundred miles north of Hanoi millions of Asians were discovering, albeit in chaotic circumstances, nationalism and self rule. The moral force of the Kuomintang was ridiculed in *L'Impartial,* but membership in the nationalist party was no laughing matter. To belong to the Cholon chapter of the Kuomintang was an act of subversion. To give financial support to the cause was practically considered treason, even for Chinese citizens.

Besides Paul's own money, much of the start-up funds for the new paper came from Cholon. The leaders of the banned Kuomintang chapter were convinced any emancipation in Vietnam could only be a promise of support for China's ultimate liberation. Getting the finances together took three months.

For the title of their newspaper Paul and André deliberately chose the modest, almost dull and uninspiring name *L'Indochine*. Their prospective audience was not limited to Saigon. They wanted to reach readers in Hue, in Hanoi, in Pnompenh, and in Vientiane.

Clara liked the automobile rides to Cholon just beyond the rice paddies. André, Paul, and she usually went out there during the evening cool. They were rarely invited into anyone's home, but toothless old women gave Clara a bowl of unsweetened tea when she sat down with the men. Always she was the only woman.

One night they were invited to a banquet where lukewarm brandy was served and a first toast thanked Paul for his intercessions as a lawyer on behalf of Chinese citizens and for his friendly gestures toward the Republic. Clara would have preferred an opium pipe, but she, André, and Paul were sitting there, trying to keep up with the toasts, when fireworks and firecrackers began crackling outside. "For you," said a small man with a face almost as red as a brick. "To celebrate your becoming members of the Kuomintang."

Clara thought it must have been like that for the first Christians. "They adhered to a faith, that was all," she would remember. "But their baptism wasn't celebrated with firecrackers as was our Chinese adoption. Monin had given more proof of his conviction than the two of us. We were merely hangers on. We were baptized because we looked all right and because of the friendship Monin had bestowed on us."

The small, red faced man was Dong Dai, the Kuomintang emissary in Cholon. Dai knew Borodin and told André the Russian had spent six months in British jails for inciting a riot in Glasgow before being deported. Dai was usually with Dong Thuan, a taller Chinese with a sand-colored complexion. "I quickly found they had a lot in common with Jews," Clara would say. "They were exiled, yet close to their own kind, driven to succeed because the smallest failure could mean absolute disaster." Almost every day, Dai and Thuan could give detailed reports of what was happening in Canton.

Sun Yat-sen died March 12.

The death of the national hero gave Clara and André a firsthand insight into colonial justice. With police permission, the Cholon

Chinese held a memorial service. After the ceremony several Cholon merchants decided to commemorate the occasion by taking up a collection among themselves for what the Chinese Republic needed most of all—an airplane. Six men were in charge of the community collection. One of them, Huyn Vi Kanh, was arrested and jailed—authorities said "kept under surveillance"—for having collected money for a banned political party.

It took all of Paul's considerable persuasive powers to transform the Kanh's incarceration into a deportation to his homeland.

〰 14. READ ALL ABOUT IT

Dejean De la Batie was lured away from *L'Echo Annamite* and, under Paul Monin's publishership, assumed the position of general director. To Vietnamese friends who saw De la Batie's defection as a betrayal, he retorted, "Monin's name alone is a guarantee that the new paper is pro-Annamese." Progressive Annamese should always answer the call of people who not only came with open hearts but brought with them powerful means, he said. As they worked together, Clara got to like this newspaper veteran and decisive militant who knew how to resist pressures and threats against his family. As a Jew who grew up in France, she understood his straddling of cultures and aspirations, his ambivalence. Her sympathy extended to another Eurasian, Louis Minh, the owner of a sizable printing plant who, while continuing to fulfill his government contracts, would print *L'Indochine*.

Before publication, the polyglot Clara went to Singapore to line up collaboration with one of the vastly superior English-speaking newspapers and André to Hanoi to seek the blessing, or at least the tacit neutrality, of the governor-general's office.

To save money, Clara would stay aboard the ship during the three days it was in Singapore harbor. After the seven-hundred-mile voyage south to the British Straits Settlement, Clara was ready to disembark when a Vietnamese crew member slid up to her and, with a nod toward a man standing below in the motor launch taking passengers to shore, said, "That man cop. He to follow you. You careful."

Once on the dock, she made sure the Chinese person was indeed following her before she went directly to the harbor police and told a very tall and blue-eyed Englishman she was being followed.

"What do you mean, Madame?" she was asked.

"I mean, sir, that the Chinaman is following me because it is his job, because he is part of your police force, because he's under your orders."

"I'd be very surprised. . . "

"Me, too. I can't quite see why I should inconvenience Singapore police. But it's nevertheless a fact. I'd appreciate it if you would make sure I won't see him trot behind me. If he has to shadow me, let him be discreet, at least."

"I'm sure there is a misunderstanding here, Madame. But I will make sure you're no longer bothered."

If she was followed after that, she never found out. She took a rickshaw to the offices of *The Strait Times*. The editor-in-chief grinningly admitted he had no high regard for the French press in Saigon, but he agreed to an exchange of news stories.

The next day when she was ready to take the launch back to shore to meet another editor, the undercover agent was there again. She walked directly to the harbor police. As on the day before, her complaint elicited incredulity and assurances that no one would follow her. The little comedy was repeated on the last day.

André's mission was more delicate. After a stopover in Hue and a look at the ancient imperial palace where an imperial court pretended the French had never arrived, André reached Hanoi and asked for an appointment with Maurice Montguillot, the interim governor-general since the departure of Martial-Henri Merlin. Since relatively few Annamese read French, what Paul and André had in mind was the right to publish part of their newspaper in quoc-ngu. Montguillot, however, refused to see the would-be newspaper editor. His secretary claimed that native language news sheets already gave the administration enough headaches and refused permission to print in quoc-ngu. André returned to Saigon convinced of the government's vague but nevertheless very real hostility.

Vinh, Trinh, Pho, Hin, Minh. Calling out the names in the sweltering newsroom reminded Clara of a German poem her grandfather recited when she sat on his knees in Magdeburg.

Phan Chu Trinh was the elder statesman sitting in on editorial decisions and giving them all the benefits of his vast experiences. Since the French had commuted his death sentence and allowed him to return, the former photographer was Vietnam's only authentic political figure not in exile or in prison.

Trinh's association with the paper was discreet, and he preferred meetings that took place in Paul Monin's bungalow. Here he would talk late into the night, consuming endless mugs of tea and playing absent-mindedly with his thin mustache. He had little faith in a proletarian revolution. With Ho Chi Minh, his former lab assistant now in hiding in Canton, he was setting up an organization called the World Federation of Weak Nations. A constitutional assembly would be held in Canton in June.

The first time they met André couldn't help asking Trinh what he thought of the French.

"There are all kinds," he answered, "good and bad people, like in all countries."

"And?"

"In general, they're perhaps better than other colonial masters."

After a few polite smiles, Trinh said, "Stop discriminating. Allow us to live under the same laws as the French. That's all we ask. Armed struggle is useless. In your newspaper you should educate the French, make them realize that Vietnam also has culture."

"We know that," André said.

"I'm not so sure you do."

"Who should we count on?" asked De la Batie.

"Ourselves. And then perhaps on those like Monin and the Malrauxs here, who can persuade and influence a few good French people of *our* humanity."

Although the French closed the school Trinh had in Hanoi before the war, he still believed in education and, with secret funds, he was sending young men to study at the Tokyo Military Academy.

Nguyen An Ninh was the out-of-work editor of the suspended satirical weekly *La Cloche Felée*. Few Frenchmen and few Annamese, said Paul, were as cultivated as this thirty-year-old bachelor. Ninh had made a short trip to Paris the year before. On his way back he had been arrested and questioned by British police in Singapore, his ship cabin ransacked and books, including copies of the Human Rights League text, confiscated. Clara couldn't help feeling better, hearing his story. At least her feeling of being shadowed by an undercover agent was not a figment of her imagination. Ninh was optimistic that the next governor-general could be persuaded to allow him to start up his weekly again. He was touchy and easily hurt, but ready for whatever sacrifices his convictions demanded.

Vinh and Hin were young intellectuals. Vinh was from Cantho in the south, the son of a tyrannical mother who had found a fiancée for him and married him off. Torn between submission and revolt against this schoolteacher harridan, who was not to know that he worked on a newspaper, he craved freedom and deserted mother and wife on occasion to spend nights with a timid young woman he loved. Vinh sought out Clara one day and told her he'd have to quit because his mother had lain down in front of the door, forcing him to step over her to leave the house.

Hin was a moody and passionate graduate student, a ticking time bomb ready to go off any moment. A Montagnard from central Vietnam, he was looking for a commitment when they recruited him. A short, strapping youth, he had been brought up by his uncle, one of the pillars of the throne of Hue. The uncle had cursed this nephew whose aspirations were too brutal for the effete leaders of the ancient court.

Nguyen Pho was a native of Hanoi, seductive and complex. He lived in a tenement behind the Saigon food market but otherwise seemed to live beyond his means.

Events in France seemed to go their way. In April the left-of-center government headed by Premier Edouard Herriot, a gifted orator and

former teacher of literature, asked the National Assembly to vote for a law to control the headlong flight of capital. The proposal was bitterly opposed by private financial and business interests as "rank socialism." When, in the face of a falling franc, Herriot asked parliament to raise the legal limit of currency circulation and to institute a compulsory one-percent loan on private capital, the Chamber of Deputies obliged, but the arch-conservative Senate refused. Whether the Senate had the right to overthrow a government supported by a majority of the popularly elected Chamber of Deputies had never been settled, and there were some who urged Herriot to refuse to step down and instead provoke a dissolution of the Chamber and appeal to the country in a general election.

Fearing the state might go bankrupt before an election could be held, Herriot resigned. His replacement was another left-of-center politician, Paul Painlevé, a brilliant mathematician from the Sorbonne who had been premier for two months during the darkest days of the war (and whose son had signed the André Malraux petition). Painlevé formed a middle-of-the-road government. His idea for getting France out of the government deficit was to impose a one-percent capital gains tax for fourteen years. His ideas on the colonies were sweet music to the ears the little crew in the Rue Taberd.

They wanted everything to be just right. Making up the first issue was exciting. The front page was pasted up, changed, and reset several times in the little newsroom where desks touched each other and assignments were decided with amiable imprecision. As for content, they felt they were in a bazaar of injustice and, if anything, facing a surfeit of stories about official high-handedness—despotism and occasional crime. They would mix international and local news with serious and light information. They had the right to reprint from Hachette publications and Clara was ready to scissor *The Strait Times*.

The first issue was set and reset during a heat wave that made tropical Saigon nearly unbearable. One noisy ceiling fan gave the front office the impression of a clammy breeze—and also made all paper not weighted down sail through the air. The new daily would be set by hand. The composing room, where they did their own proofreading, was a sweltering oven without a fan.

The first subscribers appeared in the front office, and Vinh was sent to Cantho in the south to collect an important donation.

On the eve of the first print run, the Kuomintang leaders in Cholon threw a party at which, as always, Clara was the only woman guest. In his speech Paul Monin underlined his attachment to the Chinese cause, that once the British were forced to evacuate Shanghai, Canton, and Hong Kong it would be nice to believe that the traditions of French democracy could be an ally in China's republican future. Weimar Germany and Soviet Russia had signed treaties with the Canton government renouncing extraterritorial privileges in China. France, it was hoped, would follow.

"I have little to add to all the things that have been said tonight," André said when it was his turn to speak. "We will make this newspaper together. . . . It would be wrong to say our goals are identical, but what brings us together, what unites us, are our enemies." Toasts to the republics of France and China followed.

L'Indochine—"a daily newspaper dedicated to Franco-Annamese rapprochement"—appeared, undated, on June 17, 1925. Even the weather was propitious. Afternoon showers cooled off the city just before Paul, André, Dejean, Vinh, Hin, and Pho took to the streets to give away all the five thousand copies. Clara unloaded armfuls of the eight page news sheet herself in the Rue Catinat.

There was little advertising, but lots of international news and, a novelty, lots of photos. The leading article was a Paris datelined interview with Premier Painlevé.

The head of the government had granted the interview to Jean Bouchor three weeks before his accession to power in April, but what he had to say was of interest to everyone in Indochina.

The soon-to-be premier was quoted as saying the people of Indochina "should have an advisory voice in the affairs of the colony," that since education was the best means of assimilation, the Annamese should have access to all levels of French schooling.

"The press, your newspaper, can help," Painlevé said. "Freedom to express one's opinion is the basis of civilization." *L'Indochine* was off to a commanding start.

The next day the new paper contained a defiant attack on Maurice Cognacq, the *resident supérieur* or governor of South Vietnam, written by André. This second issue was also distributed gratis, this time from rented rickshaws. Monin, André, and De la Batie handed out their piles with serious graciousness. Clara was soon surrounded by children and she joyously threw hers into crowds that she was sure couldn't read French.

The feisty little paper was the only Saigon daily to carry up-to-date news from China and to follow the rapidly escalating confrontation between Britain and the Kuomintang government. On June 18 Chiang Kai-shek, the new Kuomintang leader, ordered all Chinese crews on British ships to walk off their jobs. Five days later *L'Indochine* reported that Chinese letters of credit, certificates of deposit, and commercial paper were no longer accepted in English banks and that the national government had ordered Chinese ships to sail directly to Canton. On June 25 the paper ran a story about street fighting in Canton and the next day reported that Canton was under a state of siege and that Europeans were sending women and children to Hong Kong.

In the pages of *L'Indochine,* the events in Hong Kong and Canton were seen as proof that Asians could muster physical force to challenge a great European power and, perhaps more important, that a native government could command great moral strength. This moral force, the paper believed, was the consequence of the principle of people's right to self-determination and of "the dispersal of certain democratic ideals that France stood for."

Such views angered the establishment figures, who were convinced Chiang Kai-shek had engineered the disturbances in Hong Kong and Canton to further international communism. Monin and his staff countered with informative interviews and editorials that, indirectly, proved the *resident supérieur* right in fearing a spread of the Hong Kong-Canton fever.

Cognacq's first move was to ask André to come by the official residence. Dr. Cognacq was a former physician, who had founded Hanoi's medical school, and for young Malraux made a more formidable adversary than Lachevrotière. As governor of South Vietnam, Cognacq was in the pocket of Saigon's banking and shipping interests and a defender of the suffocating state monopolies set up by Paul Doumer a quarter of a century earlier.

The interview was brief. Dr. Cognacq said he liked to be informed about events in his bailiwick. By offering the young journalists access to people in power, the *resident supérieur* apparently tried to put a wedge between Malraux and Monin. André, however, was caustic if not sarcastic, and in the columns of *L'Indochine* reprinted part of his conversation with Cognacq. The battles lines were drawn in the name of the highest principles. The little newspaper utterly condemned a system of government based on police terror. Monin and his staff could be silly and provincial when they tilted at windmills with Lachevrotière ("since Mr. Lachevrotière is a specialist in pistol duels with the shortsighted and in epée fights with paraplegics," André wrote, "I can only hope to find a surgeon who will reduce me to a quadriplegic the day I must once more explain to M. Henry de Lachevrotière that he is perhaps a bit of a coward.") However shrill these polemics, rebuttals and counterattacks, the *L'Indochine* team redeemed itself by the sheer audacity, impertinence, and talent with which André, Clara and the rest of them plunged into hard-hitting investigative journalism.

Their first target was the Khanh Hoi Real Estate, a company formed a few years earlier to develop the Saigon-Cholon harbor complex and, less avowedly, to take over the management of the harbor. The president of the enterprise was a M. Eutrope, a civil servant who was none other than Cognacq's political adviser, while the actual director was a M. Labaste, who also doubled as president of the rice shipping Chamber of Agriculture. The contract the developers had with the city of Saigon, *L'Indochine* discovered, made the municipality responsible for all liabilities, Khanh-Hoi for none. Better than that, the entire takeover scheme was financed by the city, not by the developers.

In the June 30 issue, *L'Indochine* said the events in China were a lesson for the future, not a threat of an immediate Communist revolt. "Let us hope the governments of Europe and the United States will draw from the present events the lesson necessary to modify their attitude toward Asia and eventually arrive at a sincere and lasting reconciliation of two races which, although they are so different in color, nevertheless represent the most advanced elements of mankind." Perhaps more prophetically, an anonymous Vietnamese contributor

warned that exasperated Vietnamese, unable to wait for the fulfillment of French promises, might turn to communism.

Clara met and befriended a Frenchwoman ten years her senior.
Identified only as Yvonne in Clara's memoirs, the much-divorced
woman was tough as nails, a former seamstress and labor militant
who was the first person to make Clara realize the misery of young
working women.

When Clara's new friend told her of the horrible infant mortality
rate among the Vietnamese and of the ignorance of personal hygiene
among Vietnamese women, Clara ordered medical books from
France so she could write about it.

The small, sweltering newsroom became a center of happy con-
spiratorial effervescence. Clara and Vinh had their desks in the back,
she writing a fashion and beauty-hints column and translating explo-
sive items from *The Strait Times,* he interviewing often frightened
Annamese. A piano that a previous tenant had left behind and no one
could find the energy to have removed stood in the back, usually
with a jar of icewater on top. The next day's paper was written and
edited during the day, printed at Louis Minh's at night, and hit the
street in the early afternoon. Between 5:00 P.M. and the sudden
tropical nightfall everybody relaxed.

For Clara and André, the Saigon ritual of the late afternoon siesta
inspired their lovemaking. Clara would write that although work and
obligations modified their life style, "we nevertheless persevered in
our carnal games—such as the denials I pretended, and played with,
not in order to refuse the end result because that would be a cheat,
but to heighten the expectations so that when my desire became too
sharp, I capitulated with passionate violence, followed by a blinding
surrender."[1]

André's fiction would contain only two sex scenes, but in both the
man makes love with open eyes, watching his partner's face to see
pleasure transform her features, to surprise the depth of her being, to
imagine himself as she. After frenzied climaxes, both Perken in *The
Royal Way* and Ferral in *Man's Fate* scrutinize the afterglow on the

---

[1] Clara Malraux, *Les Combats et les Jeux.*

faces of their slumbering companions, the dying Perken to fathom the gulf separating him from the Asian woman he knows will be the last he will sleep with, Ferral to imagine himself inhabiting the body of Valerie, a free and sophisticated "new woman."

Afterward they would lie under the bedside fan. The blades whirred, shedding coolness as they talked into the oppressive twilight when it was time to dress and go downstairs for gin and bitters, rum and sodas. They went more and more often to dinner in Cholon, but the drinks were on the Continental terrace, where *le tout Saigon* was to be found around frosted glasses.

Clara developed a taste for an occasional pipe of opium. The first time, she vomited in the rickshaw taking her back to the Rue Taberd. André tried it, but, she would remember, opium demanded more passivity than he could muster.

Clara liked the opium dens, the darkness, the low bench she stretched out on, the pungent sweet smell and the limpid and compassionate detachment that overcame her. Maurice Sainte-Rose was sometimes her smoking partner.

While under the influence one night, she began an unguarded confession to André. She could live without opium, she said, but not without him. As an adolescent, she had felt she was different from other girls, and when he came into her life, he accentuated and focused that difference. "Only with you can I talk about everything. Who besides you can make me realize how much each moment can hold of events and ideas? The idea that you could die has made me realize that I love you more than anything in the world, more than myself, more than my own happiness. It's of course the drug that makes me say that, but also the presence of death."

There were evenings when André and Paul exercised on the building roof. They were both competent swordsmen and dueled with epees. So evenly matched were they that bets were gleefully laid by Clara, Yvonne, Ninh, and Pho on the outcome of the contests.

After two weeks' existence, *L'Indochine* was broadsided by Lachevrotière's *L'Impartial.* With a screaming headline, the big daily published a telegram from Premier Painlevé's press secretary denying that the chief executive "had in any way been mixed up in such an affair." Lachevrotière denounced the new paper as a fraud, a scheme put together by swindlers who didn't hesitate to take advantage of political leaders in order to fleece their subscribers.

In a front-page editorial, *L'Indochine* shot back that since its premier issue had not yet reached Paris, it was perhaps premature to wonder whether Painlevé's press secretary knew whereof he spoke. The staff would soon obtain a confirmation of Painlevé's statements. In the meantime, here was Jean Bouchor's manuscript.*

André set to work digging into Lachevrotière's past and came up with a few devastating nuggets that he joyously published under his own byline. The best one quoted Lachevrotière answering charges of blackmail before a Saigon judge. The court transcript showed Lachevrotière asking the judge to disregard the accusation because "All I was doing was practicing my job as an informer."

Although acclaimed as a consummate swordsman, Lachevrotière did not take up the challenge. Instead he set out to discredit Monin by reprinting a *China News* article on the lawyer as proof that he was a "paid adviser" to the Kuomintang. André wrote an open letter to the rival publisher on the front page of *L'Indochine* offering free subscriptions to Lachevrotière's paper to anyone who could prove that the Chinese ideogram for lawyer doesn't also mean paid adviser. When Clara found a dispatch telling how Koreans had poisoned their own wells to protest against Japanese oppression, the Lachevrotière paper accused *L'Indochine* of inciting the Annamese to follow suit.

Vinh and Clara had become close, and one day he introduced her to his secret lover, a tiny girl even more timid than he.

His mother had found out about his mistress and his job. Her imprecations followed him out the door, but he still came to work, still went home most nights to hear his mother's abuse. "How will it all end?" he wondered one night when they walked among the market

---

* Posterity would judge Bouchor's "interview" with some severity. More a collection of Painlevé's ideas than a transcript of actual remarks, the statements attributed to him certainly reflected the center-left politician's convictions. It is doubtful, however, as several Malraux scholars would agree, that Painlevé would have alienated the colonial lobby on the eve of his investiture with an accusatory interview in an as-yet-unpublished fringe paper.

stalls together. To get an answer to his own question, he asked a fortuneteller. It would all end badly, he was told.

With Vinh, Clara and André attended an evening meal in Hin's tenement. A half-dozen students sat with them on straw mats on the floor, slowly tasting the food they had brought themselves with their gifts of lotus flowers and candy for the host. Someone began to sing a long mournful chant. Vinh whispered to André that the song told of the death of the Trung sisters.

"That was two thousand years ago, and since then we've never been left alone," said Vinh. There were moments, André said, when he realized the Vietnamese thought the white man's ways were fundamentally eccentric.

When they were alone, Clara and André had impassioned discussions about their Vietnamese friends. And their own relations to them. Clara needed to focus her sympathies on warm human beings; André's solidarity was more to the ideals, to the belief that the dross of life can be purified in the fire of the mind.

"We're facing the same enemy," said Clara. "You said so yourself in your Kuomintang dinner speech. What unites us, you said, is our enemies."

André said, "The terrible difference between the Cholon Chinese, between Vinh, Hin, and us is that you and I can walk away."

Both Monin and André wanted to give their journalistic endeavor a political dimension and, together with Pho, they tried to revive Jeune Annam (Young Annam), a Vietnamese movement that had been of some consequence, especially in Hanoi, right after World War I when Woodrow Wilson led the battle for "self-government amongst all the nations of the world."

There was little reason to revive Jeune Annam. The event that Monin, André, and Pho could perhaps be forgiven for missing was the assassination attempt on Martial Merlin in Canton the year before. The incident marked the seismic shift from intellectual to revolutionary nationalism.

The Constitutionalist Party and its subtle leader, Nguyen Phan Long, occupied the middle ground of the tolerated, police-infiltrated indigenous opposition. But the center of gravity was moving off-stage, to Canton, the headquarters of Kuomintang China. Just a hundred miles north of Hong Kong, the great commercial metropolis of southern China was the natural site for Vietnamese on the run. Canton was close to the homeland yet out of reach—or so they thought—of French police, and it provided access to the aid and comfort of Russian and Kuomintang revolutionaries.

Phan Boi Chau, the grand old man of the nearly defunct Restoration Party, was in Canton. French police still had a reward out for his capture, but after his years in Japan the "scholar rebel" felt it was safe enough to move closer to the homeland. Ho Chi Minh was also in Canton, officially an assistant and translator to Borodin, but almost entirely focused on creating a Vietnamese Communist Party. Many of his followers were defectors from the Restoration party.

It was in Canton that Pham Hong Thai, allegedly inspired by early writings of Ho, threw a car bomb at visiting Governor-General Merlin. The attempt had failed, but it made a deep impression on Vietnamese exiles, who swore to fulfill Thai's goal of a "free, independent Annam."

While traveling to Shanghai in June, Phan Boi Chau, the former radical leader, was arrested and extradited to Saigon. How did French agents know that the elder nationalist was in Shanghai? Either Ho Chi Mih himself tipped off the French as to the whereabouts of Chau as a means of removing a rival and, at the same time, to receive the reward, or Lam Duc Thu, a double agent in the entourage of Ho, was the betrayer.[5]

Since February, Ho had managed to create the nucleaus of a Revolutionary Youth League of Vietnam (Vietnam Thanh Nien) and was trying to print, albeit in exile, a journal by the same name. Beyond the collaborators and friends of the *L'Indochine* team little notice was paid to the Monin-Malraux effort.

At the end of June, André received good news from Paris. The Supreme Court of Appeals had quashed his Pnompenh conviction. The victory was far from complete, however, because the decision was

---

[5] Recent scholars tend to believe Thu double-crossed Phan Boi Chau, that Ho would have opposed such action. cf. James Pickney Harrison, *The Endless War: Fifty Years of Struggle in Vietnam*; New York: Macmillan, 1982.

on a narrow jurisdictional question of infringement of court gag rules during the Saigon appeals hearing. The high court did not pronounce itself on the guilt or innocence of the defendants but referred the case back to the Saigon appellate court for retrial. In its June 28 issue *L'Indochine* carried the story, stretching the truth a bit when it said the conviction had been overturned "because coded police evidence of a confidential and political nature had been withheld from the defense."

Certain things André wrote astonished Clara. Facts were recreated, transposed, embellished, and given subtle twists. She didn't know whether to laugh or be irritated when he wrote that *The Chicago Tribune* had joined France's most illustrious writers in his defense and that Anatole France had tried, on his deathbed, to intercede on his behalf. When she confronted him, André answered that, rearranged in this fashion, events appeared more plausible, carried new authority, new meaning.

He sensed that she wanted to compete with him as a journalist. What they were experiencing, he told her, they were experiencing together. She found his answer both right and terribly glib.

ꕥ 15. CAMAU

South Vietnam had an elected representative in Paris, Ernest Outrey, a member of the Chamber of Deputies who was somewhat to
the right of the Paul Painlevé administration. He had voted against
the one-percent capital gains tax and he opposed a law of amnesty for
striking railway workers. "To use amnesty in a social conflict is as
wrong as applying amnesty in our great colonial possessions where
the natives constitute the majority," he declared, "because the indigenous population sees such a law as an act of weakness."

Always driven toward muscular and authoritarian solutions, right-
wing members of the Chamber cheered when the representative
from Cochin China declared it folly to bargain with the masses,
whether railway workers or colonial agitators. As proof he ripped
from his pocket a copy of *Le Paria*, the subversive periodical put out
by a group of African and Asian nationalists, and began reading an article signed by Nguyen Au Quoc. The author had the nerve to re-
mind his readers that the reason Vietnamese men had agreed to fight
and to die for France during the war was that the French government

promised them human rights and citizenship. Raising his voice to an indignant pitch, Outrey quoted the future Ho Chi Minh as having written "We did not want to believe that promises made by the representatives of France can be lies."

Outrey was a firm believer in Paul Doumer's doctrine that colonies should not only pay for themselves but furnish profitable outlets for capital, engineering, and construction as well. The colonies supplied raw materials, and as the owner of thousands of hectares of land in the most fertile part in Camau in the southernmost part of South Vietnam, Outrey made sure his constituents contributed economic value.

On July 27, the colonial government would auction off fourteen thousand square kilometers—more than five thousand square miles—in Camau, the richest agricultural area of the whole of Indochina. *L'Impartial* and *Le Courrier Saigonnais* gave ample space to Governor Cognacq's inspection tour of the region, stressing how the *resident supérieur* wanted to make sure the Nha-ques, the illiterate peasants, would not be exploited by settlers or plantation syndicates.

"Sounds too good to be true," said De la Batie.

To Monin and the Malrauxs, a land sale in Outrey's district promised to make the Saigon harbor-development scheme look like a tempest in a teacup, and their investigative journalism would pay dividends for the exploited Annamese.

The first hint of a land scam in the making came from a friend of Paul's in the Saigon municipal administration. A classic case of land speculation—an undeveloped industrial site, bought for peanuts and developed with city money—showed that the president of the South Vietnam Agricultural Council had lent himself enough council money to be in on the real estate speculation. Proof in hand, Monin wrote in *L'Indochine*, "The premier civil servant in Cochin China, the representative of the executive, in change of the strict and complete adherence to the law, is the first to violate it when personal interests and those of his friends come into play."

Two weeks before the announced Camau land auction, a pair of farmers from Camau showed up in the newsroom. Paul, André,

Clara, Hin, Vinh, and Pho listened with increasing interest as Tran Van Dang, a man with a thin white beard and a briefcase, heaved documents on the table and asked for help. "They want to confiscate our land, although we have not missed out on paying taxes," said Tran. "We are ignorant, we don't know administrative rules, but we know we're right."

If Tran was right—and a cursory glance at the tax receipts pulled from the briefcase seemed to bear him out—then the huge land sale was not, as Cognacq and Lachevrotière's newspaper claimed, an auction to satisfy tax liens.

Interim Governor-General Montguillot would be in Saigon the same day the auction was to take place, Paul told Tran and his companion. "We have a newspaper that reaches over five thousand readers every day. We will expose the case."

There was a hint of rebellion in Tran's voice as he rose. "We are peaceful people, like our Cambodian neighbors. Yet one day an administrator was murdered in Cambodia."

Paul got up also. "You don't have to resort to that. We will know how to defend you."

The two Vietnamese left almost reassured.

There was not much time to lose. André and Vinh decided to go to Camau immediately to dig into the story. Neither of them could drive, however, so Monin's Vietnamese chauffeur drove the Panhard convertible two hundred miles over dusty roads to the provincial capital of Bac Lieu. By obtaining copies of the actual rules for the auction, they found out that small bidders were locked out. To make sure Cognacq and the syndicate were the only bidders, the adjudicators had, contrary to custom if not the law, bundled parcels together to sell them in 600-square-kilometer (or 231-square-mile) lots. Buyers could further bundle lots and bid on several 600-square-kilometer lots, or indeed buy the whole 14,000 square kilometers in one single chunk.

André and Vinh were ready to return to Saigon with the facts when an official from Cognacq's office showed up, and everybody at the auction office was suddenly very nervous. At least a minimum of rules, it seemed, would be observed during the auction.

Meanwhile, Paul Monin wrote scorching editorials, naming no

names but intimating that *L'Indochine* knew every skeleton in every closet.

The campaign boosted circulation. Clara saw crowds surrounding newsstands when the paper arrived at 3:00 P.M., just the right time to take it home for the afternoon siesta.

For the trip back from Bac Lieu, André sat in front next to Monin's chauffeur. André liked the way Vinh and he had worked together and wanted to show him—and the driver—that a white man wouldn't always have to sit in the back. It was a long, tedious drive through endless plantations, bush, and rare villages. They were going through a stretch of jungle when the driver suddenly jammed down hard on the breaks. The car went mad and Vinh screamed in the back. André reached over to grab the wheel when the driver brought the car to a halt in a swirl of dust.

Just in front of them a steel cable was strung across the road, strong enough to overturn the car, high enough to behead the occupants of the front seat. In the stunned silence that followed, they heard the footsteps of people running away through the bushes.

When André and Vinh got to Saigon, they immediately told the newsroom they owed their lives to the chauffeur. Without his eagle eyes they probably wouldn't had returned alive.

"Was the steel cable intended for us?" Vinh asked darkly. "We guess so."

Monin, Clara, and De la Batie also had news for them.

"Montguillot is out and a socialist is in, a guy named Varenne," Clara shouted.

The news from Paris was that the Painlevé administration was replacing interim Governor-General Montguillot with a permanent appointment. The nominee was Alexandre Varenne, a former journalist and a socialist member of the Chamber of Deputies.

"I'm going to write a long piece examining the defects of colonialism and suggesting a way out," André announced on the spot. "A 'Letter to Varenne,' or something like that.

Had they had more paper and their own presses, they could have sold more than five thousand copies during the last days before the Camau auction. The Camau farmers still lost their land, but by announcing the auction and circulating the particulars of the huge land sale, *L'Indochine* at least caused a tripling of the price the Vietnamese received.

"Success brings people together," Clara would remember. "As a winning team we liked the people for whom we had fought, the people who had allowed us to measure the strength in ourselves, allowed us to realize we were up to the job, and given us a chance to prove ourselves."

Some evenings when Clara had had enough of "the boys" and sought feminine companionship with her friend Yvonne, André and Monin dressed to the teeth and visited Bienhoa, the local resort.

Getting out of Monin's automobile in their tuxedoes and sporting ebony canes, they rakishly crossed the lobbies of the better hotels to go to the bar. To the tunes of fox-trot melodies from *le dancing,* they sipped their drinks and made racy remarks about the nouveau-riche clientele. Afterward, if the rain stopped, they sometimes staged mock duels with their canes under a banyan tree, imagining situations in which they could challenge Lachevrotière to a duel.

The strong rank smell of wet grass melted with the waft from the jasmine and the hibiscus. The cicadas chirped and one of the two friends suddenly sprang into the cone of light, his cane high.

"En garde!"

André loved the swagger of the revolutionary fop, the tuxedoed defender of the downtrodden.

⤳ 16. PLOTS

There is one scene in André Malraux's most famous novel that for over fifty years filmmakers from Sergei Eisenstein to Bernardo Bertolucci have dreamed of staging, a scene that catches all the desperate hope and absurdity of terrorism. Clutching a bomb with which a wayward revolutionary plans to assassinate Chiang Kai-shek during uprisings in Shanghai, the terrorist throws himself under the wrong car.

Ch'en Ta'erh is the young revolutionary who in the opening pages of *Man's Fate* hesitates for an existential moment before plunging his knife into a sleeping man it is his duty to kill. Later, this missionary-educated former gunrunner, seduced into joining the revolution by a recruiter who plays on his illusion of heroism, draws away from his comrades, defies both discipline and doctrine, and insists on murdering the Kuomintang leader. By hurling himself in front of the general's speeding automobile he tries to give terrorism a meaning.

The botched attempt—Ch'en finishes himself off with a bullet, un-
aware that he had thrown himself under the wrong car—trigger the
savage repression that is the core of the book.[1]

Ch'en is André fictionalized rendition of Hin.

There was no tension in Hin when he told them one night in July.
Like a noble animal, Clara thought, Hin stood motionless and just
announced he had decided to do it. It would be easy. Interim Governor-General Montguillot was coming to Saigon to meet Dr. Cognacq. There would be a ceremony, a parade of some kind.

De la Batie was the first to speak. "But how?"

Hin grinned. "Playing a photographer."

"What do you mean?"

He had already obtained a press pass, he explained. He would be
standing with his camera in front of the governor-general and, at the
right moment, pull out his gun.

"You'll miss him." De la Batie winced.

"I'm a good shot."

"That's true."

Monin said, "They'll arrest you."

"And I'll be condemned to death."

De la Batie sighed and said the whole idea was crazy.

But Hin came back. "I'll do it because it must be done. Cognacq is
a criminal. Because of him land is being stolen from the Nha-ques,
because of him we're crushed by taxes."

"It won't change anything. Or if it does change anything it will be
for the worse. Finally, they'll have grounds to treat us like an
enemy."

Someone—Paul or André, Clara couldn't remember—said De la
Batie was right. He continued, saying *we* when he meant the
Vietnamese.

"If nobody does anything," Hin said, "nothing will change." Pho
said the question was not whether to do anything or not, but to do
the right thing.

---

[1] André Malraux, *Man's Fate.*

Hin shot back that to them—meaning the French—the Vietnamese will never be anything more than a gutless mass of coolies. André reasoned that an attempt on Cognacq's life not followed by a popular uprising was not only a murder but a failure.

The conversation turned to the attempt on Martial-Henri Merlin's life in Canton.

"Think how useless that was," André said.

"Still," said Pho, "when the bomb exploded Merlin crawled under the table."

"Merlin lost face," said Vinh.

"In the eyes of Annamese, maybe," said André. "In French eyes he did the smart thing."

For the first time they felt divided along racial lines, the Vietnamese sullen and bitter, the French aloof and logical.

"The few liberties we have can be taken away at anytime," said Pho. "Today we have *L'Indochine*. Ninh wants to start up *La Cloche Felée* again, but we all know any newspaper can be silenced."

Nobody spoke for a while. Quietly Monin mentioned the dreaded Colonel Darles. The murder of Cognacq would mean the triumph of all the Darles. Thinking perhaps of the discipline of Cholon's Kuomintang leaders, he added that Hin had no organization behind him.

"Organization!" Hin's voice was scornful. Suddenly he turned on his heels and headed for the door. "I don't give a damn," he bristled. "I don't give a damn."

At the door he turned and stared back at them, as if he no longer knew whether they were his friends. When he looked at Clara she knew what he was thinking—if we liberate ourselves from you it will be without your help.[2]

A ringing telephone froze Hin in the doorway. Monin reached out and answered. They all listened as the lawyer made an appointment with someone for the following week. Tension drained from Hin, but he left, to be alone.

The next day they learned that Montguillot and Cognacq would

---

[2] Clara Malraux, *Les Combats et les Jeux.*

make only a brief stopover in Saigon before heading for Hanoi. Plans for a parade had been canceled.

People came to the newsroom with tips and suggestions. The French mayor of Saigon, a pharmacist from the uplands, merchants, and landlords came to the office and, while paying their subscriptions, told of things they knew—election irregularities, graft, intimidations. A delegation trooped in to tell of justice denied.

The little newspaper was beginning to interest police, something Clara couldn't help but find flattering. There was one early warning: their postman told them their mail was being scrutinized at the central post office.

One suffocating afternoon when Clara and André were lying naked on their bed reading, he looked up from an old issue of Ninh's *La Cloche Felée* and said, "Listen to this. Ninh described in his own paper what the authorities were doing to him."

André read from the page: "The colonial government has a thousand ways of stifling a French-language newspaper it does not like. One way, for example, is to tell owners of printing plants they cannot accept outside jobs to print newspapers. Another is through the post office, having copies sent to subscribers returned with a stamp saying Not accepted by addressee.' Yet another abuse of the postal system is to open mail addressed to the newspaper to try and obtain the names of those who find new subscribers."

"They're doing that to us, too," Clara said. Several subscribers had come to the office to say officials had asked them why they were supporting a Bolshevik paper.

There were days when Clara and André had the distinct impression they were being followed. One afternoon they wanted to be certain. In a busy street they suddenly split and quickly ducked into opposite sidestreets. Sure enough, at the intersection a man stood looking confused.

Had police infiltrated them?

An informer in their midst was such an obvious possibility they should have thought of it long ago, but it was also a danger they would have to deal with. Paranoia made them reel through recent events. Was it inside information that had led Lachevrotière to fire off a telegram to Painlevé's press secretary? Was the parade for the new governor-general canceled because police knew of Hin's assassination threat? Did the authorities know *everything?*

De la Batie, Hin, and Vinh came to work bleary-eyed one day and told Clara they had spent several nights trailing Pho. Every night Pho had eaten in restaurants where a dinner cost more than any one of them earned in a week. Also, he had moved out of the tenement behind the market and into a colonnaded house.

The fraternal complicity snapped that morning.

When Pho came to the office, the poison was in all of them. André thought that if Pho avoided their eyes, Pho knew that he was suspect. A few days later, when Clara was spending the afternoon siesta alone stretched in a wicker chair on the roof, a shadow slid toward her and stopped. It was Pho saying he had to talk to her, "the first white woman who treated me like a friend."

Clara sensed the sentimental blackmail in the phrase. She didn't want to hear what he had to say.

"Clara, you have no right to doubt me. I give you my word of honor that I have nothing to do with police. Hin, Vinh and Dejean are wrong to suspect me. They have proof of my loyalty. I wouldn't betray my friends for money."

Why should I believe him? I believe so easily what people tell me. But why shouldn't I believe the others? They had solid arguments.

"Clara."

I felt his voice insist too much.

"Pho, I don't want to judge. You should talk to them."

"It's you I want to convince. I can't live with the idea that you despise me."

"Why do the others believe. . . ?"

"I don't know. They often speak out of turn, sometimes in places where they'd be better off keeping their mouths shut. We're being watched, you know that."[3]

---

[3] Clara Malraux, *Les Combats et les Jeux.*

They let Pho stay. Twenty-five years later, in 1950, Pho one day rang the doorbell of Clara's Paris apartment. He had been living in Paris, he said, earning a living as a teacher of Chinese. He was barely seated before he told her that the people they had worked with in Saigon back in 1925 had been men without character. "You were wrong in having confidence in them. They accused me of being a police informer; then, after you left, they made me managing director."

They were never to know the truth.

André had come to like Maurice Sainte-Rose, and to try to launch the wastrel Eurasian in Saigon's modest literary salons wrote a piece under his name. That anything published in *L'Indochine* could enhance anyone's reputation in Saigon's establishment circles was dubious, but the gesture was touching. The piece was a lyrical description of an almost mythical Asia, a traveler's report on Isfahan in central Iran that neither Sainte-Rose nor André had visited.

There were days when *L'Indochine* had to admit it had no news from China. An item in the July 17 issue noted that although all communications with Hong Kong had been severed, it had obtained telegraphic information in "roundabout ways." The next day the paper could tell of Hong Kong work stoppages by nearly five hundred thousand men; how all newspapers had been shut down; on a lighter note, how the English had to do all household chores themselves.

As the summer wore on, clashes between British authorities and Chinese in Shanghai and Canton left many Chinese killed. The riots provoked patriotic students to flock to the Kuomintang and to the Communist Party. Educated Chinese, weary of the long civil war, hailed the advance of the Kuomintang.

In Canton the anti-imperialist movement was masterminded by Borodin and some of the late Sun's more radical lieutenants. Although it would be another three years before Chiang Kai-shek entered Peking, his new Nationalist army was consolidating the Kuomintang's power in Kwangtung. Its victories were achieved as much by skillful propaganda as by force of arms. Wherever the Nationalist forces showed up, agitators directed popular sentiments against foreigners and against Christian schools, churches, and hospitals.

Phan Chu Trinh was proud of the fact that a Vietnamese was with

Borodin, that none other than Trinh's former lab assistant, Ho Chi Minh, was in Canton with the Soviet commissar as part-time interpreter while supplementing his income peddling cigarettes and newspapers and acting as stringer for a Soviet news agency. Ho had many names. His new Vietnamese name was Li Thui. Among the foreigners in Canton he was known as Au Quoc, Wang, or Vuong. He sometimes called himself Nilovsky and signed his news dispatches Lou Rosta.[4]

But it was Borodin who fascinated André. Here was a foreigner like himself masterminding a revolution in Asia, a man who was barely forty, a man who, when the revolution triumphed in Russia, had come home to put himself at its disposal. André sensed he could not commit himself to a cause in the same way, but he liked the fraternal stir of a revolutionary movement. Borodin was a man of action, someone who in tumultuous situations knew how to create his own usefulness.

Less than two weeks separated the news that Alexandre Varenne was the new governor-general-elect and news that sent Monin and crew into a tailspin. On July 31, L'Indochine welcomed the announcement from Paris that Varenne, a man known for his quick intelligence and capacity for work, was the nominee. His mandate, L'Indochine predicted, was sure to result in "numerous and beneficial reforms."

André greeted the Varenne appointment with a promised long piece on the current situation. "I'm not writing to condemn an individual but a policy," he wrote of the insidious limits that governors-general had put on the number of Vietnamese students allowed to continue their education in France.

Standing the governor-general's argument on its head, André said the consequence of limiting the access of students to French universities was to turn against France the highest and the best energies Annam had to offer.

"One impression stands out for whoever travels through Annam,

---

[4] Ho Chi Minh used some twenty pseudonyms in his lifetime; see James Pickney Harrison, *The Endless War: 50 Years of Struggle in Vietnam* (New York; Macmillan, 1982).

from the mouth of the Red River in the north to the Mekong delta, and that is the very names of the towns have a ring of revolt. The tomb of Le-Loi lies in ruin, but the songs that extol the somber grandeur of his life are still on the lips of all the women and in the memory of every fisherman."

Returning to the vexing limitations on students allowed to study in French universities, he tried to be sarcastic, saying France was not such an ugly and shameful country that its government has to hide it from Annamese eyes.

This attitude is not only so stupid that it makes one cry of anger, but it will provoke, in a very short time, the most dangerous attack on our colonization. What I'm asking is that France be accessible to whoever wants to go. I'm asking that the governor-general demand that his subordinates either:

—recognize the right of Annamese—right already set out in current law—to go to France; or

—submit immediately the files of people wanting to go to a special commission, to be set up in Hanoi and to be accountable for its decisions.

This would show that we know better than to turn against us, thanks to a clever scheme, one of most beautiful, most unsullied concentrations of energies that a colonial power can possibly raise against itself."[5]

André called the piece "A Choice of Energies."

He was writing the follow-up piece for the August 15 edition when Louis Minh came to the office.

He was sorry, he mumbled, but they would have to find another printer.

It didn't take Monin, André, and De la Batie long to get it out of him. Anonymous callers had told Minh that if he continued to print "that Bolshevik rag," his workers would surely be so disgusted that they would strike.

"But your workers are not against our paper," André said,

---

[5] In *L'Indochine*, August 14, 1925.

stunned. He remembered reading Ninh describing the thousand ways the government would stifle a paper it didn't like.

There was more. Cognacq's office had let Louis know it might seek a new printer for the government's printing needs.

"No printer," he sighed, "can survive in this town without government jobs."

Within the hour, Monin contacted every printing firm in Saigon. Everybody had gotten the word.

The last issue of *L'Indochine* was dated August 14, 1925. Forty-six issues had appeared since the first printing June 17. It had taken the colonial powers just under two months to silence the paper that had dared to castigate the Cognacq administration of South Vietnam, expose the collusion if not the corruption of its officers, urge Annamese to demand reforms, and had gone so far as to publicize, if not espouse, the Kuomintang cause in China. Indirectly, the pressure had started to build when Lachevrotière began a smear campaign, accusing Monin and Malraux of being Bolsheviks, a campaign increased in stridency with the growing unrest in China.

As the notion sank in that they were actually shut down, the mood in the sweltering newsroom was a mixture of dejection, revolt and cunning. Hin suggested a spectacular assault and occupation of the Lachevrotière offices and presses for the printing, at gunpoint, of one last flaming issue of *L'Indochine*. Cooler heads prevailed with the idea of finding their own printing press. Monin agreed. Their strategy should be somehow to outlast interim Governor-General Montguillot until the arrival of Varenne, scheduled for late November.

Three months was a long time. To survive they cut the enterprise to the bone. Monin's ailing wife was still in France with their young son but hoping to join her husband in a few months. In the meantime, Monin decided to close the newspaper office in the Rue Taberd and to move everybody to his half-empty villa.

Through a friend of a friend of one of Minh's typesetters, an old printing press was acquired and installed under the veranda in the villa. The press was put in working order but attempts to buy type met with the same response as efforts to find newsprint. Coqnacq's office had been thorough.

Monin's law firm would have to keep them all afloat until they could start up again. An editorial bull session decided that since Clara and André had valid passports they should go to Hong Kong and buy type so that *L'Indochine* could be launched again, preferably before the end of Montguillot's caretaker term.

Paul wrote personal letters to several acquaintances in the Crown Colony. "I'm not sure how exactly these people will welcome you," he told André as he handed him the introductions. "But a few good names may be enough."

Before the British occupation, Hong Kong Island was the notorious haunt of pirates. Its deep sheltered harbor was a base for British ships during the first Opium War of 1839-1842 and its strategic value in the path of the chief trade route to China was quickly realized. China ceded Hong Kong Island in perpetuity by the Treaty of Nanking in 1842. Eighteen years later Britain obtained possession of part of Kowloon and Stonecutters Island and in 1898 was granted a ninety-nine-year lease of the mainland area known as the New Territories.

The Chinese Republic, established with startling speed and ease in 1911 by Sun Yat-sen, caused only the progressive collapse of national unity and orderly government. The still-raging civil war had made Hong Kong a haven for both people and capital. By 1925, however, the growing success and authority of the Kuomintang was accompanied by hostility toward foreign interests. By August, when Clara and André sailed toward the Crown Colony aboard a British liner, Hong Kong was tied up by widespread strikes and a boycott that tried to exclude British trade from all of southern China.

There were more Westerners than Asians on board. The English, Clara would remember, buried their anxiety behind civil manners. Rumors haunted the deck during the eleven-hundred-mile voyage up the Vietnamese coast, past the Paracel Islands and China's Hainan peninsula. The wireless crackled at night and passengers lined up at the radio room to send telegrams and, at noon, outside the purser's office when the daily news bulletin was posted.

André felt terrorized in any language but French, and although he had a bookish command of English that allowed him to read Shakespeare in the original, he would be incapable of giving directions to a cab driver. Clara struck up conversation with a tall, ginger-haired Englishman in his forties. His name was Nabby Adams, he said, lighting a cigarette.

Nabby Adams had huge hands stained with nicotine. He was a tiger hunter, returning from a hunt in southern Annam.

"Handsome tigers in the highlands," he smiled.

Clara had a feeling he was a wealthy nobleman who had nothing else to do.

Nabby Adams lived in Hong Kong but had no interest in current events. Clara was sure aristocratic game hunters cared little about politics in lands where they went shooting, and when he leaned toward her to say the captain had just sent a wire to Hong Kong police warning them that his passengers included the reddest Bolsheviks of all Annam, it took her a second to realize he was trying to tell her something.

"You mean. . . my husband and me?" she finally asked.

The big man grinned.

It was Singapore all over again. "But how does the captain know?" she wondered.

Nabby Adams told her. "The captain just received a wireless from the French authorities in Saigon."

Clara excused herself. "I must find my husband."

"I'll see you at tea," Nabby Adams called after her.

She found André in the stern watching Chinese immigrants in the steerage below. He listened, nodded, threw his cigarette overboard, and said, "Come."

"The reddest Bolsheviks of all Annam." The phrase lingered on

André's tongue, in English and French, as they walked to their cabin. Behind the closed door they decided they'd have to destroy Monin's letters. They began by memorizing the names and addresses, repeated them again and again to each other before they went back on deck and hurled letters and their address book into the sea.

Nabby Adams had Clara and André as his dinner guests that night. The meal was first-class, but linguistically only Clara could appreciate the accompanying tiger stories.

The ship reached Hong Kong at night but didn't dock. The general strike had paralyzed the harbor. No pilots and no longshoremen were available. The first officer announced over the loudspeaker that they would ride at anchor in the roadstead until morning.

Clara and André were to spend one week in Hong Kong and loved the idea of a free night on board. They walked from starboard to port side under the bridge where wireless messages crackled and watched the double line of lights of Kowloon and Victoria. Clara felt a surge of tenderness for the man with whom she had traveled this far.

"Imagine the empire stretching all the way to Mongolia," André sighed as they watched the Peak.

"China."

"A mysterious land in decay, but also a country full of unknown possibilities."

They went to their cabin. Before going to bed, they lit a small newspaper fire in the washbasin and burned the last compromising papers.

Breakfast was accompanied by loudspeaker announcements that a tugboat would take debarking passengers to shore. When a big tug pulled alongside, the first officer was back on the loudspeaker. Passengers would have to fend for themselves. There would be no one to handle the baggage.

Passengers struggled down a gangplank to the heaving tug with their trunks and suitcases. Nabby Adams was cheerful.

"I'll have one of my boys pick up my skins," he said.

As the tugboat glided toward the docks, Nabby Adams invited Clara and André to come to dinner before they sailed back. He lived on the Peak, he said, handing them his card.

On the dock, European crew members struggled to lower the gangway. Behind them stood the serried ranks of striking dockworkers and coolies.

The moment Clara and André appeared, two Chinese porters broke ranks and ran up the gangway to take their luggage, a mutely telling gesture by a people in insurrection toward those on their side. How did they know? Ship-to-shore radio messages to police had a way of falling on unintended ears.

It was a gorgeous day. Between Victoria and Kowloon the bay was one stretch of azure shimmering under the sun and, André would remember fifty years later, jade plants hung over the fretwork on the Chinese hotel balconies along Queens Road. Smiles of complicity creased the faces of the boys at the hotel they checked into, but Clara and André found the bed unmade when they found their room. Each time they went down to the lobby a lanky Chinese pretended to study a newspaper.

"Must be a policeman," said Clara. "No newspapers have been published since the general strike began." When they went out the man with the newspaper followed.

Luck was with them. In a week-old newspaper left in the room, André spotted an ad that, Clara verified, said "Type for Sale." A telephone call confirmed that local Jesuits were the publishers of a modest newsletter. They were modernizing their printing shop and indeed selling their old type. Clara got the address.

The monastery was situated halfway up the Peak and, the plainclothes detective following them, Clara and André gamely began their ascent. Coolies, apparently always following and protecting them, caught up with them and forced them into rickshaws for the rest of the climb. As in Bangkok, Clara and André felt embarrassed to be pulled by running Asians, but the idea of leaving the undercover agent behind was too tempting.

Clara found André positively comical, crunched into the rickshaw in a near-fetal position.

'Montmartre," Clara smiled when the rickshaws pulled up on a small square that looked like Montmartre's Place du Tertre. André had to laugh at himself trying to extricate himself from his rickshaw.

The coolies grinned along with them and saluted with a clenched fist.

A narrow climb upstairs led to the monastery wall and a massive wooden gate. A Jesuit greeted them cordially and took them to a tidy little printing office.

No indiscreet questions were asked. The monks were as happy to get rid of their old type as Clara and André were to acquire it, and the transaction was accomplished in no time.

The fathers promised to have the type delivered to their Saigon-bound vessel. "Part of the type will only be available in a week," said the monk in charge of the printing shop. "We will forward those remaining cases directly to your Saigon address."

As the monastery gate closed behind them, Clara and André shook their heads in disbelief. It had been so simple. They had imagined a convoluted scenario of dogged detective work, dead-end leads, strange phone calls, and clandestine meetings with accomplices before they would find—or not find—the blocks of typeface destined to propagate allegedly subversive thoughts.

With five days to spare before the scheduled return trip, Clara and André became tourists.

They loved the picturesque, chaotic city where affluence razed racial barriers and wealthy Chinese and Europeans built villas next to each other on the Peak. The Chinese informer assigned to tail them was not always the same, but they soon learned to recognize their man. By the second day, their spy stopped pretending he just happened to be walking in the same direction and walked next to them.

English-language newspapers began to appear again. When Clara saw an entertainment-page ad for Max Linder's Three Musketeers parody, *Three Must-Get-Theres* and asked the desk how to get to the theater, the hotel porter soon gave up explaining and called over the police agent. André didn't want to go, but Clara and her spy were off.

The cinema was far away. They took a ferry to Kowloon and started to walk. After a while Clara regretted her spontaneous need to see the French Charlie Chaplin in a three-year-old movie. But her little escort wouldn't understand.

"Not far," he said.

"I'm tired, really," she said.

"Come, only ten more minutes."

She refused. She could see perplexity spread on his face. "Tomorrow," she sighed, giving in.

There was desperation in his voice when he said "Tomorrow not my turn following you."

They remembered Nabby Adams and went to dinner at his home high on the Peak. None of Nabby Adams' servants were on strike and port was brought to the terrace overlooking the harbor by boys in immaculate white. Clara couldn't quite believe it when her host told her his first name was actually Abel. "It's been Nabby since my childhood."

Other guests arrived in dinner jackets and long dresses, and Clara never got around to ask whether, in the face of the political turmoil, Nabby had found it prudent to send his wife to Europe or whether there was a Mrs. Adams at all. She did learn that the best port was to be found in Hong Kong.

"The reason, my dear, is that English servants only agreed to follow their masters to the end of the world if they could have enough port to sustain themselves. In consequence, vast amounts of port were shipped out, to age in caves dug into the rock."

To taste the special flavor that the Hong Kong caves gave the Portuguese wine, guests were invited to clean their pallates with a solitary herring.

André bought several English-language newspapers a day and followed the unfolding events in Canton and in Hankow, still held by the wiliest of the northern warlords, Wu Pei-fu. The papers freely speculated that Wuhan, midway between Hong Kong and Peking, would be the focus of the next thrust against Wu by Chiang Kai-shek's Nationalist armies. The information available in Hong Kong was light years ahead of what passed for news in Saigon. For the first time he was beginning to see the whole picture.

"I can't wait to get back," he said.

To while away the last day, Clara and André made an excursion to Portuguese Macao to take in the sites of vice. They played fan-tan, peered into opium dens, and watched teenage prostitutes.

The fan-tan game was played in a two-story house where gamblers stood leaning over an upstairs balcony railing to look down on the "banker" emptying a handful of small coins onto a table with its sides marked 1, 2, 3, and 4. After the banker covered the coins with a bowl, the gamblers bet as to what would be the remainder when the pile was divided by four by setting their stakes on the side of the square that bore the number each favored.

André put their bet in a little basket that, like a ski lift, came up to the players on a string. When everybody had placed their bets, the banker removed the bowl and, with a small stick, removed coins from the heap, four at a time. When the final batch was reached, the number of coins it contained determined the winning number, if four coins, the bettors of number 4 won five times their stake.

André kept sending money down in the basket but never won.

Had she been alone, Clara would have tried one of the inviting opium dens. Instead, they walked down alleys lined with hovels where pubescent girls waited, with their parents, for clients who would take the girls with them behind a curtain for fifteen minutes. Macao offered only games of chance, opium, and girls, and its propositions were open, frank, and negotiable.

When *The Conquerors,* André's staccato novel about revolutionaries in China during the 1925 Hong Kong general strike, became an immediate success and overnight transformed André's marginal reputation into recognizable renown, the time he spent in China in 1925 was to be the most mysterious period of his life. If he was in China, if he met Borodin and Mao Zedong, if he became one of the committee of Twelve, if he took part in the Canton uprising, if he helped patch up differences between the Kuomintang and the Chinese Communists and as a reward was named Commissar of Propaganda, it would all have had to happen between the August 14, 1925, suspension and the November 4 resurrection of *L'Indochine.*

A legend was to grow of Malraux as a people's commissar of Mao's ragged armies, hero of the 1925 Canton insurrection if not the 1927 Shanghai uprising. Over the years, André was to learn to answer inquisitive questions with half-confidences, heavy silences, and sometimes bafflingly accurate details, all adding up to the legendary persona thrust into the crucible of dangerous and significant events.

André was never above adding to the colorful apocrypha himself. In a 1933 letter to Edmund Wilson thanking the American critic for his review of *The Conquerors*, he was to write: "I went to Asia at the age of twenty-three in charge of an archeological mission. I abandoned archeology, organized the Jeune Annam movement, then became Kuomintang commissar in Indochine and later in Canton.[1]

The only piece of objective testimony to the China connection was by Paul Morand. The writer-diplomat who had savaged the postwar smart set in a trio of discerning, brazen novels was on his way through Asia to gather material for his no less observant and impudent travel books. Thirteen years older than André, Morand had just fallen in love with Helene Soutzo, a very wealthy and very beautiful Romanian princess. He was arriving in Hong Kong on his way to a new posting in Bangkok in August 1925, he would write, "exactly the same time as Malraux arrived from Canton, coming from Saigon."

Once in Bangkok, however, Morand fell gravely ill and in November was taken to Saigon and hospitalized. One day he received a visit from Malraux. "I saw him come in looking like a ghost," Morand would write, "pale, thin, looking like a haunted man, he was definitely sicker than the patients around me.[2]

Did Clara and André push the extra eighty miles to Canton after they bought the type from the missionaries? Clara was to say no. Did André meet Borodin, whom he described so vividly in *The Conquerors?* Clara was to say no. Monin and Dong Dai in Cholon knew Borodin and could have described the Soviet commissar in sufficient detail for André to assemble the rich portrait. Did André go to Canton alone from Saigon? Clara was to say no. They never had the money for the three-thousand-mile round-trip railway ticket.

What must be deduced from Malraux's documentary knowledge

---

[1] Edmund Wilson, *Shores of Light: A Literary Chronicle of the Twenties and Thirties* (New York: Farrar, Straus & Young, 1952).

[2] Paul Morand, *Papiers d'Identité* (Paris: Grasset, 1931).

of China, however, must be added to his gift as a writer. Between 1928 and 1932 he was to complete four novels, all set in Asia and three of them saluted for their quasi-journalistic authenticity. Two of them were set in a China in revolt and both were hailed for brilliantly conveying the fever, progress, and horror of revolution.

Clara and André's Saigon-bound ship was not riding at anchor offshore, but properly docked and when they arrived for boarding they saw the Jesuits' cases handsomely lined up on the pier. Distractedly they signed waybills and customs papers. Mission accomplished, they went on board.

The return trip was uneventful.

Paul Monin's big automobile and the chauffeur were the first things they saw when they docked in Saigon. Next to it, Monin and De la Batie waved their greetings.

They all saw the cases of type being unloaded, but in the customs shed Clara and André were told certain papers had been filled out incorrectly at the point of embarkation.

"Let me fill them out correctly," André proposed.

"That should have been done in Hong Kong," the agent repeated.

André was angry. The customs agent had to get his supervisor. The scene grew ugly as André insisted and the full force of the law came down on the side of customs declarations filled out at the point of embarkation.

"Hong Kong will have to be contacted," said the supervisor.

"When?" Clara tried.

"It will take some time."

André knew they were defeated. "And in the meantime, the merchandise stays here."

The supervisor smiled, "That is correct, sir."

The chauffeur drove the dejected foursome back to the Monin villa. Monin had personal news to impart. Following her lengthy convalesence in France, his wife would be coming out, bringing their twelve-year-old son with her.

A week later, the smaller consignment forwarded by the Jesuits arrived and cleared customs with ecclesiastic punctuality.

"God, type made of wood like in the sixteenth century!" André exclaimed when they opened the boxes.

It was with this second batch of type that they resurrected the newspaper.

❧ 18. RETREATS

In the checkered history of France's nearly one hundred years in Indochina—from the 1858 occupation of Danang to the 1955 withdrawal after the Dien Bien Phu defeat—Alexandre Varenne stands out as one shining example. In an appalling succession of mediocre men, this former vice president of the Chamber of Deputies distinguished himself as the governor-general who gave the peoples of Vietnam, Cambodia, and Laos their first social reforms. To Paul Monin and his crew, who so fervently believed an extension of French democracy to the colonies was the future, Varenne should be the good guy rescuing them from rout and ruin and giving them the last laugh. It didn't quite turn out that way.

The three short years as governor-general of this goateed socialist were indeed a period of timely, if less than bold, social and political reforms. Inexperienced in colonial affairs, but possessed of financial knowhow, Varenne succeeded where Merlin, the last full-term (1922-1925) governor-general, had failed. During the Varenne administration, standards for labor relations were instituted and regulations governing the minimum age for factory workers, work hours, convicts' earnings, and medical entitlements were established. Rural loan-sharking was abolished, a farm credit system enacted, and the civil service opened to all Indochinese. With the creation of regional advisory councils in south and north Vietnam,* and a colonywide Economic and Financial Grand Council, Varenne started the progress toward democracy. His timid reforms, however, managed to antagonize both Asians and settlers, the former for not going far enough, the later for being enacted at all. For Monin, André, Clara, De la Batie, Vinh, Hin, and Minh, it all came too late.

On November 3—André's twenty-fourth birthday—they began printing their resurrected newspaper. *L'Indochine Enchaînée* (Indochina in chains), as they called it, was on the street the next day, two weeks before Varenne's scheduled arrival. The missionaries' type had no accent and the first issue looked un-French.

On the third night, when Paul and André were out and Clara was alone in the improvised newsroom in the Monin's living room, she received a strange visit by five Vietnamese men clad in black robes. None of them spoke French, but with a bow—the *lai* salute most Vietnamese refused to execute when facing government officials—they extracted tiny bundles from their long sleeves. Untying handkerchiefs, they handed her their offering. It was type, a hundred characters with accents graves, accents aigus, and circonflexes. In a mute gesture of gratitude, Clara bowed in turn. The next day she learned the men were typographers and that they had stolen the type at work.

L'Indochine Enchaînée was more flysheet than newspaper, reduced in size and frequency but defiantly printed on the old press under Paul's veranda, determined to attack the outgoing regime until it drew blood. Cut down to half the size of *L'Indochine*, it was a biweekly, appearing on Wednesdays and Saturdays. According to a front-page editorial in the first issue, it was a temporary issue "awaiting the day, certainly far distant, when the government will agree to return the

---

* Chambres Représentants du Peuple en Annam et au Tonkin.

type that belongs to us." Above the list of contents was a woodblock caricature of Cognacq looking like a stuck pig.

In their editorials, Monin and André believed the colonies had reached a turning point but that it was not yet too late to reform the colonial government, although time was running out. When it came to concrete proposals, they suggested social reforms. André wrote a long piece about infant mortality, saying the government could easily reduce the appallingly high rate by a concerted propaganda effort. He said leaflets could be distributed showing how women should care for their newborn babies and that if the leaflets were expressed in pictures, so much the better.

Paul and André put all their hopes in the new governor-general. They published an eloquent open letter to Varenne, Monin predicting that the arrival of the socialist appointee "will mark the inevitable hour of reckoning." On November 19, the day after Varenne's arrival in Saigon, they wrote that "for this part of the country, Cognacq and his henchmen—Colonel Darles was nicknamed the Butcher of Thai-Nguyen—had done as much harm as a war," and pleaded with Varenne not to be blinded by the brilliance of his reception, that behind the comedy of errors lurked tragedy.

There was something moving and slightly out of touch about the twice-a-week, eight-page paper. Political positions were hardening on the left and on the right. The attitudes of moderates like Nguyen An Ninh, who was allowed to publish his satirical *La Cloche Felée* again, and Bui Quang Chiang was becoming less tolerant of France. Instead of the reforms Monin and Malraux stood for—André's galvanizing of Indochinese "energies" and Paul's belief in equality for all under a French flag—the moderates began to see the merits of still vague national aspirations. The colonial lobby and the French settlers on the right, who dismissed the Vietnamese, demanded strong-arm measures to prevent Chinese nationalism and the Kuomintang's increasing success from becoming an example.

Dejean De la Batie was the first defection, leaving them to return to Ninh's *La Cloche Felée*. The reason, he said, was that he believed a Vietnamese news outlet carried more clout. André and Clara suspected he had sensed *L'Indochine Enchaînée* was really not a viable proposition.

Varenne's first day in Saigon was sweet music to liberal ears. He appeared in a plain dark suit instead of the governor-general's uniform and announced that he refused to take part in any inaugural festivities "paid for by Annamese taxpayers." He agreed to meet indigenous spokesmen at the Saigon city hall. In front of six hundred people, some carrying welcoming placards reading "Long Live the Socialist Varenne," others expressing such sentiments as "Down with Settlers and the Strap," the Constitutionalist Party leader Nguyen Phan Long was allowed to address the new governor-general and politely formulated several Annamese demands and brought up the question of press freedom.

Varenne's answer was chilling. If press freedom was granted immediately, he predicted, and if, as a result, Vietnamese individuals would, through extravagant expression of their ideas, provoke troubles throughout the country, the resulting reactionary backlash would be of such proportions as to sweep away all progress already accomplished.

From there on it seemed to be all compromises and sellouts to the vested interests. Varenne, or his secretary, refused to meet Monin and Malraux, and it was first with sadness, then with anger, that they heard his official speeches stress that his first order of business was social reform, "not Annamese reforms," and that with regard to alleged abuses of power in the past, it was best to forget. On November 28, when Varenne left for his official residence in Hanoi, André wrote in *L'Indochine Enchaînée*, "This is the first time a governor-general has been so quick to belittle himself. . . Yesterday a socialist, today a conservative, yet another conversion under the sign of the piaster."

Varenne's administration was to be less negative than his first ten days would have anyone believe. Actually expelled from the Socialist Party for having accepted the post, Varenne managed to abolish imprisonment for debt for Asians, a tremendous relief for millions of peasants crushed under taxes and usury-interest rates. He made University of Hanoi degrees acceptable in France, reinforced real estate legislation, and created a short-lived cooperative bank.

In 1933, when *Man's Fate* had made André famous, Clara and he ran into M. and Mme. Varenne on an Arctic cruise. The former governor-general was anxious to meet the literary celebrity. But, as Clara was to write, "for a moment I was silly enough to feel that to meet Varenne and his wife somehow compromised us, silly enough to get upset when a photo was taken of the four of us against the backdrop of an iceberg. It was childish and I was the first to admit it.[1]

L'Indochine Enchaînée was no longer a political force. The shattered hopes that the new governor-general represented made André turn to resentful speculative journalism. In a violent piece entitled "In Praise of Torture," he described how, in order to extort money from a suspect, a top police official had beaten a man to point of crippling him. Because he was both "a torturer and an informer," André concluded, the official would probably be elected president of the colonial Council.

Annamite soldiers were fighting in France's latest colonial war in North Africa, and Truong Van Ben, one of the ten Vietnamese members of the Council, rose to demand the immediate recall of Vietnamese troops sent to Morocco to quash the guerrillas in the Rif region. In Paris, left-of-center sympathies were for Abd-el-Krim and his guerrilla efforts to resist French advances and, as a former Council member, Monin was in the visitors' gallery with André. When Truong Van Ben spoke, Monin shouted "Hear, hear" and André applauded vigorously, to the indignation of the majority of the Council members. The next day, *L'Impartial* called Monin a Bolshevik for supporting the return of Vietnamese troops.

There was no more money. Clara and André's Continental Hotel bill had not been paid for longer than they cared to know. Every day they feared credit would be cut off and their luggage waiting for them in the hallway. At Pnompenh's Hotel Manolis murmurs of "temple robbers" had followed them when they passed the front desk. Here, indignant European whispers promoted them to revolutionaries, Bolsheviks, or traitors to their race.

Clara felt the paper no longer needed her translations, her beauty tips and baby care columns. When she suggested to Vinh that she give personal hygiene and family planning advice to his secret girlfriend and any of her friends who might want to join an informal session, even the timid Vinh protested.

---

[1] Clara Malraux, *Les Combats et les Jeux.*

"Suppose a man sneaks in under the pretext of accompanying a woman?" Vinh asked indignantly.

Clara said she didn't understand. Saigon's streets and markets were full of women who seemed to be free enough. What taboo was she threatening?

"No Vietnamese will ever allow wife or mistress to attend get-to-gethers where such subjects are discussed," Vinh persisted.

Clara felt increasingly useless. André did, too. He remembered the Grasset publishing contract. In late November he wrote a letter to the publisher, mentioning a book in the works, and told Clara, "Now the only solution is to write one."

Clara spent several afternoons with Yvonne. Her friend had married again, a man of some means, and lived in a villa in the suburbs. Clara had no money for taxi or rickshaw. To walk was considered a disgrace for white people, but Clara walked, the only European woman along Asian sidewalks and sunbaked suburban roads. One day she decided her cork-lined sunbonnet was too stained and walked bare-headed. Better be taken for a kook than a destitute. Vietnamese kids ran after her, and Vietnamese women, sitting on the ground eating watermelon and playing cards, looked up at the strange apparition. From a European villa came the sound of piano scales. Clara imagined a young girl behind the tamarind trees, poincinas, and half-closed shutters doing her exercises and thought of her own sheltered girlhood.

Yvonne's husband came home in his chauffeur-driven automobile in the late afternoon or sent his driver to pick up his wife for an evening in town.

"I like to walk," Clara told Yvonne when she arrived and slumped down in a bamboo chair. "Besides, I'm afraid I'm putting on weight."

Her friend laughed. Clara weighed less than forty kilos (eighty-eight pounds.) Yvonne knew that because she was sewing a dress for Clara. The day the dress was ready, Yvonne forgot, or pretended to forget, to ask for money. When her husband arrived at six, he asked if his chauffeur could take Clara back to the Continental.

"Clara doesn't let herself go," Yvonne interrupted. "she doesn't want any of that ugly colonial fat on her. We should follow her example. We should accompany her back to the hotel."

That evening the chauffeur drove respectfully a few feet behind

Clara in her new dress, Yvonne, and her husband as the trio trudged back to town.

There were days when André and Clara sensed Monin drifting away from them, days when the lawyer seemed no longer to believe in the joint effort. The arrival of Monin's wife and their son Guillaume strained the intimacy. The wheelchaired presence of Mme. Monin in the big house, now turned into a printing plant, put between the two couples a distance that imminent failure could not help but exacerbate.

Clara was almost certain she was pregnant.

"Of all times," she told Yvonne, the only person she confided in.

"How is André taking it?"

"He doesn't know." Clara said her husband was not to know. A baby would be too much for the two of them right now.

For an hour she talked. She loved André, loved him because he had taught her to see, to understand, to talk. They were both different, he by his intelligence, which made it hard for him to communicate with his own kind; she by her origins. But their distinction, the way they were different from others had brought them closer, had enriched them. He might need her less than she needed him—men needed to believe there are things in life besides love—nevertheless their complicity was total. Not that he was always easy to be with. There might be a price to pay for any woman attracted to someone smarter than she, but to be without him was unthinkable.

"I must have an abortion, and you must perform it," Clara told her friend.

Monin met almost daily with Dong Dai in Cholon and both emotionally and rationally moved closer to the Kuomintang ideals. Sometimes André came with him. He loved to talk with Dai about the difference between Western and Asian concepts. Westerners had one-track minds, Dai said, all concentrated on goals and accomplishments, whereas Chinese people tried to conceive life as a whole, as a series of possibilities.

"I want to go to China," Monin told André one night when the two of them were enjoying a late-night drink in Monin's law office. "I want to join Chiang Kai-shek, join the armed struggle."

André remembered that Monin had been a volunteer in 1914, that he had been wounded in action, and—a disabled veteran with head wounds—had returned to Lyon to find his family halfway ruined. But that was more than ten years ago.

"Don't go," said André.

"We need radical solutions."

"You mean you want to justify your own need for power."

"I'm not interested in power, but in meaning. What does it all mean?"

"They need technical types, people like Borodin. Nearly all the Bolsheviks have a cult of technicians."

Monin sighed. "I'm intensely curious about the moral forces."

"What about your wife?"

"We have separate bedrooms."

That was news to André. He wasn't sure he wanted to know whether separate bedrooms mean husbandly regard for a paraplegic or the end of a marriage. He said, "You won't survive the hardship."

Monin was not to be stopped. "Varenne is the last straw for me."

After a while, he was back on Chinese politics again. Sun Yat-sen had struck bargains with certain warlords, meaning that Chiang Kai-shek wasn't really in control of the Kuomintang army.

"Each side tries to outwit the other in a fluid situation," André said.

"But Chiang and the Kuomintang are different. It's not yet another warlord riding out of some province. Chiang went to Moscow to study the Red Army and brought Russian advisers back with him. Key people around Chiang are foreigners. That's what makes me believe he may need someone like me."

André pleaded with his friend. "If the fighting won't kill you, the malaria will."

"I want to be useful."

One last cause was to unite the talents and ardor of the two directors of *L'Indochine Enchaînée* and briefly dispatch André to Pnompenh as a court reporter—the Bardez Affair, so named after an administrator in charge of collecting taxes in a section of rural Cambodia.

19. COUPLES

Remarkably, only two Frenchmen so provoked native anger as to cause their own murder. In the face of passive resistance to tax collecting in the village of Krang Leu, Bardez and his two Cambodian interpreter-guards took one of the villagers hostage during the dry season of 1925. The measure had the desired effect of making the village pay up. Once the tax had been collected, however, Bardez refused to free the hostage. This so inflamed the Cambodian villagers that they seized Bardez and his two underlings and beat them to death.

Four years later, Vietnamese nationalists murdered René Bazin, a rubber-plantation recruiter who enlisted workers through native agents in a manner reminiscent of the kidnapping of slaves by African tribal chieftains a century earlier. Conditions were appalling and, as Monin, André and Clara had seen in March 1925, able-bodied men fled into the bush when news of approaching plantation recruiters reached a village. Rubber, the second largest Vietnamese export after rice, was produced by virtually indentured workers so blighted by malaria, dysentery, and malnutrition that at one Michelin Tire Company plantation, twelve thousand out of forty-five thousand died between 1917 and 1944.[1] When the hated Bazin left his girl-friend's house in Hanoi, an agent of the Vietnam Quoc Dong Dang, the boldest of the nationalist movements, killed him.

In both cases, police rounded up all the suspects they could lay their hands on—in the Bardez affair three hundred men, in the Bazin case scores of nationalist activists and sympathizers. The killing of Frenchmen became more common during the 1930s, when the economic recession saw world prices for rice and rubber plummet and production cutbacks incited unemployed workers and hungry peasants to seize estates and take over village councils, but in the 1920s Bardez and Bazin were the only representatives of the most hated colonial activities to be murdered.

The facts were not in dispute in the Bardez affair. The administrator, who was also treasurer for parts of Cambodia, had, in the face of defiant withholding of a new tax on rice, ordered his driver to take him and his two Cambodian assistants to Krang Leu so they could collect the assessment in person.

When they drove into the village, the local population had gathered on the square. The elders refused to pay. Bardez had ordered his two Cambodian helpers to seize one of the men in the crowd. The standoff had ended with the villagers giving in. The money owed came forward, but Bardez refused to set his hostage free. A heated argument followed, and in a sudden flash of blind fury, the villagers lynched Bardez and his Cambodian helpers and, in front of the chauffeur, hacked them to death.

Troops had been sent to Krang Leu and more than three hundred-men rounded up. At random, seventeen men had been chosen to stand trial.

What had aroused Monin—and André—was the administrative decision to appoint a civil servant to hear the case instead of bringing the arrested villagers before a regular court. Seeing a chance to un-

---

[1] Stanley Karnow, *Vietnam: A History*. On recruiting and mistreatment of plantation laborers see also Paul Monet, *Les Jauniers: Histoire Vraie* (Paris: Gallimard, 1931).

mask both an odious fiscal regime and a judicial system based on informing, André rushed to Pnompenh to cover the trial.

For Clara, there was no better time to go through with the abortion.

What André saw in Pnompenh he found appalling. The prime witness for the defense was Bardez's Cambodian driver, but he had died in police custody a week earlier "while resisting arrest." The judge was openly biased, civil servants intervened constantly in the proceedings, and the villagers' attorney, a Maître Gallet, was barely allowed to speak.

On a terrace across from the courthouse, André interviewed Gallet. A waiter brought them tea. André changed his mind and instead of tea requested mineral water.

On the way across the square half an hour later, the lawyer began to swerve, held on to André, and collapsed in his arms. In a doctor's office, an elderly doctor told André that Gallet had been poisoned.

"He will recover, but he will need rest," the doctor added.

Behind them, an ashen-faced Gallet appeared in the doorway. In spite of the physician's protest, the lawyer took André's arm and headed for the courthouse.

In Saigon, Yvonne aborted Clara.

The prosecution demanded the death penalty. Gallet was denied permission to bring other villagers as defense witnesses but managed to shout that "the crime of Krang Leu is a crime all Cambodia has committed because it is the result of general discontent."

In the end, one of the villagers was sentenced to death, four were given life imprisonment, and seven others were given indefinite hard-labor terms. Five were acquitted.

In his news summary, André attempted sarcasm. What this "trial" proved, he wrote, was a need to rewrite the penal code. "I would suggest a law resting on the following principles:

1) every defendant will have his head cut off.
2) after that he will be defended by counsel.
3) the defense lawyer will have his head cut off.
4) and so on."

André was worried about Clara when he returned from Pnompenh.

She looked weak and frail. Because he could not, or would not, guess what she had done, she became demanding and aggressive. Her need to reassert herself, punctuated by what it was she found murky and ambiguous in him, made her want to take a lover.

They were in their room, getting dressed. "I need choices," she said.

He was in front of the mirror, concentrating on his necktie. "I'm not sure I understand."

"I need to do things that are my own."

He was angry. "Try to learn something," he said.

"Like what?"

"Get a degree, for example."

"With my talent for disorder?"

He ripped the knot apart. From behind him, she saw the reflection of herself. She looked awful. The way her slip hung, as limp as her hair. She needed a haircut.

He started on the knot again. He caught her eyes in the mirror. "What we're achieving here, we're achieving together," he said, controlling himself.

"Then why is our marvelous complicity turning into scenes like this?

He didn't answer.

She said, "The important thing is to know whether our dreams still coincide." She wanted to believe that they did. Why couldn't he see she loved him, that if he wasn't the only man who could give her pleasure he was the only man who'd never bore her, the only man she'd never tire of.

He persisted with the idea of her going back to school, going on to university, getting a degree. For the first time she told him that she, too, was writing.

"I know."

"Have you been going through my things?"

"Since you were little you've been writing fairy tales. You told me you told stories to your kid brother, stories that made no sense."

She didn't mention the notebook she had continued to fill with thoughts about them. Instead, she talked about one-act plays she had written. "In 'Impermanence,' my heroine asks the hero if he likes the way she is," she explained. "He says all he wants is for her to be vibrant, alive. But each time they go out she changes a little. Her eyes change color, something he hates. He's afraid she will grow taller than him."

"And how does it end?" André asked.

"All her changes make her look like every other woman. So the question is: Now that she's everybody else, won't he want her to be like no other woman?"

She had written two other playlets. In "The Game," *she* tries to please *him* to the point of dressing like the romantic notion of an ideal woman. She becomes what he dreams a woman should be. "She's his truth but her own lie. And the game continues until she becomes herself. She tells him she no longer loves him, and he strangles her."

Her third sketch was called "The Silence." The heroine is Martha, a woman who no longer tries to be someone else. Instead, she refuses to speak. For three years, Martha falls silent to the point where *he* no longer knows if she's happy. As the snow falls endlessly outside, he begs her to speak. At the final curtain she says, "The weather has turned bad, darling." Although he doesn't pay attention to what she says, he thinks everything is back to normal.[2]

"I have the same right as you," she said another evening when she brought up her writing again.

She sensed he didn't want her to write and vacillated between a desire to show him what she had written and doubts about her talent. In the end she decided not to show him the notebook she had started shortly after their Rhine excursion two summers earlier and picked up again during her stay in the Pnompenh hospital. For ten years she would write and rewrite this *Livre de Comptes* (Account-book), which was to become the story of a woman picking up the pieces after living with a too-gifted and too-brilliant man.

The underlying theme of *Adolphe*, Benjamin Constant's 1816 fictional retelling of his stormy liaison with Madame de Stael, Clara

---

[2] With a playlet called "The Old Horse," the three one-act plays remained unpublished. See Christian de Bartillat, *Clara Malraux: Biographie, Témoignage* (Paris: Librairie Academique Perrin, 1985).

says, is the man's wish to slip away and the woman's urge to hold him back. "So often all a woman has in life is her ability to love, and, frankly, if I were a man, I'm not sure how I'd feel if I was the object of such passion. What is so unfair is that we force so many women to expect everything from love."

To be a woman is more difficult than to be a man, Clara says, because a woman knows that, however honest she wants to be, she can only win by playing games.

Couples create scenes not to question their relationship but, on the contrary, to strengthen it. The purpose of such showdowns is not to break up but to give the illusion of freedom and to recharge the relationship. Some couples find their equilibrium in such fights, and whatever is said serves as ammunition for future disputes. Still others erect so many barriers that in the heat of the argument they must first shout lies to each other before they can tell the truth, and the untruth is often more important than the truth.

When Clara published *Livre de Comptes* in 1933, she deemed the book a love declaration. André considered it a betrayal.

They felt increasingly out of place. André sensed they had been Saigon too long to pretend they didn't feel the distance between them and the locals, that they didn't feel how profoundly alien they were. Still, he felt good about himself. He had not come out to exploit anybody. On the contrary, they were working alongside Asians, alongside the victims of colonization. What he was learning in Asia was priceless.

Clara wanted to stay strong, and when they talked about the Grasset contract she was sure their experience would result in fabulous books. She liked it when they were back on the skittish subject of his truths brimming over into evasions and fabulations, and he said, "Sure, I invent like that, but what I say becomes true later on."

Rainy western clouds obscured the warm sunlight. For the first time since spring, the city was drenched with more than the usual showers before the swift twilight. Another monsoon season was coming. Another Christmas. Clara and André were broke, sick, and depressed. On Christmas Eve two years ago, the Cambodian treasure hunt had veered into Keystone Kop farce, when police came banging on their cabin door, and, as 1924 wore on, into tragedy. But also into new energy. It was in the humid and pestilence-haunted wards of Pnompenh hospital that they became conscious of realities that led to their first political commitment. A year ago they had been in Paris, on the eve of embarking on a second Asian adventure that had promised sweet revenge.

Now, *L'Indochine Enchainée* was floundering and, by ironic coincidence, so was the Paul Painlevé administration in Paris. Three votes short of carrying Painlevé's one-percent tax on capital gains, the Chamber of Deputies overthrew the government. The next government was headed by Aristide Briand, a veteran of parliamentary shuffles. During the next seven chaotic months Briand formed his eight, ninth, and tenth governments, the ninth lasting three months and the last only three weeks.

In the Monin villa, the camaraderie in the improvised newsroom felt increasingly contrived, put on, and without panicking the remaining members of the little crew began thinking of other possibilities. The animated discussions, the evening swordplay on the rooftop, André and Monin's tuxedoed excursions to Bienhoa had ceased. Clara's involved talks with Vinh became repetitious. Sometimes irritating.

The central market was suddenly deserted by pregnant women. A rumor was circulating that a holy man from India was traveling from village to village in a blue car. On market days he mingled with the crowds. If he touched a pregnant woman she would follow him, although she knew she would be one of the two hundred victims that the water genie demanded as a sacrifice.

"You really don't believe this story, Vinh." Clara asked.

"I don't know," he answered, "but I prefer that the woman I love stays indoors right now.

Defeat, thought Clara, performed curious permutations on people. "All of us seemed to be our own caricature," she would say in her memoirs. "I saw myself, now madwoman, now crybaby, unable to keep up with my self-esteem, still less with my own ideals. Him? How many hours did I spend trying to understand him without hurting my idea of him, without hurting myself."

There were days when she felt Asia was a passage in their lives, a detour perhaps. She had married a writer — the Grasset contract was there to give them confidence. A book should surprise even its author, she believed. It should express what he or she didn't quite know yet.

20. ECHOES

Twelve hundred miles from Saigon, Chiang Kai-shek was on the eve of launching Republican China's biggest offensive. If the huge country was ever to become a reality, he reasoned, the Northern Expedition was to be a necessity.

The thirty-nine-year-old commander was supremely confident that he could lead the new revolutionary army to victory. To take on the vast hordes of the warlords, numbering in all over 750,000 men; however, Chiang had no more than 85,000 soldiers (of whom only 60,000 had rifles). The Communists, and especially the Russians, didn't share Chiang's optimism, but Mikhail Borodin approved the offensive.

The Second Congress of the Kuomintang, where Chiang would report on his military plans, was to meet in Canton on New Year's Day. Expectations were high and rumors rife. Despite Borodin's approval, the Russians weren't sure Chiang could win. The facts seemed to support their skepticism.

The financial demands on the Chinese colony in Cholon to help bankroll the reconquest of the homeland were reaching new highs. As Dong Dai explained to André one evening, the "overseas Chinese" were, well, assessed a tax.

"Willingly, we pay, of course," he smiled. Perhaps more than their brethren in China, overseas Chinese such as he understood the dilemma.

"If our country is to ever to emerge from this messy revolution, money has to be raised. Lots of it. What is interesting, of course, is that we Chinese, just like the Vietnamese, are inveterate gamblers. Illegal gambling is a fact of life in Saigon."

André wasn't quite sure where Dai was taking the conversation, but as usual he enjoyed his erudite friend. In fact, he was thinking of making Dai a protagonist in the book he was beginning for Grasset.

"So why not legalize gambling?" Dai asked.

André had no firm opinion on the subject. Playing fan-tan in Macao had lightened his purse of a number of Hong Kong dollars.

"The idea is in the air," André admitted. "People are talking about decommissioning the navy ship *Paul Lecart* and transforming it into a floating casino."

"I believe Paul Monin has come out in favor of legalizing gambling," said Dai.

"Oh?"

"Calling it a lesser evil than alcohol and opium."

"Paul Monin's entire life is a moral protest."

But Dai wouldn't drop the subject. Governor-General Alexandre Varenne was, in principle, in favor of controlled gambling because it would channel the proceeds to charities instead of corruption. The way the Cholon leaders saw it, some of the charity money could help underwrite revolution in China.

André knew the word for that—skimming—but listened as Dai told him about the Great Wide World in Shanghai.

"On the ground floor you have a department store, one floor up you have a theater and a restaurant," Dai explained. "On the next floor you have gaming halls, and still higher up a brothel. Or maybe it's the reverse. In any case, that's progress. I can certainly imagine a casino in Cholon, all mirrored walls, full of noise and laughter."

"You can't win in fan-tan," André said.

Dai smiled. "The thing is that Varenne hasn't made up his mind."

André wanted to tell about his experience with fan-tan in Macao, but Dai said pointedly: "Varenne is delaying his decree legalizing gambling. I understand certain navy officers who thought they might get a license to run the *Paul Lecart* have been told to keep their mouths shut."

"Typical," grunted André.

"The point is to seek a higher authority than the governor-general."

For a man with a gift for taking quick and forceful possession of ideas and for formulating them in dazzling propositions, André was particularly dense that December evening. It was only after Dai had made pointed allusions to Prime Minister Painlevé, who had granted an interview to Monin and Malraux's newspaper, and to the celebrities who had lent their names to André's cause that he realized he was being propositioned.

Dai offered to arrange for a collection among Cholon's merchants to pay for André and Clara' passage back to France in return for André contacting people who could perhaps favorably influence the casino decision. The proposition was flattering. André didn't know Painlevé or anyone in the corridors of power, but the proposition was an unexpected life vest tossed to a drowning couple.

The moment André told Clara about Dai's proposition she jumped with joy. Long into the night she talked about the lovely familiarity of home, of four seasons, April showers and mimosas in bloom, delicate summers in painters' towns along the Seine, brisk walks in autumnal woods. She talked about the pleasures of biting into familiar fruits, of rediscovering old friends. She was sure that, once in Paris, they would find a solution to their difficulties.

Reservations were made for them aboard a liner leaving for Marseille the day before New Year's Eve. Clara was already packing.

There was an attempt on Paul Monin's life. The lawyer woke up one night to see the mosquito netting rustle on one side of his bed and the shadow of a Vietnamese lean toward him with an open razor. Monin careened off the other side and so surprised the assailant that the man ran to the balcony, jumped into the garden, and disappeared into the night.

Monin told everybody in the morning—Clara knew only André's Gilette safety razor and for a while couldn't figure out how it could be used as a murder weapon—and all agreed the would-be assassin must have been paid by the police to arrange a murder that would look like a suicide.

The attempt on Monin's life became the opening scene in *Man's Fate*. "Should he raise the mosquito netting or should he strike through it?" was the opening sentence. In a rectangle of electric light from a neighboring building, Ch'en holds both a razor and a dagger and hesitates for a second, wishing the supine figure on the bed will wake up because it is easier to kill someone who defends himself. He decides to use the dagger only.

> With a blow that would have split a plank, Ch'en struck through the gauze. Sensitive to the very tip of the blade, he felt the body rebound towards him, flung up by the springs of the bed. He stiffened his arm furiously to hold it down. Like severed halves drawn to each other, the legs sprang together toward the chest; then they jerked out, straight and stiff. Ch'en should have struck again. The body, still on its side, was unstable and instead of being reassured by its convulsion, Ch'en had the impression of pinning it down to the bed with this short blade on which his whole weight rested.
>
> Through the great gash in the mosquito netting, he could see very clearly the eyelids open—had the man realized?—the white eyeballs. Around the dagger the blood was beginning to flow, black in the misleading light.

Provoked rather than frightened Paul Monin saw the attempt on his life as a last straw. Suddenly the underhanded colonial rule, based as it was on intimidation, informing, and long knives in the night, appeared odious and repulsive to him. To die in the hands of a hired assassin was too stupid. More than ever he resented Governor-General Varenne's back-pedaling as a slap in the face and, in a flush of renewed ardor, looked instead toward China for personal fulfillment. Six months ago, the Cholon leaders had opened their purses and their hearts to him and made him their friend. They had initiated him—and Clara and André—into the Kuomintang.

Monin told Dang Dai he wanted to be a member of the Cholon deputation to Canton. A total of 258 delegates would attend the Second Kuomintang Congress. Compared to the colonial politics of containment, compromise, evasion, and downright hostility toward even a promise of reform, the Kuomintang congress looked providential. The delegates, who included Communists, would elect the thirty-six members of a new central executive committee. Monin leaned toward socialist ideals, but he knew little about communism or theoretical politics. He had a firm grasp on principles, on human rights. He was a man of action, a believer in renewal, a lawyer. Surely there was a place for someone like him.

André wrote a piece for *L'Indochine Enchaînée* justifying his return to France. Using the editorial *we*, he said:

> With speeches, meetings, newspaper articles and leaflets, we must agitate. We must persuade the working masses to sign petitions in favor of the Annamese. Those among our writers who still possess generosity—and they are numerous—must address themselves to those who love them. The voice of the people must insist that their masters explain the heavy burden and the pained agony that weigh too heavily on the plains of Indochina. Can we obtain our freedom? Too early to tell. But we will at least obtain some liberties. That is why I leave for France.

With lordly prodigality, Maurice Sainte-Rose dispensed Christmas Eve dinner and gifts. Indulgent of the weaknesses of others, Maurice ordered champagne to celebrate Clara and André's forthcoming return to civilization. They all went to midnight mass in Cholon, Maurice to pray through the pink mist of his own hospitable champagne, André to get a sense of Christianity à la chinoise, and Clara moved at the expressions of faith by women with cheongsams split to their thin thighs.

The happy friendship that had united Monin and André and had made Monin, André, and Clara the three musketeers of Saigon journalism was unraveling. Neither Clara nor André would say whether the cause of their falling out resulted from the failure of their venture, political disagreement, money matters, or a latent rivalry between the two men, but when it came to say goodbye, Monin was not there.

The lawyer who had welcomed them on the Saigon dock almost a year before did not accompany them to the ship. Dang Dai and Dong Thuan were there, handing Clara a box of dried litchis, the fruit from southern China. Prophetically, the figures on the box were a pair of dancing girls dressed in red.

Clara and André stood in the stern as the steamer slid into the shipping channel and Saigon's low silhouette receded in the afternoon mist. They had behind them two failures. The carved devatas of Banteai Srey were still in Cambodia, and Indochina's colonial system was as burdensome as ever.

But they brought with them the heartbeat, the sound and smells of a fully lived experience on a fabulous continent. Although limited to Indochina and short side trips to Bangkok, Singapore, and Hong Kong, their ordeals were nevertheless the core of the confrontation between Eastern and Western ways. What they had witnessed up close were the antagonists in a struggle for an Asia emerging from centuries of torpor and Western aggression.

To escape the adult chatter and children's shouting in the second-class stateroom, André took refuge in a deckhouse and in his fleeting longhand began to write the first fragment of *La Tentation de l'Occident,* a book about the Asian vision of the world and a theme that was always to preoccupy him—the individual versus society. His protagonist's discovery of Asia is lyrically cinematic. Snow falls over China and the islands, and the vision of falling snow fades into the white gown of a princess with a red jewel between her lips, frozen cicadas falling off trees, and magicians burning scented wood. Every spring covers Mongolia with Tartarian roses, white flowers with crimson hearts, as caravans of tall camels cross the steppes carrying loads of round bundles that open like pomegranates when the caravans halt. The scene changes to men in a sunlit courtyard making magical gestures as they describe the buildings they have known in Turkestan and Tibet. The elders in turn give way to European adventurers who have married Mongol women and become generals in the Manchurian armies, fierce and despotic men. The adventurers fade into the portrait of a cunning and all-powerful emperor stretching his thin, transparent hand over all the Chinas—China at work, China full of opium and full of dreams—a blind man sitting huddled in the Forbidden City. He is followed by still older shadows of Tang emperors, the din of their courts where all the world's religions and superstitions clashed. This is followed by images of warriors waving weapons adorned with horsetails, of generals who have died in their tents after sixty victories, and of a frosty night falling on ancient triumphs.

21. IDEAS

The France Clara and André returned to in the early spring of 1926 was quite different from the country they had left to go art-hunting in Cambodia nearly three years earlier.

The postwar euphoria was giving way to apprehension and confusion. Politically, France was torn and weakened by waltzing governments succeeded each other in chaotic fashion, none lasting long enough, even if it had the will, to come to grips with the country's problems.

By temperament and affinity André Malraux might have been expected to join the now-flourishing surrealist movement, or, like Paul Monin, turn toward radical militancy. Instead he was drawn toward the more elitist milieu surrounding his publisher Bernard Grasset and, in less than two years, to gravitate to the inner circle of Gallimard, the most important French publishing house. Although he remained a friend of the painter Philippe Soupault, the writer Robert Desnos, and the dissident Marxist theoretician Pierre Naville, he continued to dislike the surrealists for their noisy clannishness and personally loathed Breton's authoritarian leadership.

Clara and André found a smart brand new apartment at 122 Boulevard Murat, not far from Mme. Goldschmidt's townhouse. They couldn't afford it and lived in dire poverty, both hard at work, he finishing *La Tentation de l'Occident* and writing magazine pieces before plunging into *The Conquerors,* she translating and, for a short time, teaching music.

Clara hated the empty rooms and, to be able to invite some of their old friends, she furnished the rooms with crates and boxes and threw curtains and fabrics over them. André didn't want to invite anybody. Certain acquaintances had deserted them and they were indebted to others, financially and emotionally. She insisted that André meet Leo and Madeleine Lagrange, the attorney couple who had helped her after Monin returned to Saigon nearly two years before. On her own she went to see Marcelle and René Doyon in their book emporium. Marcel Arland was someone they avoided. It's difficult to be friends with people to whom you owe gratitude, said André.

When a printing firm offered to work on ninety day credit and artists said they could wait to be paid, André started a limited edition of slim art books under the name Sphere. Louis Chevasson, who had dabbled in journalism since his return from the Saigon court appeal, joined the publishing venture. André's inventiveness and Chevasson's commitment, however, were not enough to make Sphere flourish, and André launched a second imprint. In homage to the fifteenth century Italian scholar Manutius Aldus and his family of printers, the new imprimatur was named Des Aldes.

André spent long days at Clara's crate table laying out his art books. He had a knack for choosing paper and typefaces, for clipping and pasting and making up dummies. In the end André sold his little enterprise to Bernard Grasset, who took over in order to help his author. Within a few years, André's knowledge of editing and familiarity with the actual manufacture of books would draw the attention of Gaston Gallimard, who would make André his artistic director.

Grasset published Clara's translation of *Tagesbuch eines Maedchen,* an Austrian book by an anonymous authoress, and a little later Gallimard accepted her translation of Freud's *Über infantile sexual Theorien.* She also translated several texts by Christian Grabbe, a nineteenth-century playwright discovered by the Berlin expressionists. A few years later she turned to English and translated Virginia Woolf's *A Room of One's Own*.

The estrangement between Clara and her family remained total. Her younger brother Paul had married and become a father and Clara once caught a glimpse of her mother taking her grandchild to the Bois de Boulogne in a new baby stroller. André's family, on the other hand, moved in on them. With her daughters, Grandma Adriana Romana took an apartment a few blocks from Clara and André. He fell into the habit of lunching with the three women until Clara's wifely pride and her low tolerance for feminine gossip and insidious meddling made her put a stop to it. André's father suddenly found his second wife—and mother of his now-adolescent sons—incompatible. While waiting for a divorce, he invited himself for dinner at Clara and André's every Wednesday.

Clara was not happy.

She had not gone through what she did in southeast Asia to be hemmed into the role of exemplary daughter-in-law, attentive to what neighbors might say and implicitly accountable for her comings and goings. André vetoed her suggestion that she take a job by saying "Why exhibit our poverty?" and threw icewater on her literary ambitions with a wounding, "Better be my wife than a second-string writer." Angry at herself and her own semi-failures, she lashed back at André. She became intolerant, resentful, irritable, and vindictive. She realized that her resentment only underscored her inadequacy, and hated that the price for living with him was her own erasure.

A long illness brought them close again. Rheumatic fever nearly paralyzed André. For three months he stayed in bed in their furnitureless apartment, too weak even to reach the toilet without Clara's help. The medical bills wiped them out financially, but the long months together reminded them of Pnompenh when dengue fever had felled her and he had slept in her hospital room. Again they lived on each other and on hope.

Dedicated to Clara, *La Tentation de l'Occident* came out in August. Although it reflected the mood of 1926, the yearning for both order and escape, the book was only politely received. For its author, however, it opened the pages of the best magazines and the doors to the more important literary circles, where, inevitably, Malraux was someone "back from China."

André was invited to the 1927 Pontigny encounters, the annual summer symposia organized in the former Burgundian cloister by the philosopher Paul Desjardins. (At the 1924 gathering Marcel Arland had gathered the signatures on Clara's hastily drawn-up petition).

Clara wanted to go. André thought it was an all-male affair. They had a fight.

Getting off the train in the nearby village, she found herself greeted with suave condescension by Desjardins "My dear Madame," he said with honeyed elegance, "you are very young. Your husband is very young, and I understand how susceptible, how anxious you must be." Since she didn't answer, he continued. "André Gide will be spending a few days with us. If that would upset or in any way annoy you, please let me know."

Politely Clara said, "I'd be happy to meet Gide." She would have said she was quite sure her husband's sexual preference was feminine, but that even if he and the grand old man of letters were to jump into bed together, that was all right with her, because the two of them had always loved transgressions, had stolen statues together, were currently publishing erotic art, signing I-owe-yous they weren't sure they'd be able to honor, smoking opium on occasion, and helping young persons get abortions. "In my mind," she would write in her memoirs, "I was stuttering, 'You see, if we're playing your game right now, we're just pretending.' "[1]

In the conference debates, she had to admit, Desjardins was brilliant. But, she would sum up, this was a place where "God was not yet dead, Marx was barely born, Freud provoked overbearing smiles, and only Nietzsche bothered a bit." The sale of the Aldes imprimatur allowed Clara to buy snakeskins and Arab cassocks and André to agree to return a few dinners. To the people they invited to their spare but supermodern apartment Clara innocently insisted their

---

[1] Clara Malraux, *Voici que vient l'été*.

furniture had not yet arrived from Saigon. The Malrauxs showed off what was one of the first automatic garbage chutes in Paris.

Clara's cuisine—meatloaf with curry was one repeated specialty—often left people with mixed reactions, but André forewarned their guests before they sat down, Oriental style, on floor mats, that there were restaurants down on the corner for those requiring gourmet food.

They renewed their friendship with Claire and Ivan Goll. Nino Frank, a young Italian journalist who had introduced Ivan to James Joyce and knew *everyone* in posh arts circles, was a perspicacious observer who came to dinner. He had first met Clara and André at the Golls and in his *Memoire Brisée* was to leave a vivid sketch of them; she soft and squat, with a strong nose, pretty dream-eyes, and an air of affectation; he direct and open, with a very young face, long hair, and hint of a sad and vaguely begging smile. They met again a few days later:

> The Malrauxs are in love with the dreamy Italy of Stendhal and Sanseverina. Clara talks easily about herself—her good luck, her opium, her preference for bathtubs, and going out in foursomes. I'm more interested in him. There's something hungry, impatient and troubled about him that almost jars with his canny, whipsaw writing. His pleasant affectation, his Parisian gourmet's decorum (we're dining at Montagne or Place des Victoires where he enters respectfully), his somewhat delicate intellectualism, then, suddenly, flashes of ideas and words, quickly checked, because Clara fades in, anxious to speak. Immediately, he shuts up, his gaze admiring and complicitous; while she uses the gesture of dinner table talkers who want to make sure they aren't interrupted.[2]

More exotic friends than Nino Frank were the wealthy Orientalist Maurice Magre, whose poem André had declaimed at the shipboard party off the coast of Africa, and his mistress, Suzanne Paris. Magre lived a clockwork Jekyll-and-Hyde existence while smoking his eight pipes of opium a day. He was a model husband until 2:00 P.M.,

---

[2] Nino Frank, *Memoire Brisée* (Paris: Calmann-Levy, 1967).

when for the next twelve hours he left home for Suzanne's studio loft.

After sunset, this Oriental erudite and this failed actress withdrew into a work of dreams and hallucinations, propelled by an inexhaustible knowledge of classical travel *récit* and Asian history. The Malrauxs often joined them for dinner. Later, they all climbed to the studio loft. While Maurice, Suzanne, and Clara stretched out with their opium pipes, André told fascinating tales, stimulating Maurice to tell others. If André told of Timur Lang, the Samarkand king who ravaged Iran, Baghdad, and Delhi before dying on a march against China, Maurice told about Genghis Khan's body being returned to the capital of his steppe empire by his sons on a litter with drawn curtains so the soldiers wouldn't know he was dead, this following his defeat on the frozen Yangtze River, where Toongun horsemen had hacked Genghis' bowmen to pieces because they didn't know how to stand on ice. Maurice and Suzanne were later to travel to India to attend an ashram and to return both edified and bemused by Buddhism. Clara and André were to remain their friends until Maurice's death.

Edgar du Perron—Eddy to his friends—was new friend to whom André would dedicate *Man's Fate*. A mixed-race Dutchman of Creole, Dutch, and Javanese descent born in Indonesia, Eddy was a little man with big brown eyes who looked much younger than he was and whose childhood and youth in the East Indies made him see European affairs with bemused bewilderment. He was a writer of breezy irony and studied detachment that shielded a despairing pessimism and a feeling that he was more spectator than actor in his own life. He had a special admiration for Stendhal, whom he resembled physically, and shared with André a fascination for Asia.

Clara and André saw Eddy almost every day during the spring of 1927 when Chiang Kai-shek disarmed pro-Communist trade unions in Shanghai and neither Stalin in Moscow or Chou En-lai and Mao Zedong dared take action. The Shanghai massacre began at dawn April 12.

The slaughter of the Communists brought up the inner struggle between Stalin and Trotsky. Both Marx and Lenin said only the proletariat can create a Communist state, meaning in the case of China that the indigenous Communist Party should support the nationalist revolution and, at some future time when a Chinese proletariat existed, overthrow the nationalist regime. Mao Zedong would one day prove that a peasant revolution could impose communism, but in 1927 this idea was Marxist heresy.

Stalin's "correct" pro-Kuomintang policy now seemed to lie in ruin, and Trotsky was trying to organize the angry opposition to it. The events were hotly debated in Clara and André's circle of friends. André was sure the Shanghai massacre would force the Soviet Union to reverse its policy. "The question," he said, "is not to define the revolution, but to make it happen." He was writing the first draft of *The Conquerors*, in which Pierre Garin was called Starin, a name evidently derived from Stavrogin, the willful revolutionary who lost faith in revolution and hanged himself in the last pages of Dostoevsky's *The Possessed*. Dostoevsky had been one of André's favorite authors since his teens. Now he carefully studied the 1871 novel. He also found inspiration in a new movie: Sergei Eisenstein's *Battleship Potemkin*, the triumph of the new Soviet cinema.

One December day in 1927, Clara ran into her mother. After a moment's confusion, they embraced. Everything seemed simple. Madame Goldschmidt took her daughter home to the big house Clara had known since childhood.

When Clara told André about meeting her mother and their tentative reconciliation, he listened in silence.

"Henceforth," he said with finality, "I no longer consider myself responsible for you."

The words sent her reeling. She had never had the impression that he, or anyone, was responsible for her. She had helped him, helping herself at the same time, but she had never believed she was accomplishing a duty or felt superior. Did he think she was less at his mercy because she had made up with her mother? Did he have to be richer than she in order not to feel poorer?

For New Year's, Mother sent Clara five thousand francs, which she had the strength to return "precisely because I could use it."

After another cold interlude, mother and daughter settled into an uneasy peace.

• • •

The Conquerors changed everything.

Written in the present tense, in a terse, notational style, the story of the hard yet deeply vulnerable Pierre Garin asserting himself amid revolutionary strike action advanced cinematically from one scene to the next. The use of headlines and radio flashes—reminiscent of John Dos Passos' collages of newsreel headlines, phrases from popular songs, and "camera-eye" points of view—added to the dramatic immediacy, staccato and sweep of physical action in a fluid revolutionary situation. The book, which Grasset brought out in the spring of 1929, put an end to Clara and André's shoestring existence and transformed André's marginal reputation into recognizable renown.

⌒ 22. SILK ROADS

André's fabulations and "mythomania," as Clara would later call it, was part of his talent. To friends and acquaintances he began to fictionalize their Asian past. In some of his accounts the Banteai Srey caper became politicized, with Clara's German background the cause of murky suspicions; in others she no longer existed. As the accounts of the treasure hunt grew in color and daring, it seemed increasingly incongruous that a tiny and apparently fragile female could have taken part in it. In some retellings of the Saigon newspaper venture her contributions were attributed to Vietnamese collaborators, in others her intercession with the Paris literati became an effort undertaken by Vietnamese and Cambodian leftists.

In the name of their total commitment, Clara had cut herself off from her family. She had accepted misery, illness, and humiliation. And now he denied her the experiences she felt justified the pain she inflicted on her mother and the bruises she had endured herself.

But André felt no need to excuse himself. He not only insisted he had every right to transpose personal experiences into fiction but also believed that, rearranged in this fashion, events appeared more plausible. Myths, he said, were neither true nor false, but a way of investing people's lives with meaning. To "invent," to re-create and transpose, was to turn experience into consciousness, and that was as essential to him as adventure in faraway places was a means of self-discovery.

She had the feeling he was destroying that in her which he had found interesting, and when—in order not to be an echo or a mirror—she fought back, she hurt him where he was the most vulnerable, in his pride. She admitted he was her superior. "I listened to him, I admired him, I told myself: he takes up the entire space," she would say. "He was my delegate to the world which no longer reached me except through the fog of a steamed-up window. Finally, Zelda Fitzgerald and I both suffered because the men we had been smart enough to choose were too brilliant. Once the choice was made, we were asked to surrender the intelligence that had made us choose them in the first place. Neither of us could. She went mad. It could have happened to me."

Best-sellerdom allowed for distractions. They decided to visit another Asia. They sailed from Marseille aboard a freighter, the only passengers, and after calls at Italian and Greek ports, entered the Black Sea and disembarked in Batumi, in Soviet Georgia. The first night in the Soviet Union was spent in a dim and crowded tavern, where a dwarf in a top hat led a low-voiced chorus of smelly men in an elegiac singalong. The whole thing, Clara and André told each other, was more Dostoevsky's Eternal Russia than the new USSR they had expected to see.

After a train ride across the Caucasus Mountains and a stopover in Tbilisi, which looked like a plundered Nice, they reached the oil city of Baku on the Caspian Sea. They would have loved to cross the Caspian and follow the ancient Silk Road to Samarkand, the fabled city once captured by Alexander the Great and another time by Genghis Khan, now a mere town in the Uzbek SSR. However, the Intourist official said they weren't supposed to be traveling around Russia by themselves. After a few days they were granted an exit visa and on a tiny steamer crossed the iridescent-green Caspian Sea, lunching on deck with the German ambassador to Teheran. The Shah had just abolished the veil for women, he told them.

Persia—Iran—captivated them. So much so that they returned the next year and again the following year.

The last novel of the three-book contract with Grasset was both meditation on death and heroic retelling of the Banteai Srey expedition. The publication of *La Voie Royale (The Royal Way)* brought out the Pnompenh trial and appeal. When *Candide's* star critic André Rousseaux interviewed him, André admitted the story was autobiographical while insisting on the attenuating circumstances of his case—the nonclassification of archeological sites in Cambodia and the fact that no court had actually ruled on the issue. Rousseaux came away baffled. Instead of the fascinating anarchist he had expected to interview, he had had to listen to endless pleas from someone obsessed by "bourgeois order."

"I cut the interview short and ran," Rousseaux reported in his magazine. "I had expected for a moment to skirt pure anarchy and despite myself I admired his lucid and gloomy despair, the horrible and sublime beauty. I must admit that pure anarchy doesn't exist, except in M. Malraux's books."[1]

The novel was a success, although its acceptance did not match the electrifying reception accorded *The Conquerors*.

Banned in the Soviet Union and Mussolini's Italy, *The Conquerors* was a dud in English. Winifred Stephens Whale's awkward translation, published by Cape at Aldous Huxley's suggestion, sold very poorly both in England and in Harcourt Brace's American edition.

In November 1930, the elderly woman who cleaned Fernand Malraux's apartment came to see Clara and André. She didn't know how to say this. Monsieur was very unhappy. Recently she had heard him muttering that he was going to take his own life.

To change Fernand's mind, Clara and André invented an elabo-

---

[1] *Candide,* November 13, 1930.

rate story. Claude, Fernand's younger son by his second wife, was suffering from a contagious disease, they told him. Roland, Claude's brother, would have to come and stay with Fernand.

The strategy seemed to work. The presence of his adolescent son cheered up Fernand, but after a while he became dejected again. A few days after Roland returned to his mother for Christmas, Fernand opened the gas valves. When the cleaning woman found him the next morning, his face was serene and his hands were on a book on Buddhist concepts of the afterlife. He was fifty-four years old.

During the summer of 1931 Clara and André were back in Iran. Isfahan was a *Thousand and One Nights* enchantment, yet completely without relation to the city André had described in the travel piece written under Maurice Sainte-Rose's name. The palace of Shah Abbas was immaculately beautiful and the *maidan*, the great dusty square surrounded by glowing mosques, had scarcely changed since the city had been the capital of a great empire. Clara—and her husband with her—was adopted by the local Jewish community. André went on a metaphysical binge and sat under flowering pomegranate trees in miniature gardens talking with Sufi masters and mullahs.

They continued east to Afghanistan, a country they found austere. In the streets of Kabul the women wore the *chador*. Clara found the absence of feminine faces atrocious. They went to visit the local bazaar on a Thursday. The Afridis were easy to distinguish from the city-dwellers. They were wiry men with shaved heads and full beards who spoke a strange tongue called Pakhtu. After nearly a century of British effort to conquer them, they still lived outside the control of any organized government. In a narrow alley a giant Afridi, insane and therefore sacred, came toward them, singing a plaintive ballad. André pushed Clara toward the shops and resolutely reached into his pocket as if to grasp a hidden revolver. The crowd saw the gesture and formed a circle around them.

"Keep walking," he told Clara. "Not too fast. Watch the displays as if your presence here is totally normal!" As they advanced the crowd yielded, finally leaving them on a small square with two blind beggars. The French consul suggested they refrain from going to the bazaar alone, especially on Thursdays, when the primitive Afridi tribespeople, who lived on both sides of the Khyber Pass, came down from their mountains.

"We just came from there," said Andre.

"In that case, what can I tell you?"

The consul invited them to ride with him in his small truck to Ghanzi, a town two hundred miles south of the capital, that he had arranged to visit. The tires blew out in the desert. They were down to their last bottle of water, when, looking like something out of a Buster Keaton movie, a Model T cleared the horizon. The governor of Ghanzi had worried and sent his son out to look for the consul.

Their arrival was celebrated with a twelve-course dinner, each course served with rice. When Clara wanted to see the local bazaar, she was accompanied by twelve barefoot soldiers. The Ghanzi population had not yet seen a European woman.

They discovered that the Silk Road, the trade route that had linked China with the West since the third century B.C., divided east of the Caspian into a northern branch through Samarkand and a southern route that followed the Amu Darya River into Afghanistan. After circling the borders of the Takla Makan Desert, the two routes rejoined in Tun-Huang in northwest China.

They crossed the Khyber Pass into British India and, in Peshawar, decided to escape the heat by scaling the Himalayan foothills to Kashmir. Srinagar looked like a Swiss village, with houseboats floating on its pristine, cool lake. They rented a houseboat that came with seven male servants. At the local bazaar André saw a shoemaker who, while waiting for clients in need of shoe repairs, either sculpted little Buddhas himself or sold Buddha heads he found in the surrounding hills.

"Do you have any others?" André had Clara translate.

The man could do dragons.

"Ask him if he knows where we can find ancient dragons, ancient stones." They ended up buying, for a modest price, a Karnak sculpture. Karnak was in Egypt, but André was soon fabulating on the existence of a road from Egypt to India that was no more, an ancient road running through Syria, Persia, Afghanistan that a changing climate had buried under an advancing desert. "Aren't you back in Cambodia again?" Clara laughed.

"Baghdad was not always surrounded by desert. Remember Mesopotamia, the hanging gardens of Babylon."

They were back in the foothills of Kashmir the next year and the year after that.

Afghanistan was in the middle of a civil war in 1931, with one usurper just boiled in oil, but André was fearless. He was sure he was on the scent of the missing link between classical Greece and Buddhist India, the crossroads where the twain did meet, where Christianity in the West and Buddhism in the East transformed Apollo into Jesus and Siddhartha. It was the haunting Silk Road again. The ancient route had served both as a commercial bridge between East and West and as a conveyer of artistic and religious customs and convictions. "If Christendom is dominated by the tragic picture of an execution—Jesus on the cross—Buddhism, a religion primarily of the conquest of immobility, is expressed by the tranquil picture of a meditation." he would write one day.[2]

Dominated sporadically by nomadic tribes and the Chinese, the Silk Road fell under Islamic Turkish rule and then under Mongol domination, only to be forgotten in the fifteenth century after the opening of a sea passage between Europe and India. Up in the mountains where the fierce Afridis lived, André managed to buy terra-cotta sculptures from a recent excavation near Tashkurghan.

It was night when the Afridis delivered the clay heads. Andre ran his flashlight over the acquisition. The torso had the bowed head, turned slightly. of the crucified Jesus, and it also had Buddha's lowered, but not yet closed, eyelids. Nobody had ever seen a bowed head in Indian art. Wasn't this intuitive proof that Alfred Salmony and André had been right, so many years ago, in suspecting a shared nervous system that linked all people together?

"As I always say, I may bungle once," he whispered to Clara, "the second time I make damn sure I succeed."

With native helpers, Clara and André got the Graeco-Buddhist heads across the Khyber Pass to Peshawar, down the Himalayan

---

[2] Andre Malraux, *Les Voix du Silence* (Paris: Gallimard, 1951); translated by Stuart Gilbert, *The Voices of Silence* (New York: Doubleday, 1960).

foothills to Rawalpindi and, with oxen pulling an engineless Model T Ford part of the way, to Lahore. André would never forget the descent from Kashmir, camels lost in fog and braying to each other, the sandbars along the Indus further down, thornbushes full of grasshoppers as big as shrimp. And the people, men in rags but superb horsemen, women in veils in front of clay huts built on the sand. "Outside not a leaf, inside not a stick of furniture," he would write in *Antimemoires,* "only walls, the sky and God." They continued on to Bombay, where Clara's English got the bodhisattvas through British customs and aboard a freighter sailing for France.

They themselves continued east—around the world.

India captivated them. "There is something at once bewitching and bewitched in Indian thought which has to do with the feeling it gives us of climbing a sacred mountain whose summit constantly recedes," André remembered. They felt India was the most religious and most affectionate country, with superstitions swarming like mayflies around temples. They found Benares a melancholy garden and its crowd silent. They studied erotic temple sculpture, and in the Hanuman temple saw monkeys pursuing mysterious errands around a sacrificial stone and heard once more the story of Buddha's promise to the monkeys that if they behaved well, one morning they would wake up human.

From Burma, Clara and André went to Hong Kong and, finally, Canton, Hongchow, and Shanghai—nothing, André had to admit, like the cities described in *The Conquerors.* After Peking they boarded a train and traveled north for days, suddenly into colder weather and Mongol faces. On a platform they saw twenty young men in Western dress, shouting ecstatically and jumping up and down. Someone managed to translate into pidgin English that war with Japan had just broken out and that the young draftees were dancing for joy.

After Korea and Japan, North America—"discovered backwards"—Vancouver, Seattle, San Francisco, and a train ride across a United States deep into its Depression. In New York their money ran out and they spent two very poor weeks, walking everywhere as they had done in Hanoi seven years earlier while awaiting a telegraphed currency order from Gaston Gallimard.

The revelation here for André was the Metropolitan Museum. While Clara discovered speakeasies and the mixed pleasure of drinking alcohol out of coffee mugs, Andre stalked through the Far East and primitive art rooms of the giant museum. He lingered in front of the Khmer displays. Who was Perry Lewis, the bronze-plaqued donor of a four-armed bodhisattva? Privateer with a taste for art? Who were Margery and Harry Khan? An American lady who had married a Pakistani grave robber? An esteemed Afghan gentleman who had married a Ziegfeld Follies chorus girl? Wealthy collectors always professed the noblest of motives and the highest of ideals. Works of art, they liked to say, also belonged a little to those who rescued them. It was already eight years since Clara and he had loaded their loot aboard the riverboat in Siam Reap. "Gift of Clara and André Malraux." Maybe museums were the only places where anything could escape death.

When Gallimard's money reached the Western Union office, where they had become twice-a-day visitors, they bought fresh clothes and had themselves invited to several parties.

On the ocean liner steaming across the Atlantic toward Cherbourg, Marshal Henri-Philippe Pétain, hero of Verdun and within nine short years the head of Nazi-occupied France, was at the head of the captain's table. And André celebrated his thirtieth birthday.

The Graeco-Buddhist sculptures arrived from Bombay. Gallimard, who was trying to lure André away from Bernard Grasset, suggested the Tashkurghan heads be exhibited at the Gallimard corporate headquarters. André wanted Clara to be in charge of the art show. If an amateur should decide he or she couldn't live without a Graeco-Buddhist statue, André wasn't against selling a piece or two, if the offered price was hefty enough.

The publisher managed both to acquire the author and to exhibit his art.

André asked art historian Josef Strzygowski, whose epic theories placed the dawn of Western art in Armenia or the steppes of Russia, to write the exhibition catalogue. The Austrian scholar was somewhat surprised when told the heads came from a region traditionally considered beyond all Greek influence but valiantly set to work on a series of hypotheses. Clara had little talent for selling, and to her humiliation she saw her role pared down, and a secretary assigned the full-time responsibility for the exhibition. One day when the secretary was absent, Clara convinced a provincial curator that his museum could not be without an example of the hybrid Afghan art.

When, proud of her commercial initiative, she told André, he retorted, "I won't admit that my wife turns herself into a salesgirl."

The retort cut her deeply. It also made her re-examine their life. She was first of all *his* wife, but to what end? During the years in Vietnam, the question of the space she claimed as her own had never come up, perhaps because she was so much a part of the Banteai Srey quest and the newspaper venture. She had always believed she was entitled to be herself. Now, his success seemed to imply that she had to reduce her living space. For the first time she saw gray hairs and wrinkles in her mirror. She tried a couple of lovers, one-night stands that she told herself were not to hurt him but would help her feel alive.

The fall of 1932 marked the death of André's grandmother, Adriana Romana, and, a few months later, his mother, felled by an embolism.

Clara became pregnant that fall and Andre wrote the book that would make him world-famous. *La Condition Humaine (Man's Fate)* was written in large part in his friend Eddy du Perron's suburban house in the pretty Vallée de la Chevreuse. To tell the complicated events leading up to Chiang Kai-shek's massacre of the Shanghai Communists, he relied on notes taken the previous year during his and Clara's round-the-world trip, on newspaper clippings and on talks with Georges Manue, a journalist friend who had covered the 1927 events from Shanghai and Nanking and had even interviewed Chiang.

As in *The Conquerors*, the characters in *Man's Fate* are a motley of expatriate revolutionaries, multinational executives, and a few sharply drawn Chinese. As is not the case in the earlier novels, people here have families—wives, husbands, sons, and in-laws.

André delivered the *Man's Fate* manuscript at the end of the year. Gaston Gallimard was deeply impressed by the novel; André Gide was not on the first reading. Malraux wanted the publisher to push for the Goncourt prize, but Gallimard felt the powerful action, the exotic locale, and sometimes disconcerting lyricism might go over the heads of the literary jury members.

La Condition Humaine was serialized in six issues of *NRF* magazine from January through June 1933 and was in the bookstores by September. The triumph was immediate, lasting, and international. *Man's Fate* was an instant classic. Ilya Ehrenburg, *Izvestia's* Paris correspondent, prefaced his review by saying it was already in its twenty-fifth printing in France. "It is not a book on the revolution, it is not an epic, but an intimate journal, an x-ray of the author himself fragmented into several characters," Ehrenbourg wrote. In America, Edmund Wilson wrote in *The New Republic* "I don't know of any modern book which dramatized so successfully such varied national and social types. Beside it, E. M. Forster's admirable *A Passage to India* appears a little provincial; you even—what rarely happens nowadays to the reader of a French novel—forget that the author is French." If this wasn't enough to coax an American publisher into bringing out a translation, Leon Trotsky fired off a letter to Simon & Schuster saying "only a great superhuman purpose for which man is ready to pay with his life gives meaning to personal existence. This is the final import of a novel which is free from philosophical didacticism and remains from beginning to end a true work of art."[3]

The book had one enthusiastic reader in Russia: Joseph Stalin. The novel was not too flattering about China policy, at least as it had been practiced in 1927, but to the Russian leader, Andre was one of two good Frenchmen (the other was the socialist politician Pierre Laval). In China, the defeated Communists were on the eve of their famous Long March. In Germany, the book came out as Adolf Hitler blamed Germany's communists for the Reichstag fire that allowed him to seize power. Until the 1960s, rumors would persist that Malraux's Kyo character was based on Mao Zedong's second-in-command (and active participant in the doomed Shanghai uprising), Chou En-lai.

---

[3] Isaac Deutscher, *Trotsky*, Vol. III: *The Prophet Outcast: 1929-1940* (London: Oxford University Press, 1963).

In December *La Condition Humaine* and its thirty-two-year-old author received the Prix Goncourt, following a unanimous vote by the jury. The prize, the jury said, not only crowned *Man's Fate* but the whole of the three Asia novels, including *The Conquerors* and *The Royal Way*.

André loved the prize and the glory—and Clara with him. Not everything was perfect between them, but on March 28, 1933, they were the proud parents of a little girl. "At least she was intelligent enough not to be a boy," André said, bending over the hospital crib. "I'd have a hard time getting used to a caricature of myself."

Clara thought of naming her Adriana, after the baby's paternal grandmother, but André asked Clara if she'd find it silly to name her Florence, "in memory of the city where we were happy." Clara was overwhelmed with joy. With tears in her eyes, she held the baby and said, "Florence, Flo—that's German for flea, almost."

It was an eventful year for the new mother and the celebrity author. Nazism ended the German Goldschmidts' wealth, and Clara's nineteen-year-old cousin arrived with his teenage "Aryan" fiancée, the first of the family members that Clara and André helped settle in France or emigrate to the Americas. Because of Paul Goldschmidt's reckless investments in French companies doing business in Vietnam and because of a final devaluation of the Poincaré franc, Margrete was practically ruined. Maurice, her eldest son, and the Magdeburg uncles managed to hide the extent of the ruin from her by sending money from Germany, but Paul continued to skid into disastrous financial adventures. In 1933 the revenues from the German investments stopped and Margrete had to be told the truth.

She sold the already-mortgaged townhouse. Emotionally, she was far from stable. There was a measure of irony in her moving into a six-room flat on the ground floor of Clara and André's apartment building at 44 Rue du Bac and being discreetly supported by the son-in-law she had begged her daughter to divorce.

Clara and André had been married ten years. Little Florence was a happy surprise, but little else was going right in the relationship. Their adventures in Asia and, in André's case, the novels they inspired, had been thrilling. Asia, to them, had been an exotic world in which they progressed from romance through crime to political awakening. They evolved from treasure-hunters to resident co-conspirators in a commitment to a free press. The central theme of their Asia was colonialism, one people ruling another, its delusions and smarting ironies. The shock of what they witnessed had done more than anything else to stimulate their growth as human beings. After that, life in a Parisian apartment was something of a bore.

Like many people, they were better at handling adversity than success. If he wrote her out of his novels, it was because he could never forgive her for reminding him of who he had been. When, much later in life, she wrote her version, the Asian years took on a wistful, sometime sardonic resonance that the youthful saga never had.

She had been the first to be unfaithful, to have a shipboard affair with Charles G. Now it was his turn.

Louise de Vilmorin was an ardent poet, intimate friend of Coco Chanel, and the wife of a Wall Street banker. A year younger than André but matching his verbal gift, she was as aristocratic as her name and lived with three brothers in the family chateau in Verrières in the southern outskirts of Paris. The lovers didn't hide, but flirted outrageously across tables whether they were at Maxim's or at Marius's, the parliamentarians' Left Bank restaurant, and as an in joke Chanel had Louise model a bridal gown in her collection. When they met, even Clara was impressed, saying she was jealous of so much graceful lightness.

In retaliation Clara went to Palestine to spend a week with a twenty-year-old Sabra, a sun-tanned student from Haifa who said he couldn't live without her. André came to Marseille to greet Clara on her return. She was touched and they were reconciled.

Caught up in his celebrity, André dazzled a young Gallimard editor, Josette Clotis, who signed letters and an occasional magazine piece Jo Clo. The fame, the pitch at which André lived, his tales and adventures and what she later called "his combination of intelligence, egotism and sometimes hypersensitive vulnerability," totally captivated the twenty-one-year-old editor, who loved expensive clothes and all shades of blue.

Clara hated Jo and tried to foist her off on Roland, now a handsome nineteen-year-old. As Clara would write,

She leaned over my crib and said, "I want to have a baby like that, too." I advised her to see my brother-in-law; she preferred to stick to her own idea, which, as with so many obsessions, finished by coming true.[4]

Clara's many quarrels with André found their way into her notebook. Eleonore and Adolphe's conjugal scenes in Benjamin Constant's hundred-eighteen-year-old novel *Adolphe* echoed in her own writing as she pondered. But Clara made no move to leave André. She also loved the pitch at which they lived, and feared boredom and mediocrity in other men. Gide and Malraux were the spearhead names protesting the Leipzig trial of two leading left-wingers for the burning of the Reichstag. They went to Berlin to meet with Hitler and, although the Reichkanzler never deigned to meet the two French intellectuals, his minister without portfolio, Hermann Goering, did.

Clara and André went to see Trotsky during his French exile in 1933. When André was invited, as one of the few Western non-Communists, to attend the All-Soviet Writers' surreal congress in Moscow in 1934, they both went. André gave one speech that made party members uncomfortable. Sergei Eisenstein, fast becoming a nonperson in the Soviet Union, wanted to make the film version of *Man's Fate*. Vsevolod Meyerhold wanted to stage it at the Moscow Revolutionary Theater, with Sergei Prokofiev writing the music. Eisenstein came to the National Hotel every day to talk about a screenplay that, instead of the novel's live-to-fight-another-day ending, would have machine guns attack Chiang Kai-shek, filling the screen. Maxim Gorki wanted Andre to collaborate on a vast encyclopedia. But nothing came of anything.

For hours they stood on the top of Lenin's Tomb, a few feet from Stalin, watching an interminable parade. At one point Clara whispered to André she found Stalin, with his hint of an Oriental profile, his black eyes, sensual mouth, sexy and that she wouldn't mind spending a moment in bed with him.

André's nearness, if nothing else, to Stalin spread among the dele-

---

[4] Clara Malraux, *Voici que Vient l'Été.*

gates and at one of the closing receptions André was approached by a shrunken man in too-big clothes. It was Mikhail Borodin, éminence grise of the Chinese revolution and main character in *The Conquerors*. "Since you are on such good terms with the authorities," Borodin said in a low voice, "perhaps you will be able to put in the right word to help me get an apartment with central heating."

Inveterate travelers, Clara and André didn't return to France at the end of the Writers' Union Congress but stayed another four months in the Soviet Union. They traveled east to Novosibirsk, but could not get permission to see the fabled city of the Silk Road, Samarkand.

23. THE REST OF OUR LIVES

It was 1935, ten years since André had told the Cholon Chinese on the eve of the publication of *L'Indochine* that if they didn't have the same goals they certainly had the same enemies. The rise of Nazism gave Clara and André the same friends as well as the same enemies.

Clara and André's involvement with refugees from Hitler's Germany made André abandon a novel about oil, to be set in Soviet Asia, and to write *Le Temps du Mepris (Days of Wrath)*. This long short story about a German Communist organizer who is arrested when he deliberately walks into a police trap to save his comrades, his internment by the Nazis, and his near-miraculous escape to Czechoslovakia contained none of the ideological conflict of *The Conquerors* and *Man's Fate*. In 1935, however, it was the first French report on Nazi police repression.

Twice a week Clara and André's apartment in the Rue du Bac was the meeting place and focal point of Parisian intellectual energies. Clara was a member of numerous committees, perpetual translator at meetings, and helpful behind-the-scenes intermediary for new streams of socialists, Communists, and/or Jewish refugees making it to Paris, and Gide made her the treasurer of a fund for refugees.

"The money he entrusted me with was considerable," she would remember. "He never asked for an accounting." They spoke more than freely, Gide wondering whether she had slept with one of the handsomer refugees. "You've got the sexual drive of a man," he told her one day.

During the summer, when Mussolini openly prepared to invade Ethiopia, Clara and André rented a house in the Loire Valley. Nino Frank, the Italian journalist who had first met them at the Goll's in 1926, came to visit them and little Florence. Clara had bought a secondhand four-cylinder Rosengart car and when it was decided to go for crayfish one evening, Frank came along. "She drove in her own inimitable way, to the tune of her husband's sardonic remarks," the Italian wrote. The little car couldn't quite make the uphill slopes, and at one long hill they all had to get out in the rain and push. "As usual, Malraux was patient and ceremonious toward Clara, but with an indefinable added irritation, heightened by the insistence of Clara, queenly behind her wheel, that he was somehow responsible for the Rosengart's death throes."

André cut short the wet Pouilly vacation to be in the center of efforts to organize an antifascist conference, a kind of Parisian answer to the previous summer's Moscow conclave. When in June the International Writers Congress convened in the sweltering old Mutualité Hall it brought together an extraordinary cohort of intellectuals, ranging from Romain Rolland and Aldous Huxley to Bertolt Brecht and E. M. Forster. André and Ilya Ehrenburg got the Soviet ambassador to fire off a telegram asking that Boris Pasternak and Isaac Babel, the two writers the French proletariat supposedly loved most, be sent to Paris. Both authors arrived totally bewildered, Pasternak to declaim a poem, which André read in translation, Babel shuffling onto the platform unable to take the conference seriously, telling Jewish jokes, captivating everyone by his modesty and gentleness, to be wildly applauded at the end.

Clara went to Germany with a lawyer and a Protestant minister in 1934 to protest the trial of twenty union leaders. When they got to Wuppertal, in the industrial Rhineland, the lawyer, the preacher, and the famous author's wife were barred from the courtroom—it had been decided that the trial would be held in camera. Outside, Clara mingled with the defendants' wives, all working-class women sullenly watching their men being rushed in. Ten minutes later, the three French nationals were being told to follow a plainclothes detective to the police station. Clara spoke German too well not to raise suspicion, but to the question "When did you leave Germany?" she bluntly lied "I was born in France." After verification with the French consulate in Cologne, the trio was released and even granted an interview with the presiding judge. With Clara translating, the French lawyer and the judge had a surreal discussion about new German jurisprudence—which, the judge said, made an act a misdemeanor even if it had been committed before a law making it an offense had been passed. The twenty defendants were on trial for having belonged to a union before 1933, when it was legal to belong to one.

The United States had turned toward reform by electing Franklin D. Roosevelt in 1932. In April 1936 France went to the polls in heavy rain and in a record turnout elected a Leftist coalition. The advent of the Popular Front was welcomed by the masses as a thrilling victory promising long overdue social and economic reforms and by the dismayed right as bringing France to the brink of Red revolution. The head of the coalition government was socialist Leon Blum, a man prey to self-doubts, self-criticism, and given to airing his soul-searching in public. His undersecretary of state was Leo Lagrange, Clara and André's attorney friend.

With the Spanish Civil War, André's legend came true. In this conflict, in which the great issue of democracy versus fascism seemed to be at stake in the elected Republican government's resistance to Francisco Franco's attempted armed forces coup, he came to incarnate the heroes of his novels and, by energetic and intelligent intervention, tried to influence the course of revolutionary events. Here he was not just a journalistic camp follower like Ernest Hemingway and the rest of the literati; he commanded an international air squadron and wrote his last big novel, *L'Espoir*—which, to echo *Man's Fate*, became *Man's Hope* in English.

It was the first novel to grow out of Malraux's firsthand experiences. It was his triumph over himself, the triumph of objective truth and reality over fantasy and myth. Influenced by Tolstoy's *War and Peace*, screenwriting and journalism, the big powerful novel was the story of the first nine months of the war, a broad canvas where all attempts at concentrating the action on a single protagonist is abandoned for the epic sweep, with many people engaged in the complex struggle between the ideal and the possible. As an anarchist leader tells an intelligence chief, "The communists want to *do* things. You and the anarchists, for different reasons, want to *be* things. That's the drama of all revolutions like this one. The myths we live by are contradictory—pacifism and the need to protect ourselves, effectiveness and justice and so on."

Clara came along with him to Spain. When they landed in Madrid, the government held the extreme northwest corner of Spain, Madrid, and Barcelona, while lightning coups had put Seville and Cordoba into the hands of the Falangists, as the rebels called themselves. Clara was moved by the sight of armed militiamen and -women, all dressed in the same work clothes, patrolling streets and building barricades, but believed it was a lost cause. Not so André.

Flying back to Paris for meetings with airplane manufacturers—even his brother-in-law Maurice Goldschmidt was helpful—and air ministry officials, André pleaded for aircraft and made long-distance phone calls from his Rue du Bac apartment all over Europe and America. In October, the Air France manager in Barcelona saw a whole squadron of fighter aircraft fly in from France commanded by Malraux, "lean, gaunt and eyes flashing." André had a chat with him and an hour later a quarter-million gallons of aviation fuel were "transferred" to Republican registry.

Beating an arms embargo that France, England, Germany, Italy, and the Soviet Union agreed upon to deny weapons to both sides in the civil war (and Hitler and Mussolini immediately violated to supply Franco), André managed to get more planes into Spain. The Republican government was more than grateful and, making André a "coronel," gave him the right to form and command a wing of foreign mercenary fliers. The unit was immediately baptized the España Squadron.

André's fame as a writer, his far-flung contacts with influential people, the respect Republican leaders showed him gave him an ascendancy and an influence that impressed his little army of pilots and mechanics. The España Squadron airmen were French, German, American, Italian, Russian, and one Algerian.

Clara was sometimes with André in Madrid, sometimes in Paris. André Gide, who had just returned from Moscow and caused consternation in leftist ranks by denouncing Soviet mentality as being more stultifying than the climate in Hitler's Germany, visited the Malrauxs in the Rue du Bac in 1936. André had just arrived from Madrid and was soaking in a bath while three-year-old Florence was tearing petals off a dahlia to make a "salad," as Gide noted in his diary. Clara was brooding. She had proclaimed complete sexual freedom by sleeping with one of André's airmen, and André had announced the marriage was over.

When André went on a whirlwind fund-raising tour of the United States for the international brigades, his companion was not Clara but Josette Clotis. They arrived in New York in February 1937. Although the Roosevelt administration tried to maintain a "moral embargo" and Congress actually had two resolutions banning arms shipment, American liberals were fervently behind the Loyalist fight against fascism. Nearly three thousand Americans were fighting in the brigades. No one granted André an interview in Washington, but the audiences he addressed in New York and Philadelphia and at university rallies at Harvard and Princeton before flying to the West Coast were more than sympathetic.

André arrived in Los Angeles, clutching a copy of *The Maltese Falcon* and asked if he could meet Dashiell Hammett. *Le tout Hollywood* contributed to the cause. Hammett was not prepared for Malraux's enthusiasm and compliments on his writing, which, André said, Hemingway had copied. Hammett's ladyfriend Lillian Hellman wanted to hear about Spain. She was soon to join Joris Ivens, the Dutch documentary filmmaker, and Hemingway in Spain. Back in Paris, André persuaded Gaston Gallimard to bring out Hammett's entire oeuvre in French.

Clara entered a dark period of her life. The favorite uncle from her Magdeburg childhood passed through Paris, en route to South America—where he would die of homesickness. In 1938, her mother took her own life. The suicide sent Clara into an emotional tailspin. Margrete Goldschmidt's health had been declining, but Clara couldn't help feeling that if her own life had been different, her mother would still be alive. "Why am I always a loser?" she cried.

•   •   •

With Josette, André spent the late summer of 1939 studying medieval art in southern France. The ignoble end of the Spanish civil war, the crushing defeat of the Spanish Republic in the hands of Franco's fascist forces while the Western democracies did nothing, turned him inward.

He wanted to write a book that would grasp the whole of art in one intuitive sweep and see art not as the expression of beauty but as an age-long attempt at defying human destiny. Art, he believed, was not the result of social conditions, but of pressure from within each artist and as such was testimony to the transcendence of the human adventure. Like the Graeco-Buddhist heads Clara and he had brought back from Afghanistan, Romanesque sculpture was art in transition, leaving behind it the frozen forms of Byzantium and anticipating the Gothic cathedrals and the warm humanity of the Renaissance.

Germany's invasion of Poland on September 1 and the French-British declaration of war on Hitler two days later was almost anticlimactic. Josette and André returned to Paris, he thinking of joining the Polish army ("Can you see me wearing a shapka?" he asked his old friend Louis Chevasson), but Poland was crushed in one week and the war settled into a long lull that was called the phony war.

André wanted to fight. He had commanded a squadron and as a gunner-bombardier had personally flown sixty-five sorties that included combat with both Italian and German warplanes. Because of his "cardiac trouble" noted in the military record following the 1922 induction physical in Strasbourg, however, he was rejected.

Pulling strings, the thirty-eight-year-old Malraux managed to get into an armored unit, and while waiting the call-up moved into a furnished apartment to settle his civil affairs. The tank regiment appealed to him because it had been his father's unit in the First World War and because he felt armor could play a decisive role in the new conflict. As he joined his unit in Provins, fifty miles east of Paris, Josette became pregnant.

The magnificent tank battles that were to become just-as-magnificent pages in a new novel occurred hundreds of miles from Provins. By June 1940, when Erich von Manstein's armor outflanked the Maginot Line by dashing through Belgium and striking into the heartland of France, Marshal Pétain's hastily formed government, soon to set itself up in the spa city of Vichy, accepted Hitler's terms for an armistice. André was one of ten thousand German prisoners.

The Nazi sweep of France saw Clara and seven-year-old Flo take refuge first in the countryside in south-central France, and, when the armistice divided France into the German-occupied northern and the southern Vichy zones, in Toulouse. As Josette gave birth to a boy she named Pierre-Gauthier, André escaped from the prison camp and, totally destitute, joined her on the Riviera in December 1940.

Josette's father was the mayor of a village between Cannes and Toulon, and with their newborn son, André and Jo were taken in. Their "situation" as unmarried couple, now with an illegitimate child, was not the kind of arrangement that enchanted provincial families. Money and escape from the Clotis' family home became André's major obsession. No money could be sent from Gallimard in German-occupied Paris, but the Riviera was full of empty villas. Together with Jo and their little boy, Andre managed to move into an English painter couple's villa in Roquebrune Cap-Martin.

Clara and her daughter found refuge with Madeleine Lagrange, now a widow, and Jean Cassou, the Spanish-born novelist and curator of the Paris Museum of Modern Art she and Andre had gotten to know in Madrid when he had come to salute the Popular Front.

Clara and André met in Toulouse January 18, 1942—a date she would never forget—to ask for a divorce.

"I don't want the son I have with Jo to be illegitimate," he said.

"I wouldn't mind if my daughter was illegitimate," Clara answered, "if only she didn't have a Jewish mother."[1]

Leaving him, she wept. She was forty-five years old and told herself she would have to forget him, try to live without the shadow he cast on her life. In anger she wanted to throw off the surname that had been hers since 1923 and almost walked into a city hall to register herself as "the Jewess Goldschmidt." But the name Malraux was a shield and, to save herself and Flo from obvious finger-pointing and deportation, she kept the name and, as an extra precaution for her daughter—had the girl christened.

---

[1] Christian de Bartillat, *Clara Malraux*.

•   •   •

The war liberated Clara. Responsible for Flo and herself, she lived in hiding for four years. To avoid being a humiliated Jew, as she would say, she joined the resistance and felt herself slowly reconquering her identity. André's legend and charisma made him a natural underground leader. In 1943, shortly before Jo gave birth to a second son in a Perigord hideaway that Louis Chevasson and his wife helped find for them, André joined and became a commander of a brigade fighting the Germans in Alsace in 1944-1945.

Meanwhile, everybody died around André. Jo, waiting with the infant sons for war's end in the Perigord château, put her visiting mother's luggage aboard the local train and, when it pulled out, jumped down. Hampered by the thick-soled wartime shoes she fell between two cars and died ten days later. During the last days of the war, André's two half-brothers died senselessly, Roland in the hold of a freighter full of Nazis trying to flee to Sweden, young Claude executed after being caught in a sabotage attempt aboard a German ship in the Seine estuary.

De Gaulle made André minister of information in his first postwar administration, a government that lasted two months. André turned toward art and wrote *The Voices of Silence*, a vast synthesis of art as its own absolute, as a bond linking all people across the chasm of time and culture, as the triumphant form of human expression.

Clara published her first book. *Portrait de Griselidis* took its title from the classic tale of the king who marries a shepherdess and who, to try her faithfulness, invents a series of monstrous tests.

Clara found Griselda's story, told both in Boccaccio's *Decameron* and Chaucer's *Canterbury Tales,* a timeless example of a woman's inner need to be with a man she can look up to. Set in Indochina, *Griselidis* (which was never translated into English) is the story of Roger Perrouin, a doctor to Vietnamese natives whose career is jeopardized by a drug charge, and Bella, a woman who admits she is not so much in love with Roger as she is "intoxicated" by him. The novel has several harrowing sentences. Bella tells Roger that since he is irreplaceable to her, he can't abandon her. "To think how big a man's responsibility is when he brings out in a woman needs that only he can satisfy." And perhaps the deepest expression of the Griselda dilemma: "To be possessed of an intelligence that can only be fulfilled when in contact with a stronger mind, to be incapable of functioning alone in life or with someone inferior, that is the true feminine drama."

Clara and Andre were divorced in 1947. André married Marie-Madeleine, Claude's widow, to give his two small sons and his brother's widow's newborn son a home and stability. In 1961, when his sons Gauthier and Vincent were twenty-one and eighteen respectively, they were killed in a car crash.

Clara never remarried. She found meaning in her writing and in the shared destiny of the Jews. "Jewish without knowing why," she said, "I am a Jew now because I knew the deep reasons." She was in Jerusalem at the creation of Israel in 1948. With the publication of the first volume of her autobiography in 1963, she gained recognition on her own.

If in 1945 provisional president De Gaulle had offered Vietnam gradual independence and sent a general to Haiphong to drink a toast with Ho Chi Minh, the French government coalition of Communists and Socialists and De Gaulle's own party reneged in the name of a million Catholics in Indochina. Ho cried betrayal and overnight increased his guerrilla forces from thirty thousand to sixty thousand. From 1946 to 1950, Ho and his forces lived according to Mao Zedong's maxim: "If the enemy is strong avoid him; if he is weak, attack him." As a guerrilla movement the Viets harassed the French expeditionary force without being able to tear away control of the country. Mao's victory in China changed the Asian picture and, from 1950 on, Ho disposed of a veritable army and sanctuaries in China. Over the next four years, French garrisons fell like dominos, from the Chinese border to the Hanoi delta, with French commanders trying to save the situation by pulling back toward Hanoi and other coastal cities. The field commander said it would take half a million men to win. Paris sent only 130,000, of whom barely 40,000 were French. Many were Germans, some barely repentant Nazis in the Foreign Legion; the rest were Algerians, Tunisians, and Moroccans who would soon put to practice at home the lessons in guerrilla warfare they were learning in Indochina.

"If you ask me how we will save Indochina," André told De Gaulle, "we won't. All we can save is a kind of cultural legacy, a set of values. But we must vomit the idea of an 'economic presence' of which the principal newspaper in Saigon still dares to headline 'The Defense of *French* interests in Indochina.' We must start the revolution that is both inevitable and legitimate ourselves. Abolish the usury loans, mostly held by expatriate Chinese anyway, which are crushing the farmers. Sure, Asians need European specialists, but they don't need to have them as masters. All they have to do is pay them. I'll go further. In order to make Indochina a friendly country, we must help Ho Chi Minh. It'll be difficult, but no more difficult than it was for Britain to help Jawaharlal Nehru."

When De Gaulle returned to power in 1958, André joined the cabinet. For nearly eleven years he was Secretary for Cultural Affairs and as such tasted what few intellectuals ever come to enjoy—the power to experiment in culture. He sent the Louvre's treasures on globetrotting tours—accompanying *Mona Lisa* to Washington and making friends with John and Jacqueline Kennedy—and scraped centuries of grime off Paris monuments. He initiated an unprecedented inventory of France's artistic legacy, started new archeological reserves, had Marc Chagall paint the Opéra ceiling and Coco Chanel decorate a wing of the Louvre. He launched his *maisons de culture,* multipurpose art centers designed not only to extend Paris standards to the provinces but also to foster an interpenetration of the arts by combining facilities for drama, music, film, and exhibitions. Modern industrial societies, he said, must break the stronghold of money on culture and see to it that the majority of citizens are not always flooded with trash.

Clara gained renown for her six volumes of memoirs which chronicled the Indochina adventure à deux, told of her thankless task in rallying support for the accused art thief awaiting trial in Pnompenh, of the couple's emotional liabilities and progression from self-centered calculation to combative engagement in a French Indochina now slipping away into history. The successive volumes tell ingeniously of André's early misogyny, hurtfully of the Goldschmidts' money, and courageously of Clara and André's long breakup, her difficult progression as a woman, and the rich political and cultural texture of modern France.

The Secretary for Cultural Affairs diplomatically refused comment except to defend her. When a journalist suggested it might have been more tactful had she published her memoirs under Goldschmidt, he snapped, "She has earned the Malraux, you know."

Colonialism—and its liquidation—made André and his daughter opponents. In 1958 Malraux told De Gaulle France wouldn't keep her colonies, but a dirty war kept French soldiers—and settlers—in Algeria. In 1960, twenty-seven-year-old Florence Malraux was one of an imposing number of artists and writers to protest the De Gaulle administration's pursuit of the Algerian war. Her name on the list of opponents to the regime created a sensation.

Clara wrote accounts of her travels to Israel and Indonesia in the 1960s, finding the Israelis incarnating an impossible dream and Java its opposite, a sweet, savory mix of races and religions that should logically be humankind's end-game.

Legends have long lives. In choosing André for a first mission to Peking in 1965 (De Gaulle had broken Western ranks a year earlier and established diplomatic relations with China) the French president thought he was sending the old comrade-in-arms of Mao Zedong's revolutionary armies.

André disappeared into the People's Republic in the midst of its Great Leap Forward, ostensibly on a low-key visit as De Gaulle's private envoy, actually on a mission on behalf of President Lyndon Johnson to feel out the Chairman and the Chinese leadership's thinking and intentions regarding an early end to the Vietnam war. Malraux was to devote forty pages of his *Antimemoires* to his meeting with Mao, giving the dimension and frisson of this historical character who in André's view had influenced the lives of more people than anyone in this century with the possible exception of Lenin. André flew back to Paris with a stopover in Pnompenh, where he hadn't been since he had covered the Bardez Affair in 1925. A year later Mao launched the Cultural Revolution.

André renewed his relationship with Louise de Vilmorin and plunged into a voluptuous if autumnal liaison. De Gaulle did not approve, but Louise distracted André, poked fun at him, and made him laugh with her verbal spark. He moved into her château in Verrières.

As André and Louise were about to spend a winter vacation in Morocco, she died after complications from a common cold. André was too grief-stricken to go to San Francisco for his daughter's marriage to filmmaker Alain Resnais, but he met the newlyweds on their return to France. As an in-joke, Resnais, who had adapted Marguerite Duras' *Hiroshima Mon Amour* for the screen, made references to his father-in-law's meeting with Trotsky when he made his film *Stavisky*.

Flo did much to reconcile her parents. Clara went on television to say life with a genius had been fabulous and to complain that she was assailed by Malraux Ph.D. writers and researchers. "My passion has always been to make knowledge progress, and I discovered happiness in art," she said. Had age brought them closer? "He conveyed his genius to me; I gave him my point of view. If I lived so long with this difficult companion, it's because we caught up with each other, because we came to share a certain philosophy of life."

André Malraux left power when De Gaulle did. André wrote bestsellers about De Gaulle and Picasso, long discursive transpositions of intimate conversations. He was flown to Washington in 1972 to brief Richard Nixon before *he* made his historic voyage to China, and thought of seeking his own blazing death in Bangladesh's armed secession from Pakistan. But Indira Gandhi had no intention of giving any part of the victory to any Western international brigade.

He approached old age still in love with the beautiful and tragic dimension of man's fate, watching his own metamorphosis with bemused detachment. "When you have seen several schools of art come into existence and disappear, you realize that a body of work, not to talk about a human life, undergoes a metamorphosis. I know what *Man's Fate* was when it was published and I'm sure it's not the same thing now. It would be interesting one day to analyze the odd inner life of a work of the mind."

"My memory has a hard time remembering personal detail. I have read what has been written about my books, not about my life. I don't remember my childhood; I don't remember, except by deliberate attention, the women I have loved, or believed I have loved."

France, he said, had never captured the hearts and minds of the people of Southeast Asia because France, like the United States, Russia, and even communism, had lost its sense of manifest destiny. "The main facts of our time are not events, not even such admittedly shattering occurrences as the advent of the nuclear age, but the shift in the way we think, in the relentless way we question who we are. We are at the end of the empires because the sense of manifest destiny is disappearing." America showed the world the new and "essential" idea that modern nations live on an abstraction of their political institutions.

"When the ballot box was invented two hundred years ago, the Third Estate was, when opposed to nobility and clergy, a crushing majority. We have kept the words, but with a one percent majority, governments don't govern; they make deals. Democracy has become its own abstraction and is therefore unlikely to last another two hundred years."

Suicidal tendencies, vertigo, hints of aphasia, and (out of public view) convulsive dizziness followed by fainting spells sent him to the hospital in November 1972 with a collapsed peripheral nervous system and threatened paralysis of the cerebellum. He recovered and wrote *Lazarus*, a long meditation on the edge of life. Another volume on art followed and yet another one was planned, but on November 23, 1976, two weeks after his seventy-fifth birthday, he died. The cause was pulmonary embolism. The lung condition was a relapse from a chain-smoker's cancer, for which he had been operated on three months earlier.

By 1979 Clara had published the last two volumes of her memoirs. With a television crew, she made an aching and poignant pilgrimage to the town where she had been happy as a child—Magdeburg. At the Jewish cemetery in the rebuilt East German city she found her grandparents' grave. Trailed by the film crew, she looked for the ancestral house near the railway station, found only a construction site that she wasn't sure was the right place anyway, but created a crowd of curious locals.

"But isn't that Clara?" a man said, coming toward her.

"Who are you?" she asked."

"I'm Hans."

"I thought you were your older brother."

"My brother died a few years ago."

That, and the taste of a pastry from her childhood when her grandmother took her to the *konditorei* and presented her as "my little granddaughter from Paris," was the extent of her physical contact with the past.

She celebrated her eightieth year sitting still for an interview book with the novelist-biographer Christian de Bartillat. "I've traveled all my life and I've wanted to travel still more. Jules Laforgue believed that the worst punishment that anyone could suffer was 'to die without having seen the planet.' My idea was to go as far as possible when I was still young. With André back then, we were both crazy. We really left without knowing how we'd get back."

Were it to done all over again, would she live the same life again? "I'd have liked to see still more people, different countries. I have only one regret, that I made my mother suffer, especially at the time of the Cambodian adventure."

Did she have any advice for young people? "No. I might simply say don't remain spectators. Take part in what goes on. Share it, feel it. That's what used to be so awful in women's lives, to be the ones who looked on from the balcony."[2]

She lived with her cat and mementos, which included one of the Graeco-Buddhist heads she and André had bought from the Afridis and smuggled out through India in 1931. She liked the idea that the carved head represented melting-pot art, the mixing of people and cultures. "I'm a walking testimony to cultural cross-breeding," she would tell visitors. "Although French comes naturally to me, I express myself correctly in four languages. I've done a lot of translations; it's an excellent way of transmitting someone else's thoughts. I've seen myself caught up in the ideas of the people I translated.

"A language is also a rhythm, and to learn another language is to learn another rhythm.

"All art begins with rhythms that start in the human body. A woman's breathing is not the same as a man's. It's what I mean when I say that one day we'll have a truly different feminine literature."

She lived another two years. She was visiting friends in the country and took a book to bed with her December 15, 1982. They found her in the morning. Her heart had stopped and the book was on the nightstand.

---

[2] Christian de Bartillat, *Clara Malraux*.

〰️ 24. THE OTHERS

Shortly after Clara and André returned to France in 1926, Paul Monin went underground in Saigon and, via the Cholon pipeline, to Canton.

The second congress of the Kuomintang elected thirty-six members to the new central executive committee, including seven Communists. Mao Zedong, who became directly responsible for propaganda, was one of them. On February 1, Chiang Kai-shek was elected inspector general of the revolutionary forces.

The Communist members raised no objections to Chiang's military plans. After the congress, however, Mikhail Borodin was suddenly recalled to Moscow, and in his absence the Communists began saying the northern expedition was doomed to failure.

The warlords' armies outnumbered the Kuomintang forces. They were better armed and better trained, but they were provincial in outlook and liable to shifts of personal loyalty. After six months of fighting, the ranks of the Nationalist armies had grown from 80,000 to 264,000 disciplined men. By February 1927, Hangchow, the capital of Chiang's home province, fell to the Kuomintang forces. Shanghai and Nanking were theirs a month later and gave the Nationalists control of ten provinces of south and central China.

Nothing is known of Paul Monin's activities in China. The simmering quarrel between Chiang and the Chinese Communists exploded and made the first half of 1927 crowded and confused. In Shanghai and Canton the Communists made determined efforts to set off uprisings. Monin resurfaced in Saigon toward the end of the year to die destitute, as André had predicted, of malaria. He left behind his gravely ill widow. His son Guillaume became a journalist.

Mikhail Borodin was back in China as Shanghai fell to the Nationalist forces in March 1927, largely as a result of a revolutionary strike by eight hundred thousand workers organized by Chou En-lai and others. Stalin wanted to restore Kuomintang unity, even at the sacrifice of the more extreme Chinese Communists. Borodin played both sides and lost when, in April 1927, Chiang Kai-shek struck. Accounts of what happened in Shanghai were wildly contradictory. Each side accused the others of being in league with local gangsters. Chiang's supporters went into action, and when the Shanghai coup was over, hundreds of labor leaders and militant workers were shot in street fighting or executed in purges that followed an abortive general strike. Chou En-lai was one of those arrested and sentenced to death, but he escaped with the complicity of a divisional commander.

Borodin was discredited as the Soviet commissar in China. Stalin did not hold Borodin responsible for Chiang's massacre of his Communist allies, however, and Borodin returned to Moscow to become People's Commissar of Labor. He was steadily demoted and from 1932 had the comparatively unimportant job of editing the English-language *Moscow Daily News*.

Borodin did not get an apartment with central heating despite André slipping a word to Stalin. Borodin's relative obscurity as newspaper editor enabled him to escape Stalin's purges, but in 1949 he was arrested in one of Stalin's anti-Semitic drives and died in a Siberian labor camp two years later.

．　　　．　　　．

There is a measure of irony in the fact that the French establishment labeled Paul Monin and the Malrauxs "the reddest Bolsheviks in all Annam" when the two were essentially for a French assimilation, for the higher ideals of France's *mission civilisatrice*.

At a time when, from his exile in Canton, Ho Chi Minh and his Thanh Nien youth party were recruiting hundreds of followers inside Vietnam and laying the groundwork for a thirty-year war for independence, Paul and André had, in their newspaper, expressed the belief that colonialism was a kind of moral obligation that advanced nations owed less fortunate people.

"I have known a period when Europe was sure of herself, sure of bringing other continents the advantages of the civilized world," Clara would say at the end of her life. "Today this seems laughable, and we feel guilty. Of course we provoked injustices, but we also subdued other wrongs. In general, we have been softer conquerors than those of yore, the Romans for example. In fact, I now believe we were less giving than we thought at the time, but that we were also less guilty than we now believe we were. Today's young know the world is relative and should therefore be more tolerant, yet what we are witnessing is a rebirth of fanaticism."

As a theme in human evolution, colonialism—one people ruling another—is not without its delusions and smarting ironies. In order to despise colonialism a person must have something to compare his or her culture to, a knowledge of *other* people; that is, ironically, he or she must possess an overview that only colonialism affords.

For hundreds of years before the French conquest, Vietnam tried to establish its overlordhsip of Cambodia. After the departure of the French and the Americans, the Vietnamese are still at it. The killing fields of the Pol Pot regime of the 1970s slaughtered urban, educated Cambodians on a scale not seen since the genocidal attempts against Armenians and Jews.

Reflecting current French thinking on colonialism, Gilbert Conte believes that although nothing is more subject to the ambience and atmosphere of the times, colonialism is probably a constant in human history. Whether we like it or not, one people ruling and influencing another is an age-old phenomenon. Different circumstances have either favored progress or resulted in appalling disorders. In the rearview mirror, the only interest consists of seeing how we change.[1]

Under the management of Nguyen Pho, the suspected police informer, *L'Indochine Enchainée* struggled on for a few more issues before it quietly folded in February 1926. The demise was marked in Henry de Lachevrotière's *L'Impartial* by accusations that André Malraux and Paul Monin had pocketed years of advance subscriptions.

After his denial years later, when he appeared in Paris at Clara's Rue de l'Université doorstep, Clara met him on a bus once more, then heard he had died.

In March 1925, Phan Chu Trinh died. Nguyen An Ninh, the publisher of the satirical weekly, organized a national funeral for the elder statesman that frightened the white settlers. Ninh was arrested. On his release he founded a Trotskyite Communist party and disappeared.

In an offensive timed to coincide with Hitler's conquest of France, the Japanese swept into Vietnam from China in 1940 and crushed the French administration. They pushed on, driving the British from Malaya and Singapore, the Dutch from Indonesia, the Americans from the Philippines. An Asian nation had destroyed European colonialism.

Disguised as a Chinese journalist, Ho Chi Minh slipped into Vietnam, his first return in thirty years. The time had come, he told a few confederates, to fight both the Japanese and the French. At the collapse of Japan in 1945, he proclaimed the independent republic of Vietnam.

De Gaulle reimposed French rule. Lachevrotière was killed in

---

[1] Gilbert Conte, *L'Empire Triomphant, 1871-1936* (Paris: Denoel, 1988)

1950 by a bomb thrown into his car by Vietcong commandos while he was on his way to the Saigon tennis club.

When Charles de Gaulle and André Malraux sat watching the snow fall outside the former president's house in Colombey at the end of their lives, De Gaulle said politicians put together territories they don't know how to hang on to, defend interests they later betray, and that fate works in unsuspecting ways.

During the critical seventy-two hours of André's 1972 hospital stay with a collapsed peripheral nervous system and threatened paralysis, what he remembered of the Asian adventure was the military brass band playing Verdi in Pnompenh's main square at sunset.

The Rue Catinat became To Do (Liberty) Street during the American Vietnam war. The triumphant Vietcong renamed it Dong Khoi (General Uprising) Street. Now, thirteen years after the last Americans fled in helicopters from their embassy roof, the Vietnamese government is restoring the Continental Hotel to its palm courted colonial splendor in the hope that it would again be the choice lodgings for the discriminating traveler in Southeast Asia.

When Bernardo Bertolucci told the Peking government he wanted to film *Man's Fate* in China, he was told that was not possible. The Chinese government had totally sanitized and mythologized its revolution. According to current Chinese history, no foreigners took part in the 1927 Shanghai uprising. It was suggested that the director do *The Last Emperor* instead.

The block of sculptures that Clara and André hacked from the Banteai Srey ruins were put back into the temple walls. They remained there until 1970, when the shrine was destroyed in a Vietcong-Khmer Rouge attack on the Siem Reap stronghold of the Lon Nol government.

BOOKS BY CLARA & ANDRÉ MALRAUX

CLARA MALRAUX

Portrait de Griselidis. Paris: Colbert, 1945.

Contes de la Perse. Paris: A l'Enfant poete, 1947.

La Maison Ne Fait Pas de Credit. Paris: Bibliothèque Francaise, 1947.

Par de Plus Long Chemins. Paris: Stock, 1953.

La Lutte Inégale. Paris: Julliard, 1958.

Java-Bali Paris: Rencontre, 1964.

Civilisation du Kibboutz. Marseille: Gonthier, 1964.

Venus des Quatre Coins de la Terre. Paris: Julliard, 1972.

Le Bruit de Nos Pas. Paris: Grasset, 1963-1979.
  1. *Apprendre a Vivre.* (1897-1922)
  2. *Nos Vingt Ans.* (1922-1924)
  3. *Les Combats et les Jeux.* (1924-1925)
  4. *Voici que Vient l'Été.* (1926-1935)
  5. *La Fin et le Commencement.* (1936-1940)
  6. *Et Pourtant J'étais Libre.* (1940-1968).

An English translation of selections of the first two volumes, translated by Patrick O'Brian, appeared as *Memoirs* (New York: Farrar, Straus & Giroux, 1967).

Rachel Ma Grande Soeur. Paris: Ramsay, 1980.

ANDRÉ MALRAUX

Lunes en Papier. Paris: Galerie Simon, 1921.

La Tentation de l' Occident. Paris: Grasset, 1926.

Les Conquérants. Paris: Grasset, 1928; *The Conquerors*, translated by Winifred Stephens Whale. New York: Random House, 1929.

Le Royaume du Farfelu. Paris: Grasset, 1928.

La Voie Royale. Paris: Grasset, 1930; *The Royal Way*, translated by Stuart Gilbert. New York: Smith and Haas, 1935.

La Condition Humaine. Paris: Gallimard, 1933; *Man's Fate*, translated by Stuart Gilbert. New York: Smith and Haas, 1934.

Le Temps du Mepris. Paris: Gallimard, 1935; *Days of Wrath*, translated by Haakon M. Chevalier. New York: Random House, 1936.

L'Espoir. Paris: Gallimard, 1937; *Man's Hope*, translated by Stuart Gilbert, Alistair MacDonald. New York: Random House, 1938.

Les Noyers de l'Altenburg. Lausanne: Editions du Haut-Pays, 1943; *The Walnut Trees of Altenburg*. translated by A. W. Fielding. London: John Lehmann, 1952.

Scènes Choisies. Paris: Gallimard, 1946.

Esquisse d'une Psychologie du Cinema. Paris: Gallimard, 1946.

Le Musée Imaginaire. Geneva: Skira: Volume I: *La Psychologie de l'Art*, 1947; Volume II: *La Création Artistique*, 1949; Volume III: *La Monnaie de l'Absolu*, 1950.

Saturne, Essais sur Goya. Paris: Gallimard, 1950.

Les Voix du Silence, Paris: Gallimard, 1951; *The Voices of Silence*, translated by Stuart Gilbert. New York: Doubleday, 1960.

Vermeer de Delft. Paris: Gallimard, 1952.

Le Musée Imaginaire de la Sculpture Mondiale. Paris: Gallimard,

1952-1954: Volume I: *La statuaire;* Volume II: *Des Bas-reliefs aux Grottes Sacrées;* Volume III: *Le Monde Chrétien.*

La Corde et les Souris. Paris: Gallimard: Volume I: *Antimémoires,* 1967; *Anti-Memoirs,* translated by Terence Kilmartin. New York: Holt, Rinehart and Winston, 1968; Volume II: *Les Hôtes de passage,* 1976; Volume III: *Les Chênes qu'on Abat,* 1971; *Felled Oaks: Conversations with Charles de Gaulle,* translated by Irene Clephane. New York: Holt, Rinehart and Winston, 1972; Vol IV: *La Tête d'Obsedienne,* 1974; *Picasso's Mask,* translated by June Guicharnaud with Jacques Guicharnaud. New York: Holt, Rinehart and Winston, 1976. Volume V: *Lazare,* 1974; *Lazarus,* translated by Terence Kilmartin. New York: Grove Press, 1978.

BIBLIOGRAPHY

Aub, Max. *Sierra de Teruel*. Mexico: Editorial ERA, 1968.

Audoin, Philippe. *Les Surréalistes*. Paris: Seuil, 1973.

Baker, Carlos. *Ernest Hemingway: A Life Story*. New York: Scribner, 1969.

Bartillat, Christian de. *Clara Malraux: Biographie, témoignage*. Paris: Terres des Femmes, Perrin, 1985.

Blend, Charles. *André Malraux: The Tragic Humanist*. Columbus: Ohio State University Press, 1965.

Boak, Denis. *André Malraux*. London: Oxford University Press, 1968.

Bodard, Lucien. *The Quicksand War: Prelude to Vietnam*. Boston: Little, Brown, 1967.

Contes, Gilbert. *L'Empire Triomphant, 1871-1936*. Paris: Denoel, 1988.

Crespelle, Jean-Paul. *Chagall*, translated by Benita Eisler. New York: Coward-McCann, 1970.

Doyon, René-Louis. *Memoire d'Homme*. Paris: Connaissance, 1953.

292

Ehrenburg, Ilya. *Memoirs: 1921-1941,* translated by Tatiana Shebunina. Cleveland: World, 1960.

Flanner, Janet. *Men and Monuments.* New York: Harper, 1957.

Frank, Nino. *Memoire Brisée.* Paris: Calmann-Levy, 1967.

Friang, Brigitte. *La Mousson de la Liberté: Vietnam: du Colonialisme au Communisme.* Paris: Plon, 1976.

Frohock, Wilbur Merrill. *André Malraux and the Tragic Imagination.* Stanford, Calif.: Stanford University Press, 1952.

Galante, Pierre. *Malraux,* translated by Haakon Chevalier. New York: Cowles, 1971.

Garnier, François. *Max Jacob: Correspondance.* Paris: Editions de Paris, 1953.

Gide, André. *Journals,* ed. Justin O'Brien, New York: Knopf, 1951.

Karnow, Stanley. *Vietnam: A History.* New York: Viking, 1983.

Kazin, Alfred. *Starting Out in the Thirties.* Boston: Little, Brown, 1962.

Koltzov, Mikhail. *Diario de la Guerra de España.* Paris: Ruedo Iberico, 1963.

Lacouture, Jean. *André Malraux.* Paris: Seuil, 1973; translated by Alan Sheridan. New York: Pantheon, 1976.

Madsen, Axel, *Malraux.* New York: Morrow, 1976.

Mounier, Emmanuel. *Malraux, Camus, Sartre, Bernanos.* Paris: Seuil, 1953.

Picon, Gaetan. *André Malraux.* Paris: Gallimard, 1945.

Schlesinger, Arthur. *A Thousand Days: John F. Kennedy in the White House.* Boston: Houghton Mifflin, 1965.

Shirer, William. *The Collapse of the Third Republic: An Inquiry into the Fall of France in 1940.* New York: Simon & Schuster, 1969.

Sulzberger, Cyrus L. *A Long Row of Candles: Memoirs and Diaries, 1934-1954.* New York: Macmillan, 1969.

Teulières, André. *L'Indochine: Guerre et Paix.* Paris: Charles Lavauzelle, 1985.

Thai Quang Trung, *Hanoi - Moscou: Un Couple Inséparable*. Paris: Hachette, collection Pluriel, 1984.

Vo Nhuyen Giap. *Guerre et Peuple*. Paris: Maspero, 1968.

INDEX

295

ABOUT THE AUTHOR

Ever since he met André Malraux in 1974 and wrote the first American biography of the great French novelist, Axel Madsen has wanted to return to the fascinating story of André and Clara Malraux's youthful adventures in Asia.

The son of a Danish father and a French mother, Madsen was born in Los Angeles, California. He studied piano at the Paris Conservatoire but, after the death of his mother, abandoned the piano and supported himself as an organist and gallery owner while attempting his first (unpublished) novel. At 22, he started working at the European office of the *New York Herald Tribune*, where he was an assistant to Art Buchwald and the shipping and finance editor. In the meantime, he wrote a screenplay for Alain Resnais, who, coincidentally, is married to Clara and André Malraux's only child, Florence. Since then, Madsen has worked for the Montreal bureau of United Press International and written scripts for Canadian and American television and feature films. He also served as unit publicist for "Butch Cassidy and the Sundance Kid" and "Patton."

Madsen is the author of two novels and and twelve nonfiction works, including biographies of directors Billy Wilder, William Wyler and John Huston, Yves Saint Laurent, and Jacques Cousteau, and a dual biography of Jean-Paul Sartre and Simone de Beauvoir.

His most recent book is *Gloria & Joe: The Star Crossed Love Affair of Gloria Swanson and Joe Kennedy*. Currently at work on a biography of Coco Chanel, he divides his time between his Pennsylvania mill house and his home in the Hollywood hills.